FINDING
Directions West

THE WEST SERIES
Aritha van Herk, Series Editor

ISSN 1922-6519 (Print) ISSN 1925-587X (Online)

This series focuses on creative non-fiction that explores our sense of place in the West - how we define ourselves as Westerners and what impact we have on the world around us. Essays, biographies, memoirs, and insights into Western Canadian life and experience are highlighted.

No. 1 · Looking Back: Canadian Women's Prairie Memoirs and Intersections of Culture, History, and Identity **S. Leigh Matthews**

No. 2 · Catch the Gleam: Mount Royal, From College to University, 1910–2009 **Donald N. Baker**

No. 3 · Always an Adventure: An Autobiography **Hugh A. Dempsey**

No. 4 · Promoters, Planters, and Pioneers: The Course and Context of Belgian Settlement in Western Canada **Cornelius J. Jaenen**

No. 5 · Happyland: A History of the "Dirty Thirties" in Saskatchewan, 1914–1937 **Curtis R. McManus**

No. 6 · My Name is Lola **Lola Rozsa, as told to and written by Susie Sparks**

No. 7 · The Cowboy Legend: Owen Wister's Virginian and the Canadian-American Frontier **John Jennings**

No. 8 · Sharon Pollock: First Woman of Canadian Theatre **Edited by Donna Coates**

No. 9 · Finding Directions West: Readings that Locate and Dislocate Western Canada's Past **Edited by George Colpitts and Heather Devine**

FINDING
Directions West

Readings that Locate and Dislocate Western Canada's Past

Edited by
GEORGE COLPITTS AND
HEATHER DEVINE

THE WEST Series
ISSN 1922-6519 (Print) ISSN 1925-587X (Online)

© 2017 George Colpitts and Heather Devine

University of Calgary Press
2500 University Drive NW
Calgary, Alberta
Canada T2N 1N4
press.ucalgary.ca

This book is available as an ebook which is licensed under a Creative Commons license. The publisher should be contacted for any commercial use which falls outside the terms of that license.

LIBRARY AND ARCHIVES CANADA CATALOGUING IN PUBLICATION

Finding directions west : readings that locate and dislocate western Canada's past / edited by George Colpitts and Heather Devine.

(West series, 1922-6519 ; no. 9)
Includes bibliographical references and index.
Issued in print and electronic formats.
ISBN 978-1-55238-880-8 (softcover).—ISBN 978-1-55238-881-5 (open access PDF).—ISBN 978-1-55238-882-2 (PDF).—ISBN 978-1-55238-883-9 (EPUB).—ISBN 978-1-55238-884-6 (MOBI)

1. Canada, Western--History. I. Colpitts, George, 1964-, editor II. Devine, Heather, author, editor III. Series: West series (Calgary, Alta.) ; 9

FC3206.F55 2017   971.2   C2017-900110-8
                                          C2017-900111-6

The University of Calgary Press acknowledges the support of the Government of Alberta through the Alberta Media Fund for our publications. We acknowledge the financial support of the Government of Canada. We acknowledge the financial support of the Canada Council for the Arts for our publishing program.

This book has been published with the help of a grant from the Alberta Historical Resources Foundation, made possible by the Alberta Lottery Fund.

      Canada Council   Conseil des Arts
                                              for the Arts   du Canada

Copyediting by Peter Enman
Cover design, page design, and typesetting by Melina Cusano

Table of Contents

Illustrations · vii
Acknowledgments · ix

Introduction: Migration and Transformation in the Canadian West · 1
GEORGE COLPITTS AND HEATHER DEVINE

1. Spatial Deployments to Synchronic Witnessing: Reiterations of Contact in Museum Spaces · 19
KIMBERLY MAIR

2. Discombobulated Remnants?: Preserving LGBTTTIQ Histories · 39
CHERYL AVERY AND SHELLEY SWEENEY

3. J.Z. LaRocque: A Métis Historian's Account of His Family's Experiences during the North-West Rebellion of 1885 · 59
HEATHER DEVINE

4. Colonizer or Compatriot?: A Reassessment of the Reverend John McDougall · 93
WILL PRATT

5. Exploring the "Thirteenth" Reason for Suffrage: Enfranchising "Mothers of the British Race" on the Canadian Prairies · 111
MALLORY ALLYSON RICHARD

6. "Develop a Great Imperial Race": Emmeline Pankhurst, Emily Murphy, and Their Promotion of "Race Betterment" in Western Canada in the 1920s
   Sarah Carter — *133*

7. "The Country Was Looking Wonderful": Insights on 1930s Alberta from the Travel Diary of Mary Beatrice Rundle
   Sterling Evans — *151*

8. A Blueprint for Range Management: The Anderson Grazing Rates Report of 1941
   Max Foran — *179*

9. Mountain Capitalists, Space, and Modernity at the Banff School of Fine Arts
   PearlAnn Reichwein and Karen Wall — *203*

Bibliography — *233*
Contributors — *255*
Index — *259*

Illustrations

1.1 First Contact mural image, Syncrude Gallery of Aboriginal Culture
1.2 Henday fur trade diorama, Syncrude Gallery of Aboriginal Culture
1.3 Inside of Jonathan Hunt's House

2.1 National Gay Conference 1975
2.2 *Sensible shoes news*
2.3 *Perceptions*

3.1 Joseph Zépherin LaRocque
3.2 Mrs. Lucy LaRocque and Mrs. Mary Devine
3.3 LaRocque's trunk of documents
3.4 LaRocque's bundled letter File
3.5 A LaRoque typewritten letter
3.6 *Ahchacoosahcotatakoopit* (Star Blanket)
3.7 John Hawkes, Saskatchewan Legislative Librarian

4.1 The Reverend John McDougall
4.2 John McDougall and Indigenous participants at the Calgary Fairgrounds, ca. 1910

5.1 "Everybody Votes but Mother"

6.1	Nellie McClung, Emmeline Pankhurst and the Edmonton Equal Franchise League, Edmonton, 1916
9.1	Banff School of Fine Arts campus as first imagined in the mid-1940s
9.2	Banff School of Fine Art's "Colonel Wood Memorial" (sic) building sketch 1946
9.3	Student Chalet for summer occupancy
9.4	Campus composite layout, 1947
9.5	Studio Building
9.6	"Typical Chalet" proposed in 1947

Acknowledgments

The editors acknowledge the financial support made available for the *Directions West: 3rd Biennial Conference on Western Canadian Studies*, 2012. Grants by the Social Sciences and Humanities Research Council, the US Consulate General (Calgary), the University of Calgary's Faculties of Art and Graduate Studies, the Network in Canadian History & Environment (NiCHE), and the Alberta Historical Resources Foundation were greatly appreciated, as was the work of many faculty, supporting staff, and graduate students before and during the conference.

Fred Glover, PhD student, University of Calgary, provided excellent copyediting and editorial assistance in creating the final manuscript. The editorial assistance of Francine Michaud is also appreciated.

The editors would like to express their gratitude to the Alberta Historical Resources Foundation for providing a grant supporting this book project.

Introduction: Migration and Transformation in the Canadian West

George Colpitts and Heather Devine

The articles selected for this anthology reflect the innovative and myriad scholarly approaches characterizing the *Directions West: 3rd Biennial Conference on Western Canadian Studies* held at the University of Calgary in June 2012. The collection speaks to the transformative effect that westward migration has had on the people and places that characterize the region we call Western Canada.

Calgary's location at the junction of the Great Plains and the Rocky Mountains is a natural starting point, or destination, for migrants journeying between the Pacific Ocean and the remainder of Canada. How the plains and the mountains are perceived by migrants – as formidable barriers to cross, or as passages to more westerly or easterly travel – depends solely on individual worldview and experience. For Indigenous peoples such as the Blackfoot (the *Niitsitapi*), travel along the eastern slopes of the mountains and into the Northwestern Plains was a regular feature of life. The seasonal subsistence rounds focused on bison hunting and collecting available plants and berries, medicines, and ceremonial materials. Therefore the Niitsitapi were required to visit – and revisit – certain places to perform ceremonies, retell stories, and sing songs that would ensure "the continued vitality of the rocks, springs, trees and animals, and by extension, the physical and spiritual health of the entire community, both living and dead."[1] The mountains were not unfamiliar, peculiar, or necessarily hostile barriers. Rather, they were part of a larger holistic experience of

1

constant movement between places of spiritual, subsistence, and aesthetic importance. The region, seemingly, gained its very life in the movement of its people.

For the non-Indigenous visitors to the same region, perceptions of the region have evolved over time. In the eighteenth and nineteenth centuries, the region and its inhabitants were evaluated through a British colonial lens, first as a site for harvesting furs and later as a physical impediment to the expansionist ambitions of the American state. The fur trade itself was in a constant state of flux, responding to the vagaries of international and regional political and economic forces. At the apex of this liminality was the *engagé*, whose labour as a canoeist and as a freighter of goods was also seasonally driven.[2] The development and abandonment of trading posts and transportation routes, the strategic reorientation of harvesting practices, and the redirected demand for specific types of "country produce" altered regional ecosystems and shaped the very existence of its inhabitants.

Tensions arose between newcomer and Indigenous perceptions of the area. Peter Fidler's mapping of "fixed" Niitsitapi spaces along the eastern slopes of the Rockies, based on interviews with Niitsitapi elders, reflect a broad territorial range, including Chief Mountain in present-day Montana, Arrow Mountain in Wyoming, or even Heart Mountain, discernible from Calgary. These landscape features, while helping to define a territorial space, were perhaps more important as navigational guides for the extensive travel of the Siksika, Kainai, and Piikani peoples through their traditional lands. The structure and symbol systems of the few surviving Indigenous maps of the region reflect the moving and changing perspective of travellers as they see the horizon on all sides and encounter specific physical features in the landscape as they moved – a river, a hillside of Saskatoon bushes, some sandstone cliffs, a former camping place or battle site.[3]

Even in Fidler's time, Niitsitapi travel maps were being used to fix the region for purposes of Empire. European mapmakers seized on Fidler's geographic points to anchor the weight of competing commercial and political interests. In the age of imperialism, way stations were attached, sometimes very erroneously, to European maps that would became the critical imaginative fixatives for British or American empire builders.[4] Indeed, Indigenous "go-to" maps were regularly transformed into "place" maps to be used for the military, economic, and cultural subjugation of the region. Western traditions of mapmaking are biased toward observing the world as a series of static points on a one-dimensional surface, rather than capturing the motion-contingent perceptions of Indigenous travellers, who viewed their natural surroundings as holistic environments and used points in the geography according to their navigational needs. On-the-spot navigational techniques, such as those used by Indigenous people, use the changing perspectives offered to a traveller, say, on a river to know how to travel along it: how its channel islands appear to "move" one way or the other in their approach, for instance. This approach to mapping does not "fix" the landscape on paper, but allows a traveller to move through it without necessarily staking claim to it as a place.[5]

Even the "West" as viewed by present-day scholars seems effaced when the region's very ephemeral geographic boundaries are tested in any degree. The "Prairie West," as the conference program bore out, becomes the lower Fraser of British Columbia, Washington's Coeur-D'Alene, Oregon's Vancouver. Whatever is relationally fixed on one map and purported to be a "state of being" in one coordinate system becomes uprooted when other references are added, certainly when Indigenous experiential mapping complicates the picture. Western Canadian history and literature, then, shifts restlessly as a constant.

That the Prairie West was a site of occupation and permanent settlement has been well explored by scholars. The thrust of "place" studies in Western Canadian historiography, as of late, bears out this attachment to a particular locale in which human traditions, identities, and modes of production develop.[6] Places are not just conceived by residents but, as Sandhya Ganapathy has pointed out, are also constructed as "translocal" and imagined localities. In her study of Alaskan "places," Ganapathy noted, "places" gained meaning as residents developed their landscaped environments over time, and as outsiders, visiting sports people, and foreign natural resource developers contributed to their definition as well.[7] Place studies have also benefited from better understandings of western "bioregions," where historical narratives emerge from the interplay of particular ecologies, local modes of production, and market-driven connections.[8]

The West, therefore, was more than a place of permanent occupation. It was imaginatively shaped by individual, group, or corporate movement across it. That movement and migration offers an alternative reading of the West's very history. Since much Canadian historical writing has centred upon the development of the region as a British colony, the actual displacement, movement, and identity of some migrants, such as English newcomers, has often been unexplored in the literature. Even at the time, English migration supported by emigration societies and formal government programs was viewed as a means of easing social and economic tensions in Britain, or to provide stability and balance to a region in the throes of absorbing large numbers of "foreign" or "non-British" migrants.[9] As well, the common immigrant experience shared by British and non-British alike undermined the certainty of a regional, national, and political narrative that all newcomers could embrace. Moving through or beyond a region, immigrants who come, and go, challenge the story arc of claim and conquest.[10] In their recurrent waves of immigration even to the present, newcomers continue to raise questions about the West as a destination. Is a newcomer coming to really settle here or move on? What interests does he or she have in this region as a home? Is the newcomer going to conform to the dominant society's customary rules and ways of life, or challenge them?

The West, of course, was not only a destination in a conventional sense. Immigration programs sometimes failed to target or attract what were considered the right sort of people; newcomers differed so much from Canada's "founding peoples" that they were sometimes characterized as "misfits" and "malingerers."[11] As history attests, a good portion of newcomers simply did not stay put, or took up temporary employment, work contracts, or a variety of different types of labour that kept them on the move. There was a lot of rental accommodation in the "settler" West, epitomized by the boarding house, which was a common feature of the region's communities. Even those who intended to stay fixed to one place often changed locations. They sometimes went, quite literally, "off the grid" in Dominion Lands Surveys, with frequent homestead abandonment, unfinished "proving up," and hurried cross-border flight. Westerners devised exit strategies in their very engagement with a locale, whether in the Indigenous, fur trade, ranching, farming, industrial, or post-industrial era.[12] Resource booms and busts, whether in coal mining, oil bonanzas or, more recently, oil sands mega-projects, have continued to hasten a modernist migration experience characterized by movement into the region during good times and migration out during the bad. Historically, resource industries have thrived on mobile and transient workforces. More recently, the distances such workers have gone to exploit the opportunities in resource sectors have simply increased. Alberta's oil sands projects by 2014 were attracting the comings and goings of some 30,000 Newfoundland tradesmen and skilled workers, their sheer numbers supporting ten flights weekly from St. John's WestJet terminal to Fort McMurray. As telling, perhaps, is not that modern air services support work-related travel now continental in scale, but how quickly the same services can end – in WestJet's case, abruptly in 2016, with the slump of oil prices.[13]

Migrants came alone to the West. But they often retained ancestral collective identities, and their migration, whether temporary or long term, constituted diaspora communities. In the past, the difficulties faced by ethnic groups in establishing homes, and in dealing with incidences of marginalization or persecution, left them in a state of apprehension that kept them moving, even within their intended place of destination.[14]

The conference sessions revealed a multiplicity of individual and corporate "identities" that emerged and/or evolved as a result of westward migration. A cursory examination of the essays in this volume reveals a number of intersecting themes. Western Canadian studies are still fundamentally rooted in archival and literary sources that provide an historiographical "home" for westerners in the past. However, the first contributions in this volume make clear that the very basis for understanding the people of this place is influenced by currents of archival practices, cultural dictates, and politics. As Kimberly Mair argues in her study of "spatial deployments" in museum display, the West's historical representation can privilege certain people, newcomers, and ways of knowing in such galleries as the Syncrude Gallery of Aboriginal Culture in the Royal Alberta Museum in Edmonton, and Chief Kwakwabalasami's House at the Royal British Columbia Museum. The organization of objects, their witnessing by visitors, and the asymmetric power embedded in documentary evidence about the era of contact in the West would suggest the historical representations of "place" that have survived may not be as accurate, or as universally accepted, as one would like. Rather, representation is loaded with meaning and normative understandings of the past. In the Edmonton exhibit dedicated to that celebrated fur trade traveller, Anthony Henday, Mair critically observes the way that the exhibition design compelled the museum visitor to focus on Henday instead of the Siksika camp in which he finds himself. Even the camp, represented in a diorama painting, was visually depicted based on the observations of an eyewitness traveller, whose multiple accounts of the same events and place vary widely. The didactic power of the display, the dating of the objects on display, and the emphasis on the problematic Henday journal itself transforms museum visitors into witnesses of a perpetually recreated moment of contact. In the alternative case of the "Kwakwabalasami House," Mair clearly perceives a much more complex museum place. Not rooted to a single moment in time or providing authoritative interpretive anchoring, the house plays host to visitors who remain ultimately and respectfully separate from the site's deep cultural meanings.

Mair's questions as to how historical texts such as Henday's can be accepted as authoritative allows for fresh interrogation of Western Canada's official story-scripts, vernacular histories and, ultimately, the archives themselves. The underrepresentation of certain groups in the West's past profoundly influences historical writing. The official record provides only a fleeting glimpse of some groups and much more of others, suggesting that the nature and extent of interactions between Indigenous peoples and newcomers, for example, has much to do with how records have been preserved.[15] Unfortunately, simply turning to the oral tradition to "round out" a perspective of place does not in fact remedy the distortion that written records and the archives preserving them already create concerning the region's past.

The need to challenge western history as it has been fixed, mapped, or documented is addressed directly by archivists Cheryl Avery and Shelley Sweeney. In their study of regional archival practices, they reveal the attitudes, unofficial protocols, and strong personal determinants over what is, or what is not, collected in archives. The gay and lesbian experiences, as well as those of sexual and gendered alternatives, are "discombobulated" in the record, or effaced altogether. As a result, the archive, which is expected to serve as a permanent sanctuary for a region's records, is incomplete. Although archival protocols are changing and some collections have grown to include LGBT memories and records, the regional narrative itself, in respect of this community, and by extension many more, becomes erroneous by omission. The article highlights the need for archivists to challenge existing perceptions of early Western Canadian society, not only to facilitate the collection of a wider range of documents for preservation but also to ensure the accuracy and completeness of historical depictions of different eras. This paper should prompt archivists and western studies scholars to inquire further as to why the gay and lesbian experience in the West has been preserved better in British Columbia, Manitoba, and Saskatchewan than in other archives elsewhere. For westerners leaving evidence of lives that moved in and outside dominant gendered and sexual realities and engaged in quite unique experiences, the western archive still has to be broadened to accommodate these narratives in the collective memory.

Western historical writing has only recently given its just consideration to Indigenous groups, fur trade employees, and clerics whose lives more typically were not place-grounded but given over to traditional seasonal rounds, religious and social in-gatherings around wintering or summer fishing camps, and travel over large spans of western geography.[16] The Department of Interior's Dominion Lands Policy, the township survey, and agricultural, ranching, irrigation, municipal, and unorganized or organized district planning left a vast paper record. However, it does not effectively account for the migration experience still inherent in the lives of many people in the region. Their histories can attain better visibility when historians remain alert to their continued movement between jurisdictions, both national and international in scope.

While treaties and reserves created a fixed, if restricted, territory for First Nations people, the process of treaties and agricultural settlement served to marginalize their Métis cousins in a cultural and economic netherworld. After the unsuccessful Northwest Rebellion of 1885, the Métis faced significant political, cultural, and racial barriers to full participation in the burgeoning settlement economy of the post-treaty west. Many Métis were displaced from their ancestral lands due to the mismanagement of scrip distribution by the Canadian government, while others fled to remote regions to continue hunting and gathering. Their displacement occurred as equally dramatic pull and push factors in Britain and Europe drew newcomers into western agricultural lands.[17] Without access to treaty benefits, without permanent fixed abodes, and unable to produce a steady income or to pay municipal taxes, access to education and other benefits of citizenship was sporadic, or non-existent, for Métis living in the settled agricultural areas of the south. Newcomers, especially working-class immigrants, looked to social and economic networks to establish permanent places in the West, while still relying on long-distance seasonal work in mining, railway, harvester, and timber frontier areas.[18] By contrast, the Métis, long inhabitants of the region, were isolated by their French and Indigenous languages, their mixed racial heritage, and, in some cases, their inability to swiftly adapt to new business practices and social conditions. Many Métis chose to migrate northward to sparsely inhabited regions, or adopted various forms of cultural amnesia in order to integrate successfully into the mainstream. The Métis reality, given their circumstances, was shaped by uncertain squatting rights and community displacement. Even in the twentieth century their status as migrants, or diaspora people within their own region, reduced many Métis to the designation of "road allowance people."

Heather Devine's contribution to this anthology suggests the way that some Métis people coped with the economic and territorial marginalization of their communities. The case of J.Z. LaRocque reveals a family's long legal struggle to retain title to and ownership of their land, as well as the persistent lobbying required to establish relations with incoming political elites in order to maintain employment and achieve a social and economic voice in the new society. LaRocque's example yields a case study from "vernacular" sources that is crucial for a more nuanced understanding of a group often regarded as rootless, migrant, and dispossessed people. Devine suggests that the "established" histories of the West, as generated by elites and, with time, academic historians, require the balancing perspectives of grassroots historians already present in such communities as the one growing at Lebret, Saskatchewan. There, the LaRocque family's strategy of backing successive federal and provincial Liberal dynasties had helped it secure land and, later, government work. Perhaps most importantly, J.Z. LaRocque invested his time in gathering the narratives of people quite marginalized in official accounts, and in doing so left behind a personal archive impressive in its own right. He and members of his family became the unofficial historians of the Lebret area, whether the official historical community consulted with them or not. Their activities served to maintain Métis heritage and identity at a time when the policies of the federal government sought to neutralize, if not eradicate, non-British identities and replace them with a hegemonic "Canadian" ethnicity.

Will Pratt's essay on missionary John McDougall provides additional insights into how Indigenous people coped with the impact of Indian administration and reserved spaces in the western region. McDougall based his ministry to the Stoney people in the Alberta foothills west of Calgary on a foundation of stubborn paternalism and a strong initial desire to assimilate his flock. However, his growing empathy for the people appointed to his care later fuelled an interest in preserving elements of their "Indigenous" culture in the face of rapid cultural change by the turn of the century. As Pratt argues, McDougall contended with two strong poles of reference: Ottawa as a source of Indian policy which sought to situate its wards in established occupational pursuits within bordered places, and the trans-montane ecological reality of the Stoney reserve itself. McDougall attempted to reconcile the Stoneys' desire to migrate seasonally to their traditional hunting grounds on both the eastern and western slopes of the Rockies with the Indian Department's mandate to maintain treaty Indians permanently on their reserve land at Morley. Because their traditional subsistence activities were hardly fixed but necessarily mobile in certain seasons of the year, McDougall even advocated freedom of movement and wide-ranging hunting and gathering activities in the spaces reserved in the enlarged Rocky Mountains National Park, a relatively recent government initiative to "fix" boundaries in what was once an Indigenous "commons."

Settler migration westward imposed new social and political identities on Indigenous people and irrevocably altered their traditional territories, resulting in catastrophic and often tragic consequences that have remained outside the national consciousness until very recently. What Henry Nash Smith suggested in the case of American history, where "national" historical narratives came to construct the West in terms of the parent empire's progress, expansion, and prosperity, certainly holds true for Canada.[19] The personality of the prototypical migrant – ambitious, acquisitive, and exploitative – left behind a mixed legacy, however, as more recent historians of the West are quick to point out.[20] The West was not a land of equal opportunity for all, nor was it particularly democratic. Indeed, the new social history of the last thirty years depicts eighteenth- and nineteenth-century western expansion as a process that was often racist, ethnocentric, capitalist, and environmentally destructive. In fact, it could be argued that the history of western expansion, in both its Canadian and American iterations, can only be understood properly if it is viewed as a much larger colonial process of exploiting local primary raw resources to serve large-scale commercial interests – a process that continues in the twenty-first century.

The same process can be discernible in early suffrage work in Western Canada, as Mallory Richard suggests in her contribution to this collection. Richard's essay suggests that it was the very mobile and recently arrived cohort of female immigrants to Western Canada that propelled the movement for enfranchisement and other forms of social justice. But it also maintains that their claims for voting rights were based on distinctions they made between themselves as white Anglo-Canadians – those claiming permanency in the West – and the newly arrived and purportedly doubtful "citizens" who were, in the war years, denied the vote. The suffrage campaign obviously oriented itself toward white and British understandings of citizenship – and therefore permanency – in opposition to the claims of "non-white Canadians, recent immigrants, or out-of-work transients." By World War I, the intense debate about extending the franchise to wives, widows, and relatives of soldiers overseas required reformers to differentiate between supposedly "permanent" citizens and more recent immigrants whose homes, apparently, still existed elsewhere.

Sarah Carter, too, suggests that franchise claims were complicated by the visits to the West by prominent British suffragist Emmeline Pankhurst. In an article highlighting the intriguing intellectual synergy between two leading figures in the reform and suffrage movements, Britain's Pankhurst and Western Canada's jurist and suffragist Emily Murphy, Carter demonstrates the way two minds could agree, and indeed sharpen around, nativist ideas and Murphy's own promotion of eugenics. The article sheds new light on Britain's Pankhurst and, in particular, her considerable engagement with Western Canada in her post–World War I travels. In 1920 alone, she claimed to have spoken to 70,000 people and seen "more of Western Canada ... than many Western Canadians." Her whirlwind tour of 1922 took Pankhurst to no fewer than sixty-three different towns. But as Carter points out, the product of such a tour was a narrow and blinkered view of the West as it existed at the time. Also, it is clear that Emily Murphy's own ideas had some influence with Emmeline Pankhurst, despite the fact that Pankhurst was the more prominent and established activist. Carter argues that Emily Murphy's expressed beliefs about racial betterment and eugenics clearly influenced Pankhurst's own thinking in the time.

These matters touch on the very epistemological nature of journeying. Pankhurst had to travel to the West to meet Murphy, and Murphy, in turn, travelled with her own messages to England and elsewhere. Sterling Evans's contribution to this collection would bear this out. He explores the case of Mary Beatrice Rundle, secretary to Sir Clement Anderson Montague Barlow, who led a coal commission inquiry in 1935 in Alberta. Rundle was quintessentially a western traveller. She followed a tightly scheduled journey through large areas of the West with very little prior experience. Her written observations were filtered through a matrix of class, gender, and ethnic worldviews. In Evans's meticulous reconstruction of Rundle's western journey through her diary, he shares Rundle's perception of what should have been a well-understood part of the historical record: Western Canada's troubled coal industry during the Great Depression. But how much of the West, as a place, was revealed in this journey? Evans's article raises important questions about how travellers perceive their surroundings. Rundle noted some elements of the scene before her but excluded others. The most arresting feature of Rundle's journal writing relates to the writer herself; her occupational role; her gender, which restricted both her movement and her daily experiences; and, above all, her eating, sleeping, and travel as part of a well-appointed and funded British Royal Commission. Despite her extensive travel itinerary, it is revealing that Rundle seems to have written so little about the environmental disaster of the Dust Bowl. Did she not see the human consequences of the severe drought affecting large numbers of local residents, or the economic destitution marking the entire region?

Even the research topics that might lend themselves to an understanding of "place," such as ranching and mountain studies, were in fact sites of migration, change, and transformation.[21] In this collection, Max Foran explores the emergence of range management practices in Alberta. Initially, set rental rates on leased land throughout the province and liberal range practices imported into the region displaced native flora and fauna. By the 1930s, ranchers saw their industry failing and their grasslands management unsustainable. Their associations advocated a management program that paid heed to the different carrying capacities of subregions in the province, as well as changing market prices. Foran emphasizes the comprehensiveness of the commissioned study of Graham Anderson in 1939 and the forward-thinking elements of the Anderson Report of 1941. The policy recommendations themselves defied a single understanding of western grass, and ended up promoting longer leases, policies reflecting the different carrying capacities of Alberta's ranchlands and, most importantly, stricter limits on herd sizes. The western ranch as a place, then, so long associated with a rather limited conceptualization of the land, gave way to ideas and practices modified for different subregions and a changing market. The paper's great contribution, however, is found in its ironic insights into the ranching community's own limited acceptance of the very ideas that it had once promoted in the more prosperous postwar years.

In the long term, such views of western nature, not of nature as a cohesive whole, but grounded in ecological interrelationships, became accepted in the postwar period. The western paradigm was irrevocably altered in the economic and social changes occurring in Western Canada with the oil boom, international agricultural markets, and modern communications. But, as the anthology's concluding article by PearlAnn Reichwein and Karen Wall suggests, the region was not in the throes of an economic determinism by any means. Nor was its very "look" fixed. In the case of the planning and design of the Banff School of Fine Arts, the "Salzburg" ideal of architecture was thoroughly upended in favour of an internationalist and modernist alternative. The authors clarify the timing and the negotiated entry of the school into the Banff mountain landscape. They draw attention to the debate that accompanied the advent, prior to Alberta's real takeoff into oil prosperity, of an architectural modernism in the school's design at variance with the mountain profile of Banff. Under the direction of Donald Cameron, the school's flat-roofed modernist design bucked the "Swiss chalet" style that had formerly stamped Banff's town development. This new style was imported from far away – via Edmonton, where the school was originally undertaken as an out-campus of the University of Alberta – and inspired by Scandinavian, rather than Swiss, ideals. The planners of the Banff school seemed to have looked to Denmark and Sweden, and even the modernist architecture of a Kansas City art school, to both inspire and accommodate visiting art students in Alberta's Rocky Mountains.

The Canadian West was as much a direction as a destination. The literary works of two figures honoured at the *Directions West* conference, Gerald Friesen and Robert Kroetsch, provide examples of writing that, in many respects, explored the complementary themes of the west as a unique place, and the west as a destination for trickster, immigrant, or outsider experiences.[22] Friesen has challenged the certainty of the Prairie West as an enduring, imaginative, or even functional construct.[23] He has asserted the need to rethink "region" as a static concept, particularly given the rapid changes in migration, trade, and communication in the twentieth century.[24] Perhaps its history as a place of movement, change, and migration has been most evinced in its recent past. Friesen's work with Royden Loewen, for example, exposes the changing places of immigrants in Western Canadian cities, whether at first in distinctive ethnic enclaves or, more recently, in pluralistic, truly multicultural communities.[25] Whatever permanency and stability was represented in the locally focussed – and quite short-lived – family farm in the era of settlement certainly broke down in the post–World World II era, when rural areas lost their residents to cities and the entire experience of farm life was transformed due to technological and social change. Advances in the mechanization of farm machinery, which reduced the need for farm labourers, were quickly followed by the opportunities created by all-weather roads, university education in distant cities, and communications technology linking individuals to the outside world.[26]

Kroetsch, who often revisited the theme of rootedness within place, was keenly aware of the dilemmas and uncertainties facing the individual in the West without a physical or spiritual home. The figure of Hazard, in *The Studhorse Man*, as Aritha Van Herk points out, undertakes a "quest for home" but in the end the "quest is the quest itself." Even if "every journey is a journey home," the character struggles to achieve that realization.[27] In Kroetsch's criticism of the historical tradition, which he viewed as a form of writing projecting power to a particular place, and his adoption of alternative forms of history, myth, and imagination, his writing served the function of an observant, if alienated, stranger in the region's past.[28] George Melnyk, who organized the panel on Kroetsch, suggests that even the particular idiom of "Alberta writing" manifests the tension of being both a place and a process.[29] Both historical and literary studies, then, hinge on the twin realities of the West as a fixed place, an impetus for movement, itinerant experiences on the road, whistle-stop layovers, a possible final destination, or simply the act of collecting one's possessions and accumulated stories and moving on.

One iconic figure of interest in Kroetsch's work is that of David Thompson. The life of celebrated trader and cartographer David Thompson was observed in the lead-up to the conference via historical recreations of his Columbian River journeys and transcontinental canoe trips to Hudson Bay. His peripatetic career underscores the tangential directions, if not chaotic displacement, so common to individuals in the region's past. Kroetsch's extended poem devoted to Sarah Small, the wife of David Thompson, highlights the tension between the perspectives and interests of the historical traveller and stranger on the one side, and that of the original resident of the place on the other. "The West is tangled," Sarah states to her surveyor/ fur trader husband, "a sheet of paper is neat. What do you choose to write down?"[30] While she might have thought that this surveyor "would dream the short and the long in patches of light, not in shades of conquest," she finds to her dismay that "I was wrong." Speaking of her traveller husband, she says, "He dreamed a passage. He dreamed a find and its fame." But Thompson, like many westerners expressing flawed claims of permanency, was only "making a map, always, making his map of nowhere."

The anthology contributions from the *Directions West* conference, then, reveal some of the ways that individuals, groups, and corporate interests seeking a permanent, historically situated place in Western Canada found themselves caught up in an ongoing, if not perpetual, state of displacement. Even upon their arrival to their various destinations, individuals in the region's past found new journeys and new migrations before them.

These glimpses into the region's past also provide surprising insights into issues that resonate today. The environmental degradation that results from unregulated resource use, whether it be from over-grazing of lease land in southern Alberta or unfettered oil sands extraction in the north, comes to mind. The advocacy and militancy of various ethnocultural and gender minorities – immigrants, indigenous people, and women – in attempting to achieve a measure of social and legal equality in the early twentieth century is mirrored by the current struggles faced by the present-day LGBT community. Fortunately, the twenty-first century offers both the opportunity and the responsibility to uncover and share these unique historical experiences with a broad and increasingly diverse citizenry in this region we call "the West."

Notes

1. Gerald A. Oetelaar and D. Joy Oetelaar, "The Structured World of the *Niitsitapi:* The Landscape as Historical Archive among Hunter-Gatherers of the Northern Plains," in *Structured Worlds: The Archaeology of Hunter-Gatherer Thought and Action*, ed. A. Cannon (Sheffield, UK: Equinox, 2011), 69–94.
2. See Carolyn Podruchny, *Making the Voyageur World: Travelers and Traders in the North American Fur Trade* (Lincoln: University of Nebraska Press, 2006), 12; 14–17. Podruchny also presented on cultural syncretism in material Métis culture, in a panel on Plains Métis identity, 23 June 2012.
3. Theodore Binnema, "How Does a Map Mean?: Old Swan's Map of 1801 and the Blackfoot World," in *From Rupert's Land to Canada: Essays in Honour of John E. Foster*, ed. Theodore Binnema, Gerhard Ens, and Roderick C. Macleod (Edmonton: University of Alberta Press, 2001), 201–24.
4. Barbara Belyea, "Mapping the Marias: The Interface of Native and Scientific Cartographies," *Great Plains Quarterly* 17, nos. 3–4 (1997): 165–84.
5. David Neufeld, "Learning to Drive the Yukon River: Western Cartography and Athapaskan Story Maps," in *Big Country, Big Issues: Canada's Environment, Culture and History*, ed. Nadine Klopfer and Christof Mauch (Munich: Rachel Carson Center, 2011), 16–43.
6. Merle Massie, presenting 22 June 2012, suggested the importance of place in vacationing and park areas in northern Saskatchewan. Her own work draws on place studies: *Forest Prairie Edge: Place History in Saskatchewan* (Winnipeg: University of Manitoba Press, 2014).
7. Sandhya Ganapathy, "Imagining Alaska Local and Translocal Engagements with Place," *American Anthropologist* 115, no. 1 (March 2013): 96–111.
8. The expression, of course, is Dan Flores's, from "Place: Thinking about Bioregional History," in *The Natural West: Environmental History in the Great Plains and Rocky Mountains* (Norman: University of Oklahoma Press, 1984), 89–106; for bioregional applications in Western Canada, see William J. Turkel, *The Archive of Place: Unearthing the Pasts of the Chilcotin Plateau* (Vancouver: University of British Columbia Press, 2007); and James Murton, *Creating a Modern Countryside: Liberalism and Land Resettlement in British Columbia* (Vancouver: University of British Columbia Press, 2007); Shannon Stunden Bower, *Wet Prairie: People, Land, and Water in Agricultural Manitoba* (Vancouver: University of British Columbia Press, 2011).
9. Bruno Ramirez and Donald Avery, "Immigration and Ethnic Studies," in *A Thematic Guide to Canadian Studies*, ed. A. Artibise (Montreal: McGill-Queen's University Press, 1990), 77–116.
10. See Francis W. Kaye, *Good Lands: A Meditation and History on the Great Plains* (Edmonton: Athabasca University Press, 2011), 17–44.
11. W.J.C. Cherwinski, *"Misfits," "Malingerers," and "Malcontents": The British Harvester Movement of 1928*, in *The Developing West*, ed. J.E. Foster (Edmonton: University of Alberta Press, 1983).
12. See Sterling Evans, ed., *The Borderlands of the American and Canadian Wests: Essays on Regional History of the Forty-ninth Parallel* (Norman: University of Nebraska Press, 2006); and, on the reality of cross-border experience in the First Nations' world, David

G. McCrady, *Living with Strangers: The Nineteenth-Century Sioux and the Canadian-American Borderlands* (Norman: University of Nebraska Press, 2006); Neal McLeod, "Plains Cree Identity: Borderlands, Ambiguous Genealogies and Narrative Irony," *Canadian Journal of Native Studies* 20, no. 2 (2000), 437–54.

13 "Bursting of Alberta's oil bubble on display at St. John's airport," CBC News, Newfoundland and Labrador, 16 February 2016, http://www.cbc.ca/news/canada/newfoundland-labrador/airport-st-johns-alberta-downturn-1.3443452 (accessed 20 June 2016).

14 See Donald Akenson's diaspora studies, and, particularly his work, *The Irish Diaspora: A Primer* (Toronto: Meany, 1993).

15 In his own conference contribution, Lyle Dick raised questions about the insufficient paper record in a paper suggesting a "Queer Frontier" is discernible not so much on paper as in fleeting photographic evidence. Lyle Dick, "The Queer Frontier: Male Same-Sex Experience in Western Canada's Settlement Era," 22 June 2012. Valerie Korinek elaborated the case for discovering lesbian literature, certainly not viewed, at least traditionally, as a reality of the West as a place. Valerie Korinek, "'They wouldn't say they were gay if they were in bed together': The Challenges of Writing Prairie Lesbian History," 22 June 2012; Peter Boag's presentation suggests that transgendered experience and cross-dressing in the fluid social conditions of the American West has, until recently, not been recognized as a feature of the place. "'Strange Country This': The American Frontier as a Transgendering Place and Process," 23 June 2012.

16 The Francophone experience as migrants or as excluded residents as reflected by Franco-Americans and Métis, was explored in presentations by Jean Barman, Adele Perry, and Sherry Farrell Racette. Katrina Jagodinsky also compared two women's changing self-identification, depending on their situation in British or American territory in a paper later published as "A Tale of Two Sisters: Family Histories from the Strait Salish Borderlands," *Western Historical Quarterly* 47, no. 1 (Summer 2016): 1–23. A conference panel theme was devoted to "Transnational Migration: Mapping the Movements of Francophones, Africans, and Imperial Subjects in the West," 22 June 2012. The "Life along the Medicine Line: Forging, Reconfiguring and Renegotiating Plains Métis Identity" panel by Carolyn Podruchny, Brenda Macdougall, Émilie Pigeon, and Timothy Foran, , 23 June 2012, explored important themes. It was as itinerant hunters and labourers, and seasonal wintering camp adherents, not as permanently rooted settlers, that the Métis experience and identity in Western Canada took form. See Brenda Macdougall, Carolyn Podruchny, and Nicole St-Onge, eds., *Contours of a People: Métis Family, Mobility and History* (Norman: Oklahoma University Press, 2012); and Brenda Macdougall and Nicole St-Onge, "Rooted in Mobility: Métis Buffalo Hunting Brigades," *Manitoba History* 71 (Winter 2013): 21–32.

17 Jean Barman, "Ethnicity in the Pursuit of Status: British Middle and Upper-Class Emigration to British Columbia in the Late Nineteenth and early Twentieth Centuries," *Canadian Ethnic Studies* 18, no. 1 (1986): 32–51; Patrick A. Dunae, *Gentlemen Emigrants: From the British Public Schools to the Canadian Frontier* (Vancouver: Douglas & McIntyre, 1981). The experience of British emigrant women is offered in Susan Jackel, ed., *A Flannel Shirt and Liberty: British Emigrant Gentlewomen in the Canadian West, 1880–1914* (Vancouver: University of British Columbia Press, 1982).

18 A. Ross McCormack, "Networks among British Immigrants and Accommodation to Canadian Society: Winnipeg, 1900–1914," *Histoire sociale – Social History*, 17 no. 34 (November 1984): 357–74.

19 Henry Nash Smith. *Virgin Land: The American West as Symbol and Myth* (Cambridge: Harvard University Press, 1950).

20 Sucheng Chan, "Western American Historiography and People of Color," in *Peoples of Color in the American West*, ed. Sucheng Chan, Douglas Henry Daniels, Mario T. Garcia, and Terry P. Wilson (Lexington, MA: D.C. Heath, 1994): 1–14.

21 Zac Robinson, then, explored the origins and class basis of a western travelling mountaineer, and his exaggerated claims made after climbing a Western Canadian mountain landmark in "Beyond Description?: David Douglas and the Persistence of the Brown-Hooker Problem in the Canadian Rockies," 22 June 2012. See Zac Robinson and Stephen Slemon, "Deception in High Places," *Canadian Alpine Journal* 94 (2011): 12–17.

22 "Prairie Present and Absent,: A Roundtable in Honour of Gerald Friesen," 22 June 2012, with contributions by Leah Morton, Jeffrey Taylor, Royden Loewen, George Buri and Marion McKay; and "Western Canadian Literature: The Robert Kroetsch Legacy," with contributions by Dennis Cooley, Laurie Ricou, and Pamela Banting, 23 June 2012. For Friesen's understandings of the West as region, see Gerald Friesen, *The West: Regional Debate, National Ambitions, Global Age* (Toronto: Penguin, 1999); "Defining the Prairies: or, Why the Prairies Don't Exist," in *Toward Defining the Prairies: Region, Culture, and History*, ed. Robert Wardbaugh (Winnipeg: University of Manitoba Press, 2001), 13–28; *River Road: Essays on Manitoba and Prairie History* (Winnipeg: University of Manitoba Press, 1996); and "Critical History in Western Canada: 1900–2000," in *The West and Beyond: New Perspectives on an Imagined Region*, ed. Alvin Finkel, Sarah Carter, and Peter Fortna (Edmonton: Athabasca University Press, 2010), 3–12.

23 See Friesen, "Defining the Prairies," 13–28.

24 Gerald Friesen, "Space and Region in Canadian History," *Journal of the Canadian Historical Association* 16 (2005): 1–48.

25 Royden Lowen and Gerald Friesen, *Immigrants in Prairie Cities: Ethnic Diversity in Twentieth-Century Canada* (Toronto: University of Toronto Press, 2009).

26 Gerald Friesen, Afterword, in P. James Giffen, *Rural Life: Portraits of the Prairie Town, 1946* (Winnipeg: University of Manitoba Press, 2004), 202–8.

27 See Aritha van Herk, Introduction, in Robert Kroetsch, *The Studhorse Man* (Edmonton: University of Alberta Press, 2004), xvi.

28 Rosalind Jennings, "Disappearing Doubles and Deceptive Landscapes in the Writing of Robert Kroetsch," *London Journal of Canadian Studies* 12 (1996:) 20–27. Francis W. Kaye and Robert Thacker, "'Gone Back to Alberta': Robert Kroetsch Rewriting the Great Plains," *Great Plains Quarterly* 1, no. 1 (1994): 167–83;

29 See Donna Coates and George Melnyk, "The Struggle for an Alberta Literature," in *Wild Words: Essays on Alberta Literature*, ed. Coates and Melnyk (Edmonton: Athabasca University Press, 2009), x; the West, conceived as a place and process, is suggested in John Mack Faragher, "The Frontier Trail: Rethinking Turner and Reimagining the American West," *American Historical Review* 98, no. 1 (February 1993): 106–17.

30 Robert Kroetsch, *The Last Narrative of Mrs. David Thompson* (Windsor, ON: Wrinkle Press, 2007).

1

Spatial Deployments to Synchronic Witnessing: Reiterations of Contact in Museum Spaces

Kimberly Mair

James Clifford argues that the processes of research and consultation between museum staff and the communities whose history, culture, and artifacts are to be represented constitute a contact zone characterized by asymmetrical relationships.[1] Extending Clifford's observation from the realm of consultation to the spatial arrangements in museums, this chapter aims to illustrate the power of spatial elements in the design of built environments. Spatial arrangements are neither more silent nor more neutral than the textual messages crafted for didactic panels in museum displays. Since they often pose as authentic reconstructions of historical phenomena, spatial productions have a communicative force that is no less effective than textual discourse in producing a message that unwittingly resonates with hegemonic assumptions. A significant aspect of reconstructed sites is that they tend to "build the observer into the structure of events."[2] Therefore, the relative location of visitors and objects of representation is productive at the level of identification in crucial respects. Spatial arrangements of objects and visitors produce scenes of address that implicate visitors by enabling particular vantage points, animating relationships between the visitor and historical events, and sometimes interpellating visitors as witnesses.

In this chapter I will interpret two constructed sites that provide key moments in their respective exhibitions with respect to the spatial scenes of address that they produce: the *First Contact* in situ display, which was located in the Syncrude Gallery of Aboriginal Culture (SGAC) at the former site of the Royal Alberta Museum (RAM);[3] and *Chief Kwakwabalasami's House* in the First Peoples Gallery at the Royal British Columbia Museum (RBCM). I am primarily interested in the spatialization of these exhibition sites and the relative distribution of objects and visitors within and surrounding them. I will consider how both sites spatially deploy scenes of address between the visitor, the reconstructed site, and its contents with consideration of the reiterative production of contact zones, since Mary Louise Pratt insists that contact "emphasizes how subjects are constituted in and by their relations to each other ... often within radically asymmetrical relations of power."[4] Further, the discussion considers the implicit tendency – particularly with respect to in situ display practices – to situate the gallery visitor as a witness to the past.

The aim of this project is to draw attention to the power of spatial formations in cultural institutions that play a vital role in the presentation of politically subordinated cultures. This is a propitious time to give attention to the politics of museum display. As the 150th anniversary of Canada approaches, one-time funds will be directed at heritage projects. This poses an exigent opportunity to address concerns raised about the presentation of Indigenous cultures. The RBCM plans to rescript the First Peoples Gallery but is in an early stage of this process. The RAM is undergoing a major redevelopment project. At the time of writing, it has closed its exhibits as it prepares to move to a new building under construction, which is expected to open in 2017.

The Museums in Context

The two museums and their collections are vastly different in scope, method, and tone, with the RBCM having a greater emphasis on aesthetics and culture and the RAM placing a stronger accent on scientific, particularly ethnological, approaches. The audiences of the two museums are also quite different from each other, which is in part a function of location. The RBCM is situated in a destination location near Victoria's inner harbor. Hence, it attracts a far greater number of visitors, many of whom are tourists. Until recently, the RAM was located on the periphery of Edmonton's city centre and isolated from other points of interest, limiting the potential for casual "walk-in" visits. Its new building is in the downtown "arts core." The RAM resides in the capital city of one of the most politically and environmentally debated places globally: the province of Alberta. The debate revolves in part around the activities of what was the SGAC's corporate funder: Syncrude Canada Limited. It has been argued that Syncrude's projects in the oil sands are inextricably intertwined with the continuing material oppression of Indigenous peoples in the province.[5] While the SGAC gave comparatively far greater attention to the brutalities of colonial oppression than does the First Peoples Gallery at the RBCM, the conspicuous silences with respect to contemporary challenges linked to land and material ways of life may have an implicit relationship to the gallery's funding.

The RBCM First Peoples Gallery was designed in the 1970s, when the Kwakwaka'wakw (a.k.a. Kwahkiutl) were actively lobbying for the release of potlatch items seized from their villages in 1921. Confiscations resulting from the outlawing of the potlatch from 1884 to 1951 represented only part of the massive removal of artifacts from communities. Since the late 1800s, ongoing competition between rival collectors, ethnologists, merchants, and missionaries facilitated a heavy flow of objects out of the province of British Columbia to populate emerging museums in Eastern Canada, the United States, and Europe.[6] The outflow of objects eventually led to calls for the province to build a representative collection of its own.[7] The design of the current First Peoples Gallery began after the National Museum of Canada introduced a policy of democracy and decentralization in the late 1960s that coincided with local efforts of the Kwakwaka'wakw to bring material objects back home to be housed in Indigenous museums.[8] The establishment of local cultural centres, such as the U'mista Cultural Centre at Alert Bay in 1980, were already taking place during the period when the current provincial gallery was under development. This context may have necessitated a more co-operative approach from the provincial museum.[9] Despite this, as Gloria Jean Frank's observations show, the RBCM's First Peoples Gallery is fraught with curatorial practices that support a European worldview, such as: linear organization that presents active practices as though they are dead; failure to acknowledge and draw upon existing knowledges within local Indigenous communities; and the use of Edward Curtis's sensationally staged photographs as factual documents.[10]

The RAM's SGAC was designed in the 1990s and in the wake of *The Spirit Sings: Artistic Traditions of Canada's First Peoples* exhibition, curated at the Glenbow Museum in Calgary for the 1988 Winter Olympics. *The Spirit Sings* stands as a key marker of heightened consciousness of the fraught relationship between museums and Indigenous communities in Canada owing to the Lubicon Lake Cree's boycott of the event.[11] The boycott prompted the International Council of Museums to pass a resolution urging museums not to exhibit cultural materials without the consent of the Aboriginal groups to whom the objects belong,[12] as well as the establishment of a National Task Force, jointly undertaken between the Assembly of First Nations and the Canadian Museums Association, that sought collaborative strategies to present and interpret Aboriginal cultures.[13]

One might assume that the many confrontations between Indigenous communities and museums between 1988 and 1990, the Canadian National Task Force conference recommendations later that year, the Oka Crisis of 1990, and negotiations for the Native American Graves Protection and Repatriation Act (NAGPRA) in the United States might have brought about a radically collaborative approach in the planning of the SGAC in Alberta. Heather Devine observes, however, that Alberta's provincial museum more aggressively pursued acquisition of Indigenous material culture and applied a policy that was resistant to repatriation during this time.[14] The acquisition of the Scriver Blackfoot collection in 1989 is illustrative of the institution's unyielding approach to relations with Indigenous communities. The museum represented its purchase from the Montana-based collector Robert Scriver as an act of "repatriation,"[15] crudely subsuming Blackfoot communities under the province's patrimonial domain and reinforcing the Canada–U.S. border as the geopolitical demarcation of significance. Opposing the museum's purchase of the collection, George Kipp insisted that the museum should return the collection's sacred bundles "so that in 10 years an Indian won't be hanging next to the bundles."[16]

The failure to consider Indigenous artists for the production of SGAC murals during the gallery's planning offered another astonishing marker of the relationship between the museum and Indigenous communities. Four murals were awarded to artists without even extending invitations to Indigenous artists to bid on the murals. Given the international renown of Canadian Indigenous artists such as Jane Ash Poitras, the failure to consider Indigenous artists was widely perceived as having demonstrated a lack of respect and recognition. The museum director then dismissed reactions as "stereotypical."[17] Hence, the indifference of the museum served to heighten already tense relations with Indigenous groups during the planning of the SGAC. This seems to stand in contrast to what was happening in southern Alberta at the Glenbow where, after *The Spirit Sings*, new relationships were being fostered between the museum and Indigenous groups that led to a fully collaborative partnership of museum professionals and Blackfoot ceremonial leaders and teachers to plan a permanent Blackfoot gallery, named *Niitsitapiisinni: Our Way of Life*. Glenbow's gallery, which opened in 2001, was oriented to tell a story in the words of the Blackfoot and to affirm co-existence over assimilation.[18] Despite consultation processes in the planning of the SGAC, consideration of cultural property and collaboration in gallery design appear to have been more superficial at Alberta's provincial museum than at the RBCM and the Glenbow, respectively.

The above points provide some general contours of context for the comparison of two very different Western Canadian provincial museums, the RAM and the RBCM, with respect to their treatment of Indigenous cultures. This chapter analyzes the spatialization of the respective galleries, in particular, by focusing metonymically on the two key sites of address mentioned at the outset in terms of the relative arrangement of objects and texts and the diachronic spatial distribution of objects and visitors in the respective sites.

Scene of Address 1: Visitor always arrives just in time

The *First Contact* in situ display in the former SGAC at the RAM was a key site that Philip Stepney, former director of the museum, called "a turning point in the gallery storyline" that depicted "the historic meeting that set the stage for all that followed."[19] It is at this turning point in the gallery, where display shifts from a heavily linear and ethnological emphasis on ancient artifacts to dioramas, that the visitor would encounter the *First Contact* site. This complex in situ display, through which the visitor was

1.1 First Contact mural image, Syncrude Gallery of Aboriginal Culture. Courtesy of the Royal Alberta Museum, Ethnology Program.

required to pass in order to access the rest of the gallery, served to prescribe the positioning of the visitor in the gallery through the strategic arrangement of objects that gave privileged sightlines only in very specified locations.

The visitor's encounter was a museological recreation of an event described in Anthony Henday's journal, a 1754 meeting between Henday and what some historians have assumed to be a Blackfoot chief.[20] Directly across from the reconstructed meeting site was a large mural depicting the view of the presumed Blackfoot camp from the Henday party's point of view. An elaboration of the latter in relation to the dynamics of identification will follow, but I would like to begin with the constructed tipi meeting site.

Henday was a Hudson's Bay Company employee sent to persuade people of the prairies to participate in the fur trade. In his meeting with a presumed leader of the Blackfoot Nation, as depicted in this exhibit, he is accompanied by Cree guide and interpreter, Attickasish, to facilitate communications, and a Cree woman whose role is not specified. In Henday's journal, he referred to the people he met using the Cree word *Archithinue*, which means "stranger." The temporal period of the reconstruction is intended to represent negotiations between Henday and a presumed Blackfoot leader after a shared feast, the smoking of pipes, and the exchange of gifts. The arrangement of the tableau in the *First Contact* tipi site was accompanied by a soundscape that attempted to depict aurally what might have been conveyed at this first meeting. In addition to the reconstructed tipi environment and soundscape, the display included didactic panels, the mural, and a "copy" of Henday's journal.

All of the site's elements were carefully combined to deliver a coherent story line intended to neutralize the significance of this meeting in the context of colonial history. The display text, entitled "A Journey Inland," asserted: "The encounter was played by their [the Blackfoot Nation's] rules, not his [Anthony Henday's]," and invited the visitor to feel empathy for Henday as "other." The constructed scene had the figure of Henday seated next to that of the tribe's leader on the ground in the tipi, ostensibly conforming to "the rules" of the Blackfoot people. The constructed tableau of the first meeting, hence, illustrated the accompanying didactic panel "A Journey Inland," rather than the text on the panel providing context for the display as a visitor might expect.

The depiction of Henday's initial meeting with the Blackfoot was intended to represent the beginnings of the historical process that would eventually dissolve the buffalo economy that for a time sustained the Indigenous peoples of the plains in relative autonomy from the market expansion carried out by the Hudson's Bay Company. The portrayal of Henday as a passive "guest" of the Blackfoot operated also as a neutralization of this colonial process. The gallery display panels then inform museum visitors that the leader of the Archithinue did not agree to send members of his camp with furs to Hudson Bay and that Henday returned to Hudson Bay, "his mission a failure."[21] Participation in the fur trade was presented as a choice to be freely taken or refused between mutually respecting agents.

1.2 Henday fur trade diorama, Syncrude Gallery of Aboriginal Culture. Courtesy of the Royal Alberta Museum, Ethnology Program.

I would like to turn to the mural that was situated across from the tipi construction, noting that the visitor would be positioned under the tipi in this section of the gallery. While I am treating the two aspects of the *First Contact* site in reverse chronology, given that the mural depicted the scene upon Henday's approach and the tipi site depicted a formal meeting that occurred sometime following initial greetings and introductions, visitors tended to observe the tipi first and the mural second. Authority for the account of this first meeting was granted by the institutionalized cultural preference for textual documentation and its inclusion in official records. Phil Stepney observed with respect to the *First Contact* diorama that museum planners made "a conscious decision to bring elements of non-Aboriginal culture into the story at critical points."[22] While this makes sense, it remains unclear why this decision would be made in this particular instance and in a way that so heavily invites visitor identification with a non-Aboriginal protagonist, although it may reflect an institutional preference for written documents. If so, it is worthwhile to give attention to the ways in which underlying epistemological assumptions and preferences can operate over and above the explicit and careful intentions of curators, which may be at odds with the concrete power effects of disciplinary practices. The planners of this gallery did articulate care for the present in their production of the past. However, the central object that was deployed to hold the *First Contact* diorama together was a facsimile of Anthony Henday's journal, which rested on a stand that was centrally located in the foreground of the mural. The document was opened to an excerpt that described the scene that Henday reportedly saw as he approached the Archithinue camp. Yet, drawing from Barbara Belyea's study of the Henday journal, the document raises further questions regarding the coherency of the First Contact story, as given in the SGAC.

First, while Henday reportedly sent his journal to the London office of the Hudson's Bay Company, the current location of the original is not known. Second, there are four different manuscript versions of Henday's journal, and these different iterations contradict each other in significant ways.[23] Belyea observes that "the four extant texts are rife with differences and contradictions. Even entries which record the same details – for example, the entries for 26 and 27 June; 2–4, 14, 26–28 July; 6–7, 15 August; 17–18 September [1754] – differ from each other in terms of vocabulary, proper names, turns of phrase and 'accidentals' (dating, capitalization, punctuation)."[24]

Third, Henday's journal describes two hundred tents in two rows, and yet this description is not consistent with the traditional way in which tipis are understood to have been arranged. The gallery's supporting text acknowledges this perplexing discrepancy and offers a few hypotheses (e.g., trade and defence purposes) as to why these particular tents did not conform to traditional placement, which is described in plains oral culture as circular.[25] The accuracy of Henday's account, or even his authorship of this text, was not seriously questioned, even though the descriptions within it seem to be inconsistent with European cultural standards of documentation. For instance, the gallery's documentation observes that Henday did not record any of the names of the people he met on his journey. Despite all of this, the mural astonishingly reproduced the arrangement of tipis on the camp of the Archithinue in rows according to the Henday journal description. Hence, Henday's journal as an instance of simulacra – a copy of an original that is missing, fragmented, or fictional – played a key role in establishing not only the authority and discursive script of First Contact, but that of the whole of the gallery to the extent that First Contact was understood by the gallery planners as a pivotal point in consideration of post-colonial Aboriginal culture.[26]

With respect to identification, I want to highlight the significance of the *First Contact* site in terms of how it served to order visitors in relation to display elements and to co-opt visitors in specific ways. In particular, the mural played a crucial role in visitor identification. In order to see the mural fully, the visitor not only had to stand centrally in front of it but had to stand directly in front of Henday's journal. The journal and the mural jointly positioned the visitor in Henday's place of arrival, standing before the people he came to meet. This positioning implicates the visitor by inviting identification with Henday rather than with the Archithinue. Thus presented from Henday's point of view, First Contact in the former SGAC was the story of a white protagonist, who attempted to entreat the "strangers" into the economy of the fur trade. In this way, the relative locations of visitor and representation of the other, as determined by placement, were instrumental at the level of identification in a crucial way. Notably, what Alison Griffiths refers to as the "interpellation of historical witnesses"[27] was relevant to the processes of identification and contact in the SGAC, especially at the key location of First Contact. The gallery visitor always arrives just in time not only to witness this event as an amicable exchange that ends with the uncompromised agency of the Archithinue but to witness it from the place – both literal and figural – in which Anthony Henday stood.

The act of witnessing, or bearing witness, is a recurring theme in discussions of museums and memorials that deal with extraordinary and painful histories. This sentiment is noted in the following quotation:

> The presentation of one's heritage in a museum can provide an emotional opportunity for self-realization; it can provide an enduring, vivid, public testimonial to historical truths. If these historical truths are then used to foster healing, weaken stereotypical thinking and promote cross-cultural understanding, then we have truly learned from our past. If we don't, our two cultures will continue to collide and walk separate paths. Our attempt to encapsulate these aspects of our shared experience and articulate them in an exhibit was seen as one way to give *witness* and assist with the healing process.[28]

Witnessing has its major significance when the events being depicted are not yet concluded, yet willfully forgotten, and this is why we must give attention to such enactments and not just to the event that is constructed for witnessing.

Scene of Address 2: Visitor always arrives out of time

Chief Kwakwabalasami's House is located in the First Peoples Gallery at the RBCM. The Chief's House, a setting for ceremonial dance, is a relatively open space, with few structural elements. There is a simulated fire in the centre of the room and an accompanying opening in the ceiling to free the smoke, which amplifies the openness of the space. Near the fire lie two ceremonial masks. On either side of the interior of the entrance, there are story poles; at the opposite wall, which is the focal point of the house, there is a dance screen. To the left of the dance screen are two carved benches at the corner.

The Chief's House is accompanied by very little text. There is only a small plate on the wall, which would be encountered upon one's exit of the room (to the right of the dance screen), assuming visitors are moving through the space as encouraged by the overarching museum design.[29] The plate gives only the most basic contours of the house's status. Visitors are told that this house is a replica built by the chief's son and grandson; that it, and not just the house it replicates, is the site of important ceremonies.

1.3 Inside of Jonathan Hunt's House. Courtesy of the Royal BC Museum and Archives.

It indicates that there are dancers who come out from behind the screen. Nothing within the space is labelled, described, or named. The story poles are not interpreted. The visitor is not instructed about who sits in which seat. What one understands when coming upon this house is that, unless one has participated in ceremonies like the ones that are practised here, one does not *understand* it – more importantly, one does not know it. Although the visitor is invited here for a time – welcomed even – this place is not necessarily for all visitors *to know*. Instead, visitors without experiential understanding are invited to wonder, question, and imagine, but not to know.

The instructive imperative that accompanies some curatorial practices involving the description of objects for public audiences is suspended somewhat here, with significant potential for visitor interpellation. I am not suggesting that there is a politically oppositional and transformative promise in what appears to be a relatively hands-off approach in this aspect of the First Peoples Gallery. Rather, I suggest that the Chief's House stands for itself, with neither "expert" analysis (with its sense of cutting up) imposed from some external position nor explanation, and is without the imposition of nodal points of completion as to its constitutive meaning. Hence, the Chief's House invokes a sense of reverence and reflection from the visitor that was not achieved in the RAM's SGAC.

The reverential and reflective characteristics of the Chief's House, however, are not produced only by virtue of the lack of textual anchoring but also by the openness of the space and the way in which visitors can and do occupy and move through the space in multiple ways.[30] The space produces a complex site of identification, due largely to the lack of prescribed positioning of its visitors and structural constraints on their movements. The Chief's House also refrains from assuming the identity of its visitors. In observing the heterogeneous ways in which people take up this space relative to the spaces on either side of the Chief's House – with either hesitancy or appropriation, but usually sequentially both – there is a clear demarcation of spatial possibility in the Chief's House. People tend to pause once they have entered it, and then they start to move around it. The initial hesitation is noteworthy – there is a palpable sense that this is a different sort of space, one in which the institutional museum ethos is suspended. This suspension is highlighted in the immediacy of its contents and the lack of didactic panels. The ceremonial masks are neither encased in glass nor surrounded in rope. This has paradoxical effects on visitors. On the one hand, visitors initially appear to be uncertain as to how to take up the space, and exercise restraint on their movements. On the other hand, visitors do tend to relax in the space after a brief stasis in their movement. This stasis is more pronounced for visitors who arrive when the house is relatively empty. Many visitors do sit down in the space. Commonly, visitors take photographs, either of friends and family or of the space vacant of others. Some visitors try to contextualize the space, aided by the one plate, but this is not the most frequent reaction. The achievement of distance, whether spatial, temporal, or epistemological, seems to be an undesirable aim for museums. Within colonial contexts, however, aura can operate against the violences inherent in hegemonic curatorial practices that too often produce technical "experts" and then "christen" visitors who are imagined to have had something imparted to them as *knowing* subjects, while producing represented peoples as *known* subjects.[31]

The suspension of linear temporality in particular is an attribute that roughly characterizes many of the didactic panels in the other sections of the First Peoples Gallery, as artifacts are often not dated in this gallery. A gallery interpreter noted that amongst the masks, art, clothing, and other displayed items, there are often contemporary artifacts alongside the ancient ones – yet these are not denoted as such. This practice stands in sharp opposition to that of the RAM, where dating was highly privileged toward showing a cultural evolution and a technical prowess. At times, the attention to dating was so pronounced that it threatened to subsume Aboriginal cultures under the showcasing of archeological mastery. With respect to archeological practices, Heather Devine observes the influential predominance of Lewis Binford's processual archeology in the latter part of the twentieth century. Binford's approach appeals to the cultural evolutionism of his mentor, cultural anthropologist Leslie White. Devine credits First Nations protest movements – for example, the Lubicon boycott of *The Spirit Sings* exhibition – for providing the impetus for a move toward "post-processual" approaches that more readily embrace community-based and dialogically based research. Devine notes that this is significant because "[the Binford philosophy] ignored the fact that research conceived and carried out within the social and intellectual context of colonialism is fundamentally biased."[32]

Therefore, in sharp contrast to the attention to temporal precision that was expressed in the processual techniques deployed in parts of the SGAC, one finds that in the Chief's House at the First Peoples Gallery the temporality of the visitor's arrival imposes a productive distance or "aura," in part because the visitor's arrival is always out of time. That is, there is a sense that an event has just occurred. It is an event that was missed and has not been witnessed. Thus, for many visitors, the spatial operation of the Chief's House invokes a visitor subject who did not see and does not know.

The Contact Zone and the Witness

While I acknowledge that there was extensive consultation with Indigenous peoples in the design and planning of the SGAC, on the one hand, it must be noted that Clifford's work on museums focuses directly on the consultation process as a contact zone, as Pratt conceives it, one that is "usually involving conditions of coercion, radical inequality, and intractable conflict."[33] Further, consultation is not the same thing as collaboration. On the other hand, consideration of the spatialization of the in situ display of *First Contact* that was in the SGAC illustrates that it derived its testimony from Henday's journal as witness and then, through largely spatial mechanisms combined with a linguistic supplement, attempted to transfer the status of witness to the visitor through a dramatic scene of address and interpellation into Henday's place. This spatial deployment involves what could be called a synchronic form of witnessing, similar to the "imperialist spectatorship" that Julia Emberley finds deployed by the colonial archive's classificatory and normalizing strategies onto photographs of Indigenous peoples.[34]

What I am calling synchronic witnessing is quite different from the kind of witnessing that Emberley calls for, which is illustrated in the following quotation: "To unlearn and to learn as a non-Native to be a witness to colonial history and to speak to that history of representational violence means to make visible the *mechanisms* (i.e., the technologies and classificatory techniques of representation) that produce and reproduce its violence."[35] While accepting the full and crucial force of Emberley's stress on making mechanisms of violence visible and her appeal to an active, historical engagement, I would like to see a move away from the concept of witnessing altogether in addressing contact and identification in the gallery. To be clear, the kind of synchronic witnessing deployed at the Anthony Henday diorama was of quite a different order than the witnessing that Emberley invokes in her work, which can only come from a place external to the kinds of disciplinary practices that produced the First Contact site. What is striking here, given the reliance on the Henday journal to underpin the authority of this testament, is that Belyea, in her extensive work with the Henday manuscripts, seems to identify a similar mechanism in the production of these documents when she writes of the Henday entries:

The very strictness with which the empirical categories are accounted for is an indication of the degree to which the journal *prescribed* what the explorer was to observe. Its conformity with [Hudson's Bay Company factor, James] Isham's instructions shows the extent to which initial expectations guided the explorer's [Henday's] comportment as scientific explorer and trading agent. There is very little descriptive variance or spontaneous action, except perhaps in details of Henday's hunting adventures.[36]

Emberley's notion of the witness is one that is inextricably tied to the kinds of inheritance that can be hoped for from an a-disciplinary mode of address. Too often, consultation with source communities results in applying museum techniques to Indigenous contributions that are inherently coercive, even violent. The Question is: Do curatorial practices that require the visitor to act as a third-party "witness" to the event being staged result in the visitor making value judgments on the meaning of contact? Or, does the visitor become a participant? The position of witness grants authority in the first place, and it grants this authority over a fragmented, detached, and hyperreal event in the second place for which very real social formations and practices will be substituted and judged outside of the gallery. The readiness to invoke and to produce visitors as witnesses of displays that bear witness is tied to the mechanism of reiterative contact zones that redeploy and continually enact the relations of coercion and inequality that Pratt identifies with contact zones.

It ought to be noted that Clifford critiques the First Peoples Gallery at the RBCM as one that offers an overarching and "nonoppositional completeness," noting that "to identify an object as 'used in the potlatch' is not the same as showing it to be property from a specific potlatch and part of an ongoing cultural struggle."[37] The force of his critique is of political significance, and it signals the silences imposed onto the gallery. Yet this discussion suggests that some of the spatial gaps and silences found in the RBCM offer openings rather than hegemonic closures that interpellate knowing visitors or witnesses. Instead, the subversion of disciplinary practices and the edifying museum imperative can contribute to the possibilities of testament that Roger Simon has addressed, which are consistent with Emberley's conception of the witness.

Simon calls for a testament as a gift such that "no single beneficiary can be said to be capable of rendering the full meaning and significance of this testament" so that its inheritance demands "affirming its receipt through our non-indifference and reassessing its significance by reading, sifting, judging, and sorting out its possible meanings."[38] The signifying potential of the unique conditions presented by the Chief's House, given that the original's ceremonial attributes are transferred to this in situ display so that the house is in fact used for ceremonial purposes, retains a special and paradoxical status that potentially unhinges it from the overarching regimes of hegemonic representation within the hegemony of the institution, and forecloses the possibility of synchronic witnessing.

Notes

1. I would like to express appreciation to this volume's editors and readers, as well as acknowledge support from the University of Lethbridge Research Fund for the spatial studies of galleries upon which this essay is based.

    James Clifford, *Routes: Travel and Translation in the Late Twentieth Century* (Cambridge, MA: Harvard University Press, 1997).

2. Barbara Kirshenblatt-Gimblett, *Destination Culture: Tourism, Museums, and Heritage* (Berkeley: University of California Press, 1998), 47.

3. "Syncrude Gallery of Aboriginal Culture," Royal Alberta Museum. Edmonton, Alberta, Canada. This chapter is informed by mappings of the former SGAC in December 1999 and observations of visitors' movements 14-17 June, 2011.

4. Mary Louise Pratt, *Imperial Eyes: Travel Writing and Transculturation*, 2nd ed. (London: Routledge, [1992] 2008).

5. Concerning the relationship between tar sands development and material well-being see, for instance, Jennifer Huseman and Damien Short, "'A Slow Industrial Genocide': Tar Sands and the Indigenous People of Northern Alberta," *International Journal of Human Rights* 16, no. 1 (2012): 216–37, esp. 230. Also see Clinton N. Westman, "Social Impact Assessment and the Anthropology of the Future in Canada's Tar Sands," *Human Organization* 72, no. 2 (2013): 111–20.

6. Douglas Cole, *Captured Heritage: The Scramble for Northwest Coast Artifacts* (Vancouver: University of British Columbia Press, 1995); Gloria Jean Frank, "That's My Dinner on Display: A First Nations Reflection on Museum Culture," *BC Studies* 125/126 (2000): 163–78; Aldona Jonatis, *Art of the Northwest Coast* (Seattle: University of Washington Press, 2006).

7. Cole, *Captured Heritage*, 227.

8. Ira Jacknis, "Repatriation as Social Drama: The Kwakiutl Indians of British Columbia, 1922–1980," in *Repatriation Reader: Who Owns American Indian Remains?*, ed. Devon Mihesuah (Lincoln: University of Nebraska Press, 2000), 266–81.

9   Jacknis, "Repatriation as Social Drama," 270; Catherine Bell and Val Napoleon, eds., *First Nations Cultural Heritage and Law: Case Studies, Voices and Perspectives* (Vancouver: University of British Columbia Press, 2008), 75.

10 Frank, "That's My Dinner on Display," 163–78.

11 Heather Devine, "After The Spirit Sang: Aboriginal Canadians and Museum Policy in the New Millennium," in *How Canadians Communicate III: Contexts of Canadian Popular Culture*, ed. Bart Beaty, Derek Briton, Gloria Filax, and Rebecca Sullivan (Edmonton: Athabasca University Press, 2010), 218; Frances W. Kaye, *Hiding the Audience: Viewing Arts & Arts Institutions on the Prairies* (Edmonton: University of Alberta Press, 2003), particularly chapter 5, which meticulously unpacks and situates the struggles surrounding the exhibition as it was still in preparation, within a broader analysis of the shift that has occurred in the Glenbow Museum's audience over the institution's history.

12 Moira McLoughlin, *Museums and the Representations of Native Canadians: Negotiating the Borders of Culture* (New York: Garland, 1999), 11.

13 Tom Hill and Trudy Nicks, eds., *Turning the Page: Forging New Partnerships Between Museums and First Peoples*, 2nd ed. (Ottawa: Assembly of First Nations and the Canadian Museums Association, 1992).

14 Devine, "After the Spirit Sang," 229.

15 Philip H.R. Stepney and David J. Goa, eds., *The Scriver Blackfoot Collection: Repatriation of Canada's Heritage* (Edmonton: Provincial Museum of Alberta, 1990).

16 Quoted in Rocky Woodward, "Scriver Accused of Violating Trust," *Windspeaker* 8, no. 7 (1990), http://www.ammsa.com/publications/windspeaker/scriver-accused-violating-trust (accessed 20 June 2013).

17 Duncan Thorne, "Native Anger Rising over Murals," *Edmonton Journal*, 19 February 1997.

18 Gerry Conaty, "Glenbow's Blackfoot Gallery: Working Towards Coexistence," in *Museums and Source Communities: A Routledge Reader*, ed. Laura Peers and Alison Brown (London: Routledge, 2003), 240. Also, Kaye points to the exhibition *Reclaiming History: Ledger Drawings by the Assiniboine Artist Hongeeyesa* as a signal of the Glenbow's changing perception of audience and growing interest in addressing Indigenous audiences: *Hiding the Audience,* 179–83.

19 Philip H.R. Stepney, "Development of the Syncrude Canada Aboriginal Peoples Gallery," *Alberta Museums Review* 23, no. 3 (1997): 36.

20 The implication of witnessing this meeting is crucial and will be addressed later in the discussion.

21 Susan Berry and Jack Brink, *Aboriginal Cultures in Alberta: Five Hundred Generations* (Edmonton: Provincial Museum of Alberta, 2004), 32.

22 Stepney, "Development of the Syncrude Canada Aboriginal Peoples Gallery," 36

23 Barbara, Belyea, ed., *A Year Inland: The Journal of a Hudson's Bay Company Winterer* (Waterloo, ON: Wilfrid Laurier University Press, 2000), 20.

24 Ibid., 21.

25 Berry and Brink, *Aboriginal Cultures in Alberta,* 32.

26 My objection to the use of a "copy" of an absent original in this case has little to do with the strength of evidence that it provides. Rather, the point is that this story joins forces with the heavily scientific discourse of the ethnological exhibits in the gallery

that lends it the authorization of Western science and undermines, for instance, the Indigenous creation stories that were given at the entry of the gallery. For an analysis of the "500 Generations" video presentation in the former SGAC, see Kimberly Mair, "Putting Things in their Place: The Syncrude Gallery of Aboriginal Culture at the Royal Alberta Museum and the Idiom of Majority History," in *Canadian Literature and Cultural Memory*, ed. Cynthia Sugars and Eleanor Ty (Don Mills, ON: Oxford University Press, 2014), 39–52. Related to the struggle between epistemological assumptions and evidence surrounding material objects, such as clovis points (which were used to grant authority in the SGAC), see Vine Deloria, Jr. *Red Earth, White Lies: Native Americans and the Myth of Scientific Fact* (New York: Scribner, 1995), 108–10.

27 Alison Griffiths, *"Shivers Down Your Spine": Cinema, Museums, and the Immersive View* (New York: Columbia University Press, 2008), 50.

28 Stepney, "Development of the Syncrude Canada Aboriginal Peoples Gallery," 36. Emphasis added.

29 Although the Chief's House is frequently approached from the exit, the plate is located behind the visitor and is rarely observed by those visitors entering through the exit.

30 I observed this space specifically over a period of four consecutive days (12–15 June 2012).

31 Contrasted with the hierarchical and one-directional models of "knowledge" exchange are Indigenous ways of knowing that are relational, story-based, and acknowledge the significance of silence. See Julia V. Emberley, "Epistemic Heterogeneity: Indigenous Storytelling, Testimonial Practices, and the Question of Violence in Indian Residential Schools," in *Reconciling Canada: Critical Perspectives on the Culture of Redress*, ed. Jennifer Henderson and Pauline Wakeham (Toronto: University of Toronto Press, 2013), 149.

32 Devine, "After the Spirit Sang," 225.

33 Pratt, *Imperial Eyes*, 8.

34 Emberley addresses photographs in a digitized archive associated with the RBCM. In part, she shows that captions are used to impose normalizing familial orderings on those who have been photographed. Julia V. Emberley, *Defamiliarizing the Aboriginal: Cultural Practices and Decolonization in Canada* (Toronto: University of Toronto Press, 2007), 178.

35 Ibid., 179.

36 Belyea, *A Year Inland*, 371.

37 Clifford, *Routes: Travel and Translation in the Late Twentieth Century*, 137.

38 Roger I. Simon, "The Terrible Gift: Museums and the Possibility of Hope without Consolation," *Museum Management and Curatorship* 21 (2006): 195.

2

Discombobulated Remnants?: Preserving LGBTTTIQ Histories[1]

Cheryl Avery and Shelley Sweeney

Records are the foundation of any history, whether those records are published or unpublished, contemporaneous or later, oral or textual, and so on. Records created in the normal course of activity that are deemed of permanent value are acquired by a variety of archives. But much conspires against the acquisition of such records. The process from creation to preservation is filled with opportunities for loss. "Complete" collections, particularly those documenting the lives of individuals, are rare. Within this context, to have archival repositories described as "institutions that ... contain discombobulated remnants of human experience"[2] is not entirely unexpected. On the whole, disconcerting fragmentation within collections is not the result of malice, but of time and chance and human nature. But what of the broader scope – not specific collections, but documentation of whole segments of society? Our attention was drawn to the work of a graduate student at York University, whose research took him to the archives in a small town in Saskatchewan where he hoped to find evidence of the history of the local gay community. Instead he found "silences and absences," yet it was in those very spaces that the archives became "full: full of questions [and] power relations." Ultimately, the experience left him wondering about the very existence of the LGBT community's history, asking, "Where do we find ourselves?"[3]

Significant absences in the evidentiary record can only diminish us as a society, and so this chapter began as a brief exploration of that question.

The approach was twofold. We set out to determine the extent to which public archives in Canada, and those in Western Canada in particular, have retained a record of the LGBT experience. We also sought to identify and consider the various factors which have affected, or still do affect, the collection of those records. We began by examining our own institutions' LGBT resources. We then reviewed some of the responses to an earlier survey on archivists' values.[4] We further surveyed Canadian archivists to get a glimpse of current practice in acquisition, description, and access, to try to determine the relationships between archivists and donors, and to ascertain how archivists viewed LGBT materials generally. To a large extent we were influenced by our own experiences as Western Canadian archivists and were interested in seeing if our institutional experiences were common or exceptional. We also reviewed existing descriptions available on ArchivesCanada, the Canadian Council of Archives national database of archival holdings, and its constituent parts from each province and territory.[5] It is important to note, however, that archival associations in the West – from British Columbia to Manitoba, and extending to both the Yukon and the Northwest Territories – were significantly in advance of other regions when it came to creating and populating their provincial database of holdings. In part this was due to a high degree of co-operation between the western provinces; but they were also simply in the vanguard of this work. For a variety of reasons, despite its national scope, Western Canada remains better represented on ArchivesCanada than the Maritime provinces. Additionally, some significant collections – the archives of the University of Toronto, McGill, or the Canadian Lesbian and Gay Archives, for example – have not been added. This unquestionably gave our survey of holdings a western bias but has not invalidated our observations.

Not surprisingly, many of the issues brought to light by our surveys have been the subject of a great deal of scholarship in the field of archival theory. However, we discovered very little relating archival theory specifically to any identifiable type of record or to LGBT holdings in particular. The closest related study we found was a survey of an allied profession, librarians, in South Africa. In that paper, the impact of the South African constitution was instructive: the concept that "difference should not be the basis for exclusion, marginalization and stigma" has been legally upheld in various instances, importantly (in one ruling) with the observation that "acceptance of difference is particularly important in South Africa with its history of discrimination." Yet this was clearly still a point for argument and persuasion, not a foundational principle reflected in changed behaviour. More interestingly was the authors' second "motivation": the "mission of the public library to contribute to social inclusion and justice."[6] In this, there was a direct connection with archival theory. In particular, archival literature analyzes identity – specifically community identity – and its impact on the development of thematic archives.[7] Institutional mission statements, and differences between community-based archives and collections found within (often larger) "mainstream" archives, are a focus of this literature.[8] Work has also been done collating existing holdings, most notably with the Society of American Archivists' "Lavender Legacies Guide."[9] To date, no similar national, thematic guide has been created in either Western Canada or in Canada as a whole, and we found no other survey of archivists – in any country – specifically addressing the impact of the individual professional on the acquisition and accessibility of the records of an identifiable group.

A full discussion of the shifting attitudes toward the LGBT community is impossible here, but a few dates are important in terms of official Canadian policy. Homosexual activity, particularly between men, had been deemed an "offence" at least as early as 1777[10] in what is now Canada. "Gross indecency," an ill-defined term but once again specific to an activity between men, was entered into the Criminal Code in 1890.[11] In 1953 the wording was amended to be more inclusive: "*Every one* who commits an act of gross indecency with another person is guilty of an indictable offence [emphasis added]."[12] Another significant change to the law did not begin to take place until 1967, when (then) Justice Minister Pierre Trudeau famously noted that "there's no place for the state in the bedrooms of the nation … what's done in private between adults doesn't concern the Criminal Code."[13] On 14 May 1969, Bill C-150 was passed, decriminalizing homosexuality – in private and between consenting adults over twenty-one years of age. Although this did not provide full equality under the law for lesbian and gay Canadians, and certainly did nothing to diminish homophobia and various acts of discrimination, large and small, it was nevertheless a watershed moment.

The year 1969 was notable for two other events: the Stonewall Riots in New York, a "militant assertion of gay rights over [a] six-day period of rioting [against police]," and the subsequent (and very visible) establishment

2.1 "National Gay Conference 1975," Manitoba Gay & Lesbian Society Fonds, University of Manitoba Archives & Special Collections, A08-067, box 13, folder 10, item 16.

of the University of Toronto Homophile Association. Other Canadian organizations soon followed. Throughout the 1970s, however, there were continuing police raids on gay bars, meeting places, and bathhouses in Canada's major cities. A "national beacon moment" occurred on 5 February 1981, the day following one such raid on bathhouses in Toronto, when "over 3,000 protestors took to the streets to mobilize against the discriminatory arrests and unlawful invasion of these gay spaces."[14]

These events effectively politicized the LGBT individual twice: first through criminalization, then as part of a community actively pursuing human rights. Both criminality and activism have an impact on the nature of the archival record, where that record is retained, and how it is described. And whatever LGBT associations might have existed earlier, the shift in 1969 toward organized advocacy within the community also clearly created a potential dichotomy between personal records documenting an individual life and those of a social movement.

2.2 *Sensible Shoes News*: the newsletter of Saskatchewan's lesbian communities. May 2003. University of Saskatchewan Archives & Special Collections, Richards Collection HQ76.3 .C3S4

Our own institutions, the University of Saskatchewan Archives & Special Collections and the University of Manitoba Archives & Special Collections, have significant assemblages of LGBT archives. In the case of the University of Saskatchewan Archives, a former employee has been both instigator of the LGBT collection generally and a significant collector (and donor) of materials. As a long-time advocate for human rights, this individual has substantial ties throughout the LGBT community and has personally made the many introductions necessary for soliciting valuable collections. While LGBT archives are not part of the official collecting mandate of the University of Manitoba Archives, a significant and sizable collection was initiated through the donation of the Manitoba Gay

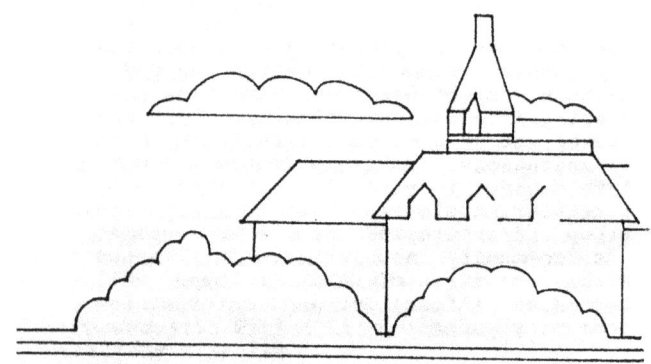

2.3 *Perceptions*, no. 1, March/April 1983: the longest continuously published gay and lesbian newsmagazine in Canada. University of Saskatchewan Archives & Special Collections, Richards Collection HQ76.3 .C3G3

and Lesbian Archives of the Rainbow Resource Centre in 2008.[15] That first organizational donation unleashed a flood of papers coming to the University of Manitoba Archives from individuals, which does not seem to be abating. Researcher response to this collecting has been swift and overwhelmingly positive: the LGBT archives are becoming one of the most popular series of private archival collections at the University of Manitoba.

In addition to our own institutions' significant LGBT archives, we were also aware of the recent acquisition by the University of Victoria's Transgender Archives, established in 2007, and the University of Winnipeg Archives and Records Centre of the Two-Spirited Collection in 2011 as indicators that Western Canadian public institutions are acquiring LGBT records.[16] The LGBT collections at these four institutions made us wonder about the nature and makeup of such collections at other archives in Western Canada and indeed the rest of Canada and, further, to wonder how those collections were acquired and what roles the archivists and the donors might have played in these acquisitions.

Two aspects of the early "Values" survey were suggestive, providing a broad framework for our more specific enquiry. First: Why might we even assume publicly funded archives are acquiring LGBT materials?[17] In most instances for *public* archives, collecting LGBT materials would require *private*-sector acquisition: Can we legitimately assume that, collectively, archivists are managing to do so in a broad and comprehensive manner?

In the "Values" survey, although just under 55 per cent per cent of archivists agreed to some extent with the statement that "archives document society as a whole," only 38 per cent agreed without qualification, suggesting most archivists are aware that the issue is complex and there may be gaps in the evidential record. As one respondent noted, this question was phrased in a manner that made the results unreliable. However, even a broad interpretation – that governments touch the lives of most individuals, so retention of government records alone document society – does not hold true for all communities, or tell a complete story. As has been noted, even early census records, so useful for much of social history, are silent on LGBT history; the question of sexual preference simply was not asked. And, for decades, most government interaction with the LGBT community was coloured by the perception of criminality, hardly conducive to a multi-dimensional record.

Many of the survey respondents indicated they had distinguished between the collective and the individual institution. That interpretation coincided with a belief that as a network, archives were acquiring broadly and documenting society comprehensively. More important, perhaps, were archivists' views on factors that might influence acquisition. A bare majority – 50.71 per cent – agreed to some extent with the statement that "archivists are in control of their acquisitions policies," but 81.69 per cent agreed that funders or sponsor agencies affected those policies. With this in mind, we would not have been surprised to see a number of respondents citing narrow acquisition mandates, or a move toward accepting sponsorial records only, as reasons why LGBT materials had not been collected.

The other interesting feature of the results of the questionnaire was a frank acknowledgement: just under 78 per cent of archivists agreed that they could not "avoid subjectivity in their acquisitions policies." Such self-awareness might in fact help mitigate uneven collecting practices, but also suggested at least the potential for some archivists to ignore LGBT records through personal bias, either consciously or unconsciously. Discrimination against the LGBT community would hardly be new.

Several historians argue that archivists have, in fact, actively destroyed LGBT history. For example, Martin Duberman writes that "all scholarship on sexuality was suspect – curtailed or suspended by archival custodians,"[18] Steven Maynard refers to "conscious and unconscious suppression of lesbian/gay materials in mainstream archives,"[19] and Gary Kinsman suggests that because "same-gender eroticism was stigmatized, historically valuable diaries and letters have not been preserved."[20] Finally, Marcel Barriault writes that "gay and lesbian materials had often been deemed by archivists to be of little or no historical value."[21] As Lisa Duggan bluntly stated, "lesbians and gay men have had their existence systematically denied and rendered invisible."[22] Clearly, archivists are thought to have been complicit in the loss of LGBT records.

The primary evidence for this is absence: researchers have failed to find early records relating to what is a known history. No written institutional policies against collecting LGBT material have yet been cited. However, there is anecdotal evidence that in some cases, suppression or destruction of relevant materials occurred. If true, then to what extent might this have happened? The appraisal decisions of individual archivists made while working through private fonds are not easily quantified; and even less so are the decisions of donors concerning privacy.

In our follow-up survey specifically about LGBT materials, we did not find significant evidence of overt bias on the part of archivists. That said, at least one of the responses was ambiguous at best. One of our questions asked why LGBT materials were not being collected, and one of the answers was, "Never been offered any. Never thought of going to look for any in the community. Don't really see the need to document this aspect of society – just as I don't see the need to document heterosexuality," which seemed to couch discrimination in liberal phrases. And, when asked if they would accept sexually explicit material (of any persuasion), at least some archivists recognized their own limits, together with the implication that had for research. For example, one respondent admitted, "I would not accept anything that could constitute child pornography ... I know this is a grey area in terms of sexuality studies, but it is not one I am willing to cross." Although the latter was not related to LGBT materials, both these responses do indicate the types of barriers archivists can create to halt the acquisition of any record. On the whole, however, there was a general sense that LGBT records were a valid area for acquisition, and no different from any other type of record in the archives' holdings. When asked if they had the same acquisition and access policies for controversial materials – hetero or homosexual – archivists overwhelmingly responded in the affirmative. "We don't make distinctions based on subject matter," one wrote.

But the sense that there was lack of interest among archivists, joined perhaps with distrust of publicly funded institutions by the LGBT community, has meant the development of private, community-run LGBT archives. An early, and initially viable, private archives in Western Canada was formally established in Winnipeg in 1988. The Winnipeg Gay/Lesbian Resource Centre was supported by the Manitoba Council of Archives and the Provincial Archives of Manitoba.[23] The centre gathered materials from a variety of sources, creating an exceptionally useful local resource. But with funding issues, the materials eventually ended up in storage – paid for by one individual – who finally donated the collection to the University of Manitoba Archives & Special Collections. Within the space of a few years the centre had gone from being cited as a community success story, to an inaccessible resource, to a problem, and finally, to incorporation within a larger institution. The largest independent archives is the Canadian

Lesbian and Gay Archives (CLGA) in Toronto, which was founded in 1973; it is largely volunteer-run and privately funded. Just how sustainable such institutions can be in the long run has yet to be determined: even the successful CLGA has had significant funding crises in the past and has been sustained largely by the extraordinary efforts of long-standing volunteers and donor bequests. And when we consider in the past decade the funding cutbacks to many archives, local, provincial and federal, such concern is not out of place.

But what of the opposite: active acquisition by public archives? Regardless of interest or willingness to house LGBT materials, only 56 per cent of archivists in our survey indicated they had LGBT materials; and only 26 per cent indicated their repository actively collected in that area. A majority (53 per cent) indicated LGBT materials had been found in personal papers acquired for other reasons; in such cases, 88 per cent indicated those materials would normally be retained. Most (61 per cent) would not consult with the donor before making the decision on retention, although many identified privacy as an issue, particularly when uncertain if the donor was fully aware of all the materials in the collection. Two comments in particular, however, stand out: "We inform donors as a matter of standard procedure in situations where appraisal leads to the *removal* of records [emphasis added]"; and "We do not destroy material that has archival value because someone does not approve of it." Both, as opposite approaches, are nevertheless essentially in agreement with another, quite firm, statement: "Retention is solely the decision of the archivist."

Curiously, if there was a suggestion of bias it was most clearly evident in the response to acquisition of "anti-gay" materials. Only 15 per cent indicated they had records of this kind – although as a means of documenting the LGBT experience, these records, which help identify the nature of discrimination and some social attitudes, are surely useful.

But there are several problems inherent simply in identifying the extent of relevant collections across the country. Not least is a changing lexicon: the Hungarian writer Karoly Maria Benkert first used the word "homosexual" in 1869, but the term did not enter into the English language until the 1890s through the work of Havelock Ellis and in medical literature.[24] "Transgender" is another, more recent, example, dating to the late 1980s;[25] and over time words such as "gay" or "queer" have transitioned from non-sexual terms, to slurs, to re-appropriation within the community.

All of these shifts have implications for description. More important for the issue of discovery, however, is the extended period when homosexual relationships were identified as criminal behaviour. At least until 1969 in Canada, that official categorization would have significantly affected how relevant resources would have been acquired, retained, and described.

For "official" sources, in particular for court records which have proven so useful in documenting gay history, descriptive records – including finding aids – are likely quite generic. Indeed, for any large record group – immigration or homestead records, for example – detailed indexes tend to follow, rather than anticipate, high researcher demand. Relevant information within sources like court records would likely not be found by specific descriptive terms provided by an archivist but by those researchers who understand the relationship between function and record and who are willing to spend time searching through the records.

The question of the archival response to personal fonds is even more interesting. Barriault suggests the loss of records was due not to overt censorship on the part of archivists but to a combination of concern over ethics, privacy, and donor reluctance: "There is much anecdotal evidence … to suggest that archivists routinely segregated records of a homosexual nature from the fonds they were processing, and returned these materials to the donors or to their heirs."[26] Few archivists would be as likely to return such records today, unless specifically requested to do so by the donor. This would bring the practice more into line with what archivists would do now with other personal concerns, such as keeping information about extramarital affairs in the papers, information which might be restricted but would not be removed.

Nevertheless, one must wonder if there were not also some archivists retaining these records, either by chance or design. The weight of being defined as "criminal" would have demanded a circumspect life to some degree, and may well have resulted in coded language being used by gay men and lesbians in some correspondence – or even in personal diaries; a language which archivists may or may not have interpreted correctly.[27] Even with clear or more explicit records, how might archivists have dealt with materials which were documenting activities then considered illegal? They almost certainly would not have signalled the fact in their descriptive records, which could have put at risk either the donor or other individuals. It seems reasonable to assume that at least some relevant records remain to be "discovered" in files, hidden under the generic rubric of "correspondence" or "diary." What is profoundly unlikely, however, is any significant action on the part of archivists to revisit old descriptions and process collections to create the "thorough, accurate cataloguing" necessary for easy discovery.[28] Indeed, when asked about their descriptive practices when dealing with any potentially sensitive materials in LGBT collections, our survey respondents admitted that "it usually just gets described at a fonds- or series-level in a general sort of way"; "we describe textual material at the folder level. Therefore, descriptions are usually vague"; and, along similar lines, "the records [are] described at the file level (subject files), and the file names don't create any issues,"[29] that is, the file titles alone may not provide any useful information for discovery of LGBT content. A number of comments were reflective not on the substance of archival description but its structure, possibly suggesting a neutral response from many archivists toward LGBT holdings. "Record the title proper and other title information based on the contents of the series, file, item, or publication" was typical of this type of response.[30]

At best we can say that specific language in archival description appears to have followed the broad shifts in public policy relating to the LGBT community. Our survey of materials accessible through ArchivesCanada revealed a relatively modern collection. We found 77 collections in total.[31] Based on the first year in inclusive dates, 68 per cent of the collections reflected materials created in 1960 or later. Only 4.16 per cent contained materials dating from before 1900. That survey also revealed a somewhat fragmentary collection: although collectively, these records amounted to 236 linear metres in total, half of the collections were 1 metre or less in extent. This amount cannot be considered extensive by any means. Although much work remains to be done in terms of adding descriptions to ArchivesCanada, unless the holdings of the CLGA are included, it does not seem likely that numerous LGBT collections will be added. British Columbia, with 22 collections, has the largest number, but this represents only 0.2 per cent of the BC holdings described online. Saskatchewan, with a smaller population and fewer archives, has 12 LGBT collections and does somewhat better proportionately, but LGBT materials still represent just 1 per cent of the total number of collections as available through that province's online descriptions.[32]

Only 14 of the 77 descriptions we found suggested collections documenting the "personal," through the correspondence, diaries, or known biography of a single individual. Another three collections – the records of an artist, a poet, and an unpublished literary manuscript – might be considered within this category as well. By contrast, 29 collections were directly related to issues of LGBT history and/or social justice, through the records of LGBT organizations specifically or within other institutions (for example, policies within religious denominations, at universities, etc.). Seven collections related to issues of health, most often HIV-AIDS, and ten were print collections (books, newsletters, or ephemera), the records of feminist bookstores, or publishers' records. As noted earlier, only four were records expressing "anti-gay" sentiment, including large collections such as the *Alberta Report* fonds, records of a weekly newsmagazine with a socially and politically conservative viewpoint.[33]

The difference between the number of collections documenting an individual and those documenting a social movement is surely a legacy of the decades of official persecution and continuing discrimination. As discussed, some early collections may actually contain evidence of sexuality not identified explicitly in descriptive records. But the opposite might also occur, in that the descriptive records might serve to narrowly focus on one facet of a person's life, emphasizing the notion of the homosexual as someone "whose very existence [is] defined by his sexuality."[34] And so to another, difficult aspect of acquiring LGBT collections: that of donor reluctance.

The graduate student whose work influenced our title asked his question – where do we find ourselves? – in the context of the small town, rural LGBT experience, and whether that history would be retained in local archives rather than in larger urban centres. As part of the constraint in establishing a local collection, he mentioned a gay lawyer who had placed an ad in *Perceptions*, published in Saskatoon since 1983 and the longest continuously published gay and lesbian newsmagazine in Canada. When this individual considered the magazine, he did so expecting it to be read in Saskatoon and Regina, Saskatchewan's larger cities – but suddenly felt uncomfortably "open" when he discovered the magazine was also being kept by his local library/archives.

The reluctance by some individuals to acknowledge aspects of their private life is exacerbated in the LGBT community through past and present discrimination, some of it violent. But such reluctance is not unique:

heterosexual donors may feel the same and, indeed, archivists may suggest the option of suppression. One donor noted an archivist had provided him with "the opportunity to excise what he called the embarrassing bits" in a personal fonds; the "letters and diaries, the intimate revelations." They were precisely the type of record, the donor noted, his "grandmother … would have consigned to the burning barrel because, she used to say, 'they are nobody's business.'"[35] Donors, too, may independently excise materials before they reach the archives; consider Henry James's statement that "a man has a right to determine, in so far as he can, what the world shall know of him and what it shall not."[36]

And increasingly, so too shall various levels of government. Rather than the "age of information," this might more accurately be termed the "age of privacy," as evidenced by both federal and provincial legislation concerning privacy generally, and its safeguards in any publicly funded sphere, in some instances with additional emphasis on health records and electronic records. But the influence of such legislation may extend these boundaries: there is little point in closing institutional records if the papers of a private individual could release the same information. Sexual orientation is not necessarily explicitly identified in all access legislation but is nevertheless normally considered the type of information meant as "personal," and therefore subject to access restrictions. When asked if they restricted personal names in LGBT archives if those names might reveal sexual orientation, archivists were evenly divided: half would restrict the information. Of those, 73 per cent cited existing privacy laws as the reason. Donors of every persuasion may have materials they consider "nobody's business," but the LGBT situation is unique. Archival literature has highlighted how uncomfortable even LGBT *researchers* may be, simply by undertaking research in public archives – Steven Maynard refers to his "trepidation,"[37] and K.J. Rawson notes the numerous "environmental cues" that signal to individuals whether or not they are welcome in an archives.[38] One must wonder, then, if archives might be considered to be not welcoming spaces for research, how easily could they be considered trusted repositories for the documents revealing the personal lives of individuals.

With so few and such relatively small collections, it seems clear that absences exist within the collective holdings for LGBT history in Canada's publicly funded archives, but the spectre of larger and growing absences is looming. The most surprising finding of our survey – certainly the most disturbing – was the number of responses which indicated archivists were taking a passive approach to collecting in general. "We are interested in this material but are not able to be proactive – we accept fonds as they are offered," wrote one respondent; another "did not have the time or resources to actively pursue" LGBT collections, despite identifying them in an acquisitions strategy. "Collecting is passive generally" was the consensus. Many apparently were willing to consider LGBT materials but only when specifically offered. It would seem the donor and not the archivist was more influential in determining the holdings of the archives. Only one respondent was proactive:

> We acquire material relating to all aspects of Vancouver's history and actively seek out archival material for those communities, such as the [LGBT] … communities, that we perceive as under-represented in our holdings. In addition, we have a good working relationship with the BC Lesbian and Gay Archives … we are proud of [our] acquisition, processing and access practices.[39]

Should this approach really stand out? Should it really be the exception, rather than the norm? Passive acquisition, to the point of inertia or complete moratoriums, is a significant issue for archives and one which clearly has implications well beyond LGBT records. Indeed, with shrinking budgets, non-existent grant funds to hire extra staff to process records, huge backlogs of unprocessed records, and overfull storage spaces, the pressure on archives is to slow down or stop acquisition entirely.

As it stands, the majority of the LGBT holdings we found on ArchivesCanada (44.11 per cent) were in university or college archives. The close ties between universities and the first LGBT movements may have encouraged leaders in the community to donate to a familiar place. This donation pattern may also reflect a willingness within universities to acquire more "special" collections, and undoubtedly reflects the growing trend in LGBT research. As one respondent noted, "Sexual diversity is a research interest among faculty hired by the university in recent years, which has encouraged the acquisition of private archives and collections of printed material that deal with this topic." Surprisingly, religious archives had the second-highest number of relevant holdings, at 20.5 per cent of the total.

Despite the fact that the federal and provincial archives are the largest in the country, their LGBT holdings were not extensive. Instead (at 14.7 per cent) they were tied for third place, together with municipal archives, the group most likely to claim a narrow mandate as the reason they had not actively pursued LGBT materials.

Several respondents did note limited mandates and particularly stretched resources when indicating why they were not collecting LGBT material: "volume of work," "do not have the resources," were typical comments. And indeed, we might look to increasing constraints from sponsor agencies willing to manage their own records but less inclined to acquire more broadly. In 2012 our largest archives, Library and Archives Canada (LAC), cut a significant number of positions in the private archives sphere but left those responsible for government records untouched. It has also long signalled its intention that "more will be done in cooperation with Canada's 800 plus archives," including the possible transfer of existing collections to those institutions "where they will get the greatest use and visibility."[40] These statements are generally interpreted by the Canadian archival community to mean the LAC will not only reduce its private-sector acquisition in the future but also de-accession a significant number of its existing non-governmental holdings and disperse them among other institutions. The trend away from active acquisition in private records is growing, exacerbated by funding and space issues affecting many Canadian archives. The question is: Will universities remain willing and able to acquire broadly as significantly larger, better-resourced and better-staffed institutions do not? *Should* archives document society as a whole? *Do* they, in fact, do this? In ten years' time these might prove useful questions to ask of Canadian archivists.

The existing LGBT holdings in Canada's publicly funded archives are not extensive, although those in Western Canada, particularly our own current institutions, are actively being added to. With passive acquisition, in particular, it is increasingly important for the LGBT "advocate/collector" to help ensure an appropriate record is preserved. Archives exist to reflect society: to ensure its authentic, reliable evidence of our lives and actions are preserved. But this is ultimately a joint project, that of donor and archivist together, and it requires public policy support. Some archivists are trying to acquire a broad spectrum of materials, despite narrowing mandates, but ultimately we cannot retain the record without at least some participation and action by individuals, organizations, and governments who understand the long-term value of retaining our shared history.

So we end where we began: asking where the LGBT community's history can be found. The answer, unfortunately, is: still fighting for recognition.

Notes

1. LGBTTTIQ refers to lesbian, gay, bisexual, transgender, transsexual, two spirit, intersex, and queer. Hereafter "LGBT." Portions of this paper were previously published by Cheryl Avery, "The Reticent Archives: Preserving LGBTTIQ Histories," *Comma* 2013, no. 1 (2014): 69–77.
2. From Bryan Ganaway's review of Carolyn Steedman's book *Dust: The Archive and Cultural History*, http://h-net.msu.edu/cgi-bin/logbrowse.pl?trx=vx&list=h-german&month=0307&week=b&msg=w3TdAIzWE3ofD77HMaHe5w&user=&pw= .
3. Joseph Wickenhauser, "Finding Ourselves: LGBTQ Archives and the Small Urban Centre," paper presented at the Knotty Encounters Interdisciplinary Graduate Student Conference, Toronto, Ontario, 3 March 2012.
4. Cheryl Avery, "Actions, Purposes and Values Survey." Hereafter referred to as "Values survey." Although useful, the results from both the "Values" survey and our subsequent LGBT survey cannot be considered conclusive. The surveys were both conducted over Arcan-L, the Canadian archivists' listserv, and were entirely voluntary; in both instances, the sample group was informative but not statistically conclusive.
5. At the time of writing, ArchivesCanada is in transition between platforms. The change is expected to enable significantly more entries to be added, and more regular updates.
6. Genevieve Hart and Ncumisa Mfazo, "Places for All? Cape Town's Public Library Services to Gays and Lesbians," *South African Journal of Library and Information Science* 76, no. 2 (2010): 98.
7. An excellent discussion of this can be found in Bill Lukenbill, "Modern Gay and Lesbian Libraries and Archives in North America: A Study in Community Identity and Affirmation," *Library Management* 23 (2002): 93–100.
8. See also Brittany Bennett Parris, "Creating, Reconstructing, and Protecting Historical Narratives: Archives and the LBGT Community," *Current Studies in Librarianship* 29, no. 1/2 (2005): 5–25.
9. See http://www2.archivists.org/groups/lesbian-and-gay-archives-roundtable-lagar/lavender-legacies-guide.
10. Gary Kinsman, *The Regulation of Desire: Homo and Hetero Sexualities*, 2nd ed. rev. (Montreal: Black Rose Books, 1996), 104.
11. Ibid., 102.
12. The wording had previously been "every male person." See "A History of Canadian Sexual Assault Legislation 1900–2000," http://www.constancebackhouse.ca/fileadmin/website/gr_indec.htm.
13. A clip of the news scrum with reporters can be viewed at the CBC's digital archives site: http://www.cbc.ca/player/play/1811727781.

14   For useful histories of the LGBT community in Canada, see Neil Richards's chronology on Saskatchewan Resources for Sexual Diversity (http://library2.usask.ca/srsd/history.php) and Graham Stinnett's essays for the Manitoba Gay and Lesbian Archives (http://www.umanitoba.ca/libraries/units/archives/digital/gay_lesbian/index.html).

15   See http://nanna.lib.umanitoba.ca/atom/index.php/manitoba-gay-and-lesbian-archives%3brad.

16   Based in part on promotional posts over Arcan-L.

17   Referred to hereafter simply as "public archives."

18   Martin Bauml Duberman, *About Time: Exploring the Gay Past* (New York: Sea Horse, 1986), xiii. Duberman suggests that in part this was due to sexuality being treated as "a shameful part of our history – diaries bowdlerized, relationships concealed, photographs and letters burned."

19   Steven Maynard, "'The Burning, Wilful Evidence': Lesbian/Gay History and Archival Research," *Archivaria* 33 (Winter 1991–92): 196.

20   Kinsman, *Regulation of Desire*, 66.

21   Marcel Barriault, "Hard to Dismiss: The Archival Value of Gay Male Erotica and Pornography," *Archivaria* 68 (Fall 2009): 225.

22   Lisa Duggan, "History's Gay Ghetto: The Contradictions of Growth in Lesbian and Gay History," in *Presenting the Past: Essays on History and the Public*, ed. S.P. Benson, S. Brier, and R. Rosenzweig (Philadelphia: Temple University Press, 1986), 284, quoted in Maynard, "The Burning, Wilful Evidence," 198.

23   The Manitoba Council of Archives is now the Association for Manitoba Archives. The Provincial Archives of Manitoba is now the Archives of Manitoba.

24   Kinsman, *Regulation of Desire*, 61.

25   K.J. Rawson, "Accessing Transgender // Desiring Queer(er?) Archival Logics," *Archivaria* 68 (Fall 2009): 124–25.

26   Barriault, "Hard to Dismiss," 225n17. In that instance, the family appeared eager to suppress evidence of a gay liaison.

27   A recent example, popularized through film, are the diaries of Yorkshire landowner Anne Lister, "uncovered" by a historian in the Calderdale archives, England.

28   Suzanne Fischer, "Nota Bene: If You 'Discover' Something in an Archive, It's Not a Discovery," *Atlantic*, 19 June 2012, http://www.theatlantic.com/technology/archive/2012/06/nota-bene-if-you-discover-something-in-an-archive-its-not-a-discovery/258538/.

29   Survey results, Shelley Sweeney and Cheryl Avery, survey on Canadian archivists' collection practices: LGBTTTIQ archives, conducted over Arcan-L.

30   Ibid.

31   Representing English-language descriptions only.

32   Figures based on Memory BC feature, "browse archival descriptions," which lists a total of 10,794 descriptions (http://memorybc.ca/;informationobject/browse); and the administrative site for the Saskatchewan Archival Information Network (SAIN), which lists 1,147 public fonds-level descriptions.

33 See John Lund, "Representation of Homosexuality in the *Alberta Report*" (paper presented at the annual meeting for the Association of Canadian Archivists, Calgary, Alberta, 15–17 May 2009), for an interesting discussion of LGBT images from this fonds.
34 Kinsman, *Regulation of Desire*, 68.
35 David Carpenter, "Private Life," in *Lights to Each Other: University of Saskatchewan Interdisciplinary Collections* (Saskatoon: University of Saskatchewan, 2004), 33.
36 As quoted in Andrew Taylor, "'The Same Old Sausage': Thomas Carlyle and the James Family," in *The Carlyles at Home and Abroad: Essays in Honour of Kenneth J. Fielding*, ed. D. Sorensen and R. Tarr (Surrey, UK: Ashgate, 2004), 126.
37 Maynard, "'The Burning, Wilful Evidence,'" 197.
38 Rawson, "Archival Logics," 127.
39 Leslie Mobbs, City Archivist and Director, Records and Archives, City of Vancouver.
40 Library and Archives Canada, "Modernization – Myth Busters," http://www.bac-lac.gc.ca/eng/about-us/modernization/Pages/Myth-Busters.aspx.

3

J.Z. LaRocque: A Métis Historian's Account of His Family's Experiences during the North-West Rebellion of 1885

Heather Devine

Introduction

Between 1867 and 1885, the Métis and their First Nations allies were the only Indigenous groups in the country to openly defy the newly established Canadian government. Under Prime Minister Sir John A. Macdonald, the fledgling government set out to secure the vast region of Western Canada in order to establish its dominion sea to sea, and to keep the region from falling into American hands. The Canadian annexation of Western Canada began with the purchase of Rupert's Land from the Hudson's Bay Company in 1869, a real estate transaction complicated by the refusal of the Métis people of Red River to allow their homeland to be sold. The Métis resistance to the actions of the Canadian government, which included the takeover of Fort Garry and the forced negotiation of land, religious, and language rights for the Métis, resulted in the creation of Manitoba. The eventual acquisition of the entire region of Rupert's Land, followed by the negotiation and signing of a series of numbered treaties with the tribal groups in what is now Manitoba, Saskatchewan, and Alberta, served to make these large areas of land available for agricultural settlement.

The government's failure to deliver on promises of land tenure to the Métis, followed by its failure to keep its treaty promises to the Blackfoot and Cree people now on reserves, resulted in a short but bloody uprising known as the Northwest Rebellion of 1885.[1] The revolt was successfully suppressed by the Canadian government, and the leader of the uprising, Louis Riel, was hanged for treason in November 1885. A series of changes to the Indian Act – most of them punitive – were made to prevent similar uprisings from taking place again. The Métis were issued scrip, a certificate payable to the bearer, for either agricultural land or cash, in recognition and extinguishment of their Aboriginal rights. Consequently, the remaining arable lands in the West were officially opened to agricultural settlement.

Life for the Métis after 1885 was difficult. Some of the Métis had troubles claiming and keeping their scrip, and by the turn of the twentieth century, these people were homeless, with no means of survival in the agricultural settlements that quickly sprang up. Some landless Métis chose to rely on hunting and gathering to survive, and soon migrated to isolated regions farther to the north and west where they could continue their traditional way of life.

But many of the Métis descendants of buffalo hunters and traders who had occupied the northern plains for generations chose to remain in the southern regions of Western Canada, despite widespread prejudice and discrimination due to their race, their religion, and their French and Indigenous languages. Moreover, the dominant historical narratives of the day branded the Métis as traitors to Canada, an impulsive, improvident, even violent people who had chosen to follow a madman.[2]

Between 1885 and 1914, an estimated three million people emigrated to Canada, and most of these immigrants were destined for Western Canada.[3] The pressure to gain access to arable land soon resulted in widespread discrimination against anyone who was foreign or non-white, did not speak English as their mother tongue, or practised Roman Catholicism. The Indians on reserves were largely ignored by the white population, as the punitive policies of the Indian Act severely restricted their movements off the reserve.[4]

By the 1920s and 1930s, a new, pathological Métis identity had entered the public consciousness, largely due to the economic and social marginalization that had accelerated since the collapse of the world economy in 1929. The Métis (colloquially referred to as "half-breeds") were considered to be a failed people, whose racial and cultural characteristics rendered them unfit to compete successfully in the New West. Their lack of formal education made it difficult for them to get permanent employment, and for those Métis unfortunate enough to be indigent, there was no free access to medical services or schooling. They populated the ditches beside the major roads, and led a precarious existence based on seasonal farm labour, handouts, some hunting and gathering, and petty crime. The transformation of the once-proud Métis into "The Road Allowance People" was complete – or almost complete.[5]

But there were other Métis who had avoided the fate of their less fortunate kin. It is often overlooked, or simply unacknowledged, that some Métis people had the resources necessary to weather the transition from a frontier to a settled society. These individuals, often part of officer families from the Hudson's Bay Company, or descended from the numerous families of independent traders in the region, had managed to establish small homesteads and secure title to their land. Some of these people also possessed a degree of formal education, and set out to adapt to the new economic reality forced upon them. Others had managed to establish kin and commercial relationships with the new arrivals, or maintained the remnants of older ties rooted in the fur trade society that once dominated the region. In order to function successfully in the racially charged, post-frontier environment of Western Canada, the "Respectable Métis," as they were sometimes called, chose to downplay their mixed ancestry publicly.[6] If they spoke Michif or Cree or Saulteaux or French, they did so at home, with their relatives and friends. Some also quietly chose not to pass along these languages to their children, as they were no longer considered useful skills. The beaded clothing, the kinnikinnick, and the buffalo guns were tucked away under beds, in boxes and trunks, and in closets. The songs and stories of the past remained in the minds and hearts of the old people, to be shared on special occasions like *Le Jour D'An* (New Year's Day). Their children went to school, became adults, and intermarried with their non-Métis neighbors.

Over time, the external trappings of Métis culture and heritage had been suppressed so profoundly that by the late twentieth century, it appeared as if the diverse Métis communities scattered throughout the southern regions of Western Canada had completely vanished from the landscape.[7] In fact, they had not. As interest in Métis culture and heritage grew after the centenaries of the 1869 and 1885 Métis uprisings, a new generation of researchers would revisit the historical documents of the nineteenth century, looking for information that would shed light on the lives of previously neglected racial and gender minorities, and provide usable data for the political and legal battles following the patriation of Canada's Constitution in 1982.[8]

Across Western Canada and into the northern United States, various cultural organizations and projects were launched to compile and preserve Métis folklore and music.[9] But what also emerged was a large body of both published and unpublished work, some written by Métis people themselves, some written by people who lived and worked alongside the Métis. These published works were not in the form of school textbooks or scholarly, "academic" histories. Instead they thrived in a largely neglected genre of literature – the field of vernacular history.[10]

Vernacular history: A definition

What is vernacular history? Recent scholarship by Western Canadian historian Lyle Dick sets out to introduce the term "vernacular history," to define the characteristics of this genre, and to provide a framework for examining non-academic sources of historical information in order that they might take their rightful place within a broader, more inclusive conception of what academics define as "historiography."[11]

The origin of the term "vernacular history" is partially rooted in existing definitions of "vernacular literature" and "vernacular architecture." Vernacular literature, by and large, refers to any literature written in the everyday speech of the common people. In terms of European literature, vernacular literature was any written work that was not expressed in Latin. Vernacular architecture is the term used to describe buildings that are built using local, traditional techniques and materials, and are not designed by professional architects.

The term "vernacular history" as discussed by Lyle Dick, is "grassroots historical practice in North America in the nineteenth and twentieth centuries."[12] Like vernacular literature and vernacular architecture, vernacular history is a product of the common people, in that it tends to be composed of information collected from, and compiled by, citizens of local communities.

> Vernacular historians have ranged from community historians to individual scholars to so-called history buffs, and their practice has assumed many forms, from informal pioneer reminiscences to highly crafted works of scholarship, exemplifying varying levels of talent, experience, and imagination.[13]

The authors of these grassroots histories may incorporate information from secondary historical sources produced elsewhere but tend to rely on their own personal experiences; original documents and interviews; creative works, such as spoken word, music poetry and visual art; and objects and ephemera collected directly from community residents.

Vernacular histories may follow some research and publication conventions, such as the third-person style of writing, citation of sources, or even formal consent forms for inclusion of personal information, but this is not always deemed necessary, or even desired, by its practitioners.

One of the major criticisms of vernacular history is that it may not display the much-vaunted objectivity of academic writing:

> Vernacular authors have often not displayed scholarly detachment; their writing has tended to be informed by direct experience and animated by a passionate involvement with their subjects of study.[14]

Another shortcoming of vernacular narratives, according to Dick, is that they are "dialogic" in the Bahktinian sense, in that the narrative may change over time according to the nature of the audience and their interaction with, and response to, the author's account. This fluidity of content in some vernacular accounts means that they lack logical coherence, which undermines their credibility as trustworthy sources of information.[15]

During the course of the twentieth century, historical production became a discrete academic specialty, and history as written by professional scholars was privileged over vernacular history in terms of its overall validity and credibility. As a result, vernacular history became marginalized and eventually discredited as a source of reliable information about the past.[16]

Dick goes on to note that while vernacular historians "share the common experience of operating outside dominant discourses of power and authority," this does *not* mean that vernacular narratives necessarily go against the prevailing dominant historical viewpoints.[17] Community historians who share the same worldview and value systems as professional scholars are often happy to incorporate perspectives that reinforce their own opinions, even to the point of excluding credible data that challenge the validity of the prevailing historical scholarship. As a result, the vast majority of local community histories produced prior to the 1970s demonstrate a relentlessly homogeneous portrait of Western Canada, where the narrative of the past starts with the appearance of the first homesteader and goes on to feature the family biographies of subsequent arrivals – all presented in alphabetical order according to surname.

More recently Lyle Dick has revisited the topic of Western Canadian vernacular history, this time focusing on the writing of early Manitoba history. His rationale for this examination is to refute the common assumption that Western Canadian historiography is a product of the period *after* the creation of Manitoba and after the founding of history as an academic specialty. Instead, he argues that there were vernacular historians resident in the Red River Settlement after the initial arrival of the Selkirk settlers in 1812–13 who were active up to, and after, the establishment of the province of Manitoba in 1870. Although these writers were not professional historians, Dick argues, their work was skilfully done, and they were motivated by "a sense of civic duty to write on issues of pressing social, cultural and political importance to their community."[18]

He then profiles a select group of vernacular historians of the Red River region; Pierre Falcon Jr.; Alexander Ross; the Reverend James Hunter; Joseph James Hargrave; and Donald Gunn. Of this group, Dick concludes that it is the works of Pierre Falcon Jr. and Donald Gunn that resonate today, largely due to their occupational and kin-based connections to the "grassroots" citizenry of the colony that enabled them to supplement their own first-person accounts of historical events with the shared experiences of their relatives, friends, and neighbours. Moreover, Pierre Falcon and Donald Gunn brought different values and attitudes to the writing of Red River history. Falcon expressed Red River history through satirical poems and songs that were entertainment as much as chronicle, first shared orally by Falcon, and then repeated or sung by his fellow Métis while lazing around campfires, paddling canoes, travelling in hunting brigades and cart trains, and settling in their cabins and villages.[19] Donald Gunn chose to challenge the narratives of his British contemporaries (many with family connections to the Hudson's Bay Company) by questioning the leadership and judgment of the Red River elite.

In Manitoba, after the Red River Resistance of 1869–70, and after Red River had been overwhelmed with Anglo-Protestant settlers from Ontario, a cadre of twenty-six prominent citizens of Manitoba established the Historical and Scientific Society of Manitoba in January 1879.[20] Many of the founding members of the organization made up the Anglo-Canadian ruling class of the new province of Manitoba. As a result, Métis accounts of the Red River Resistance of 1869–70 and the Riel Rebellion of 1885 were largely ignored, even though Roman Catholic clerics did publish religious histories of Western Canada that incorporated information on the Métis. The cohort of professional historians that existed in the universities of Ontario and Quebec, in the heartland of the young Dominion of Canada, largely maintained the status quo.[21] Because the history profession was in its infancy, this first generation of historians was quite comfortable incorporating, and building upon, the vernacular historical accounts of the respected citizens of Manitoba and Ontario, many of whom circulated in the same business and social circles as they did. These nascent academics did *not* entertain the perspectives of intellectuals outside of their linguistic and ethnic cohort.[22]

The former elites of Red River – the Francophone and Métis businessmen, professionals, and clerics – were sufficiently offended by what they perceived as "errors" in the depiction of their community's history that they formed an organization, *La Union Nationale Métisse Saint.-Joseph de Manitoba*, in 1909. They later engaged August-Henri de Trémaudan, a Québec-born historian raised in France, to research and write their community's history, and he began publishing articles and books in the 1920s.[23]

Despite the dominance of non-Métis scholars in the area of Métis historiography, it would be incorrect to assume that there was lack of interest amongst Métis people in writing their history. In fact, in the years prior to the founding of *La Union Nationale Métisse* in 1909, a young Métis man from the Qu'Appelle Valley in Saskatchewan made the decision to sell his

3.1 Joseph Zépherin LaRocque. Courtesy of Anna Marie Willey, Regina, SK.

scrip and move to Winnipeg to get an education. His name was Joseph Zépherin LaRocque.

What follows is an examination of some selected narratives left behind by one of the very few Métis vernacular historians of the early twentieth century: Joseph Zépherin (J.Z.) LaRocque of Lebret, Saskatchewan. Mr. LaRocque is perhaps most widely remembered today as one of the earliest post-1885 Métis political activists – a founder and former president of the Métis Society of Saskatchewan, and a lifelong member of the Saskatchewan Liberal Party. His ongoing political collaboration and friendships with prominent Saskatchewan Liberals, particularly James G. Gardiner, provided LaRocque with reasonably steady employment in provincial and federal government jobs for about thirty years (ca. 1914–44), including an appointment as a member of the Saskatchewan Provincial Police, and a position as a provincial fish and wildlife officer. These government posts would provide income aside from LaRocque's farming activities during the bulk of his working life.

Despite his very busy political and work-related activities, Joseph also possessed a keen avocational interest in the human and natural history of the Qu'Appelle Valley, a passion to which he was able to devote additional time as he reached middle age. He had joined the Saskatchewan Historical Society in the 1930s, and served on its board of directors for several years. He had been active in collecting and preserving original documents and artifacts of interest, many of which he loaned and/or gifted to the Province of Saskatchewan. Because of his ability to speak the Cree and Saulteaux languages, and due to his ongoing friendships with local Native people throughout the region, J.Z. was able to acquire previously unknown insights into historical events from the Indigenous perspective. He interviewed local First Nations and Métis Elders, and developed a detailed knowledge of historical sites and events, primarily those of the Qu'Appelle Valley. He shared this information in a wide range of articles that were published in local Saskatchewan newspapers, magazines, and provincial histories. As mentioned previously, J.Z.'s political connections led to administrative postings with the government, particularly as a peace officer and as a fish and wildlife officer. His background as a wildlife officer no doubt encouraged his interest in the animal, fish, and bird populations of the area, and his papers contain a number of handwritten essays on conservation.[24]

Joseph Z. LaRocque died in 1964, aged eighty-five. His collected correspondence and historical writings remained in the possession of his son Robert James "Jimmy" LaRocque until the latter's death in 2009. Since 2012, I have had the opportunity to work with Joseph LaRocque's papers, and his writings display many of the strengths (and alleged weaknesses) of vernacular historical writing. But first, some additional context on my involvement with this collection is required.

The J.Z. LaRocque papers: The legacy of a Métis Liberal

In the 1990s I paid my first visit to Lebret, Saskatchewan, in the Qu'Appelle Valley with my cousin Art. We visited our ancestors in the graveyard, went to the local museum, and later stopped by the home of Jimmy and Lucy LaRocque, long-time residents of Lebret. Jimmy, considered to be the unofficial historian of the community, was actually the inheritor of this mantle from his father, the late J.Z. LaRocque.

My personal relationship with Lebret and the LaRocque family in particular is through my mother (our Desjarlais and Klyne ancestors are from this community and buried in the local cemetery). As a young woman she also worked at Fort San (also known as the Fort Qu'Appelle Sanatorium), the tuberculosis hospital not far from Lebret. One of her friends and co-workers at the sanatorium later married J.Z.'s son Jimmy and settled at Lebret.

My first 1990s visit with the LaRocques was brief but interesting. Jimmy showed us samples of kinnikinnik, told us humorous anecdotes about our relations, and chatted about family history, community history, and his father's large collection of historical accounts.

As the years passed and I became caught up in my own Métis research projects, J.Z. LaRocque and the documents he had left behind faded from view. The existence of J.Z. LaRocque's papers was known among local historians and community members in the Qu'Appelle Valley, but the papers had never been studied outside of the family. It was well known that his son Jimmy was fiercely protective of his father's legacy, and that it was his intention to "do something" with the collected papers.

In the intervening years, my parents visited the LaRocques from time to time, as my mother was an old friend of Jimmy's wife Lucy. Then in spring 2009 I heard from my mother that Jimmy had died at the age of eighty-seven. She sent me the mass card from Jimmy's funeral, and I posted it on my bulletin board, where I often stared at it, and wondered about his papers.

Shortly after Jimmy LaRocque's passing, I asked my mother if she still stayed in touch with Lucy. She said yes. Then I asked her if she would phone Lucy and ask her about Jimmy's papers, to find out if the papers still existed. She phoned Lucy, and then she called me back to affirm that, indeed, Lucy still had the papers, and that they were in boxes and trunks. I then requested that she phone Lucy again, to ask her if I could examine the papers. And again, my mother phoned back to tell me that "Yes, Lucy says you can look at the papers, but she can't pay you to do it!." This puzzled me, as I couldn't understand why she would think that I wanted payment for looking at the collection, but I told Mom to phone her back to advise her that I wanted NO money, just the chance to look at the documents.

3.2 Mrs. Lucy LaRocque (left) and my mother, Mrs. Mary Devine (right). Photo by author.

My request to examine the collection was granted by Mrs. LaRocque via my mother. We decided to make the journey a mother-daughter "road trip" of sorts – Mom would visit with Lucy, and I would look at the documents.

My mother and I flew to Saskatchewan from Alberta in late August 2010, travelling by car to Lebret, where the papers were stored. While my mother and Lucy visited, I conducted a preliminary analysis of the contents of the boxes and trunks where the papers were housed, and asked permission to borrow part of the collection for further study.

Permission was granted by Mrs. LaRocque, and I set aside a total of four boxes of correspondence and other material (approximately six linear feet), for pickup by car at a future date. My mother and I returned to Alberta, and I completed a formal ethics application for my research project, as well as an informed consent form for Mrs. LaRocques's review and signature. The draft documents were reviewed and approved by Research Ethics, and in early September of 2010 my husband and I drove to Lebret, Saskatchewan.

3.3 LaRocque's trunk of documents. Photo by author.

Mrs. LaRocque signed two copies of the informed consent form, keeping one copy for herself. My husband and I then returned to Alberta with the LaRocque collection and the signed consent form, which completed the initial task of this project – the acquisition of the papers for study.

In early 2011 I hired a doctoral student to go through the collection, in order to document and sort the papers according to archival principles. This was deemed necessary, as the collection was in no discernible order, and it would be very difficult to review the documents chronologically or thematically without some form of preliminary arrangement.

The preliminary documentation and arrangement of the collection was completed by April 2011, and a rudimentary finding aid was prepared for the papers.

Originally my interest in the documents was strictly for the transcribed oral accounts of Métis history that J.Z. LaRocque was known to have collected from Métis Elders in the Qu'Appelle Valley of Saskatchewan. He had

3.4 LaRocque's Bundled Letter File. Photo by author.

a wide-ranging circle of friends and acquaintances among old-timers of every race, ethnicity, and political stripe.

What surprised me most, however, was a collection of documents that had been set aside by someone (probably Jimmy) prior to any outsiders looking at the collection. The file consisted of correspondence between J.Z. LaRocque and J.G. "Jimmy" Gardiner, a Lemberg, Saskatchewan, schoolteacher and farmer who became premier of Saskatchewan in the late 1920s and early 1930s, and then became federal minister of agriculture in the Liberal government of Mackenzie King. The number and variety of letters were astonishing. While there were handwritten drafts and typed carbon copies of letters that J.Z. had mailed to Jimmy, there were also *responses* to J.Z.'s letters from Jimmy Gardiner, typewritten on various government letterheads that served as visual "signposts" of Gardiner's political career over the decades. Another pleasant discovery was political correspondence between LaRocque and other Saskatchewan politicians, among them Métis and First Nations activists.

Lebret, Sask.
June 24, 1939.

Hon. W.J. Patterson,
    Premier,
        REGINA.

Dear Mr. Patterson;

    With further reference to Metis rights to landed properties in Saskatchewan, I found about 90% of them disposed of their holdings thru out the province. Those born in Saskatchewan between 1870 to 1885, including myself, received 240 acres as scrips and also had the privilege of entering an ordinary "homestead" of 160 acres. A great number took advantage of the second privilege, and again disposed of it, in most cases, as soon as they "proved up" the lands. There is only, practically speaking, the LaRocque boys owning farm lands in this district, and thanks for this to the late Right Hon. Sir Wilfrid Laurier.

    When Dad settled here in 1876, he bought out old squatters' rights from the following Metis men; Augustin Brabant, St. Pierre Poitras, and Michael Desjarlais. The Book entitled "The Company of Adventurers" written by Isaac Cowie mentions my father, on page 411, quote; "Antoine LaRocque, a considerable trader, arrived from Red River" He meant father arrived at a spot where now Fort Qu'Appelle is located. This was in 1870, and apparently he had spent much of his time in the regions of Edmonton, and Lac la Biche from 1870 to 1876 when he was persuaded by the late Father Hugonard to settle in the Qu'Appelle Valley. Originally my father intended to return to the Red River, and send us boys to St. Boniface College.

    When my father arrived here in 1876 Father Hugonard had already here (Lebret) 2 years coming from Grenoble, a province South of France. My father was bent having his sons educated and Father Hugonard promised him a school right here. The good Father Hugonard kept his promise and opened a day school for the Metis children shortly after.

    My father had acquired 3 sections of land in this district, and after the survey about 1880-1 he became the proud possessor of these properties in a legal way. However, misfortune overtook the LaRocque family in 1885. He could not read or write and to this date, I cannot figure out how he kept his accounts when he carried on such a large business. He usually had 75 Red River carts heavy loaded with merchandise, and apparently he advanced goods to trappers and buffalo hunters thru out the length and bredth of this country.

    When hostilities broke out in 1885 he kept strictly netral although he would naturally sympathise with Louis Riel. Star Blanket and the other minor Chiefs from File Hills Reservations wanted to go on the war path but wanted the open support of Antoine LaRocque. LaRocque was reputed to have considerable quantities of amunitions, consisting of gun powder and bullets. Star Blanket's plans were to kill Father Hugonard, one George Fisher, a trader, and Archibald McDonald.

3.5 A LaRocque's typewritten letter. Photo by author.

After a cursory examination of secondary historical sources dealing with Saskatchewan politics revealed no references to J.Z. LaRocque, I began making inquiries of colleagues at the University of Regina. I found, to my surprise, that local scholars who specialized in Saskatchewan political history were *unaware* of the long-standing friendship between the Métis politician and the Liberal leader. Moreover, my examination of the finding aid for the massive J.G. Gardiner fonds held by the Saskatchewan Archives revealed only *one* letter from J.Z. LaRocque to Jimmy Gardiner, written in the 1960s.[25]

While I found these political papers fascinating, I was also intrigued by the very large collection of published reminiscences and newspaper articles, and published "letters to the editor" that Mr. LaRocque had produced during his lifetime. Many of these writings documented key events from the Northwest Rebellion of 1885, as experienced by members of his family and other Métis and First Nations residents of the Qu'Appelle Valley. These written reminiscences are of particular importance. First of all, they provide additional information about specific events during the rebellion that do not appear in conventional accounts of the event. These accounts also embody many of the characteristics of vernacular histories, as discussed previously. The remainder of this examination will focus on a selection of J.Z. LaRocque's vernacular accounts of his family's experiences during the Northwest Rebellion of 1885, highlighting the unique characteristics of these documents that are not normally featured in conventional historical narratives.

The arrest of Antoine LaRocque – 1885

Antoine LaRocque, the father of J.Z. LaRocque, was a trader from St. François Xavier Parish, Red River. Like many Métis families who migrated out of the Red River Settlement after the Red River resistance of 1869–70, Antoine LaRocque and his wife Rosalie LaPlante moved westward with their children to the newly created District of Assiniboia to farm. They settled near the village of Lac Qu'Appelle, now known as Lebret, in 1875, where they operated a large farm raising cattle and horses.

Unfortunately, the Northwest Rebellion of 1885 would have disastrous consequences for the family. Antoine LaRocque was falsely accused of supplying firearms to rebels, and was arrested and jailed, despite the family's claims that Antoine LaRocque had actually persuaded local First Nations groups *not* to participate in the conflict. LaRocque was encouraged to sue the government for wrongful arrest, and proceeded to hire legal assistance to initiate a lawsuit. Unfortunately, Antoine LaRocque eventually ran out of money to pay his lawyer. To cover his legal debts, his lands were taken from him.

One version of this story is contained in a letter sent to the Hon. W.J. Patterson, Liberal premier of Saskatchewan, by J.Z. LaRocque in June 1939. Although this account is not the earliest telling of the tale, it is significant because Joseph LaRocque is using the story to illustrate some of the circumstances whereby various Saskatchewan Métis lost their lands. It is also relatively complete, in that it provides some contextual family information and also identifies the key individuals and events involved in his father's arrest and subsequent bankruptcy.

Dear Mr. Patterson:

With further reference to Metis rights to landed properties in Saskatchewan, I found about 90% of them disposed of their holdings thro out the province. Those born in Saskatchewan between 1870 to 1885, including myself, received 240 acres as scrips and also had the privilege of entering an ordinary 'homestead' of 160 acres. A great many took advantage of the second privilege, and again disposed of it, in most cases, as soon as they 'proved up' the lands. There is only, practically speaking, the La Rocque boys owning farm lands in this district, and thanks for this to the late Right Hon. Sir Wilfrid Laurier....

When my father arrived here in 1876 Father Hugonard had already [been] here (Lebret) 2 years coming from Grenoble, a province [in the] south of France. My father was bent [on] having his sons educated and Father Hugonard promised him a school right here. The good Father Hugonard kept his promise and opened a day school for the Metis children shortly after.

My father had acquired 3 sections of land in this district, and after the survey about 1880-1 he became the proud possessor of these properties in a legal way. However, misfortune overtook the LaRocque family in 1885. He could not read or write and to this date, I cannot figure out how he kept his accounts when he carried on such a large business. He usually had 75 Red River carts heavily loaded with merchandise, and apparently he advanced goods to trappers and buffalo hunters thro out the length and breadth of this country.

When hostilities broke out in 1885 he kept strictly netral [sic] although he would naturally sympathize with Louis Riel. Star Blanket and the other minor Chiefs from File Hills Reservations wanted to go on the war path but wanted the open support of Antoine LaRocque. LaRocque was reputed to have considerable quantities of ammunitions, consisting of gun powder and bullets. Star Blanket's plans were to kill Father Hugonard, one George Fisher, a trader, and Archibald McDonald, then Chief Factor, Hudson's Bay Company, Fort Qu'Appelle. Star Blanket accused these three men for betraying the Indians and Métis and he was bound to take revenge on them but wanted LaRocque's support to do it. My father always told us, he knew the Indian character too well, and he would not advise them to commit any rash act....

Star Blanket decided to move towards the Qu'Appelle Valley in the spring of 1885 and dug trenches on the top of the hills about one mile East where the cross is planted opposite Lebret. This was verified by Chief Buffalo Bow, 99 years old, when you was [sic] made Ka-Nee-Kan Otaeu at File Hills 1st July 1937. Most likely the authorities found out Star Blanket was making frequent visits to LaRocque and its an open secret to all old timers that LaRocque was an easy victim to unscrupulous would be 'spies' during the rebellion.

He stood solid to his grounds, prevented Star Blanket going on the war path, yet, he would not betray his own people. Finally the sad moment came, one night during the rebellion Col. O'Brien, Toronto, with 200 armed men went to LaRocque's trading post (where my dairy farm is now located) and arrested him. LaRocque had a revolver and he was going to use it. Mother intervened and pleaded with him to give in as otherwise, I would not be writing this 54 years after. Dad was a massive built man, standing around 6 feet weighing about 250 pounds. A general melee might have been the sad result as the soldiers would have been ordered to shoot, and being night time, astray bullets might have killed the innocent as well as the combatants.

The soldiers escorted him to Regina and kept him in Jail for 9 days on bread and water. Apparently unable to find any evidence against him, he was released. Dad told us he had to sleep on the bare floor. After his release again the dark clouds of misfortune befell on the family. A man named T. W. Jackson, I believe a lawyer, persuaded Dad to sue the Canadian Government for false arrest. I am not sure but I think Mr. Jackson was connected with the North West Council. He extracted all the cash he could from him and likely the Crown kept on asking remands. The point came when LaRocque had no more money and in default of appearing, a judgement was registered against him for the costs. Failing to pay these costs the Crown seized all his lands. Then homeless, friendless, the LaRocque family had to eke out a living the best they knew how. Necessarily we were classed as 'rebels' and looked down on as undesirables. To intensify the groans of persecution my father died in January 1894.

In 1895 the dark clouds that had been hovering over our confiscated home took a change and gradually turned silvery. The Right Hon. Sir Wilfrid Laurier then touring the West came to Lebret and attended Mass on a Sunday. I was then 14 years old and I will remember seeing the silver tongue orator kneeling at the alter railing in the little old [church] here. After Mass the distinguished visitor spoke. He made a solemn promise that if elected, he would grant full amnesty to all those that had had any misunderstandings with the Canadian Government. My late brother Alexander LaRocque, who was the eldest in the family, told Sir Wilfrid of our home being confiscated thro the arrest of our father. Sir Wilfrid took notes and not many months after his election as Prime Minister of Canada, we received a registered letter containing a clearance of our lands, and mother wept with joy and needless to say, our family always held Sir Wilfrid with the greatest of admiration....

> 'The last but not least' Since narrating all our misfortunes, we were reduced to down right poverty and in 1899 again Sir Wilfrid came to the rescue. As I was telling you when in your office recently, how I came to be a Liberal, this is how it happened. I was one of those entitled to a land scrip in 1899 and I kept mine for one year, and sold it for $300.00. With this money I took a commercial course in Winnipeg.
>
> Yours sincerely,
> Jos. Z. LaRocque[26]

J.Z.'s account of the family's fall in fortune, followed by their redemption in 1895 at the hands of Liberal Prime Minister Wilfrid Laurier, has been told and retold over the decades – in public speeches, in newspaper articles, and in the private correspondence of J.Z. LaRocque. This story, as I have come to learn, is pivotal to understanding the roots of Liberal Party loyalty in the LaRocque family. It also helps to explain the unusual, even incongruous, presence of a Métis political organizer in a mainstream political party prior to World War I.

However, the earliest published account of the LaRocque family experience may, in fact, be Star Blanket's account of the Northwest Rebellion. Star Blanket (*Ahchacoosahcotatakoopit*) was a hereditary chief and the son of Chief White Buffalo Calf (*Wahpiimoosetoosis*), a signatory of Treaty 4. Several published biographies of Star Blanket currently exist, and his resistance to federal government policies has been well documented.[27] The reminiscence below is featured in Volume 1 of John Hawkes, *The Story of Saskatchewan and Its People*.[28] Oddly enough, this account is not contained in the section of this book devoted to discussing the rebellion. Instead, it is contained in Chapter 15: "An Indian Murder Case." A few pages into this chapter is an introductory paragraph entitled "Star Blanket," written by John Hawkes:

> Star Blanket was an immovable Pagan of strong character, and there is little doubt that the old warrior was positively aching to go on the war path in the rebellion. We have seen an entirely imaginative account in print setting forth that Father Hugonard actually choked him into submission, threw such a scare

into him that he was afraid to join the rebels. The truth will be found in the following statement which was given me at an arranged meeting with Star Blanket in the Qu'Appelle at Mr. Joseph La Roque's [sic] house. Many French Metis were placed in an invidious position in the rebellion and some suggestions were at one time made against the loyalty of the well-known family of La Roque. The subjoined statement will put the late Mr. LaRoque in his true light and show that not only was he loyal but that to him and to him alone Star Blanket's neutrality in the rebellion was due.[29]

This introduction is followed by a passage entitled "Star Blanket's Statement," which would appear to be a detailed transcript of his dealings with Antoine LaRocque, as featured in the excerpt below:

Myself, Kee-was-stoo-tin and Is-koo-ches, went to LaRoque's, all dressed up in warrior style, and upon [my] entering his home he asked me, 'How are you brother? What's wrong?' I said, 'Nothing, brother: I am looking for peace, then if I cannot find it what shall I do?' He replied, 'Brother, go to the soldier's camp at Kee-pa-hee-kan-nik, and you show yourself that you are not looking for trouble by shaking hands with them. Bring no guns with you, and I guarantee they won't hurt you. Go straight to the camp and the sentry may not allow you to enter the camp grounds, and may offer to scare you with a gun, but never heed, just go by him and salute him by "How." 'Thereby I followed my brother's advice and went to the camp at the Fort (Qu'Appelle) with my two companions, and did exactly what brother (La Roque) told me to do… The C.O. asked me what I wanted. I told him I was on a peace pilgrimage and would acknowledge the Government's good will and peace by exchanging tobacco and tea. A man named McKay, a half-breed, was interpreter. The C.O. was in a happy mood when he heard this and immediately gave orders that I be given these commodities. They gave us tobacco and tea in large quantities. Then we again shook hands and we left the soldier's camp for our camp in Lebret. I must say that I was determined to have my brother's advice (La Roque's)

3.6 Ahchacoosahcotatakoopit (Star Blanket). Provincial Archives of Saskatchewan.

> whether right or wrong, which of course I intended to carry out in the extreme. But give honour to my deceased brother's (La Roque's) wise advice. If he had advised me the contrary God alone knows what might have happened, as I had a powerful band of warriors. My brother (La Roque) always advised me to avoid doing wrong, and that the Lord would give me luck. Then on my return to the camp I went again to see my brother (La Roque) and told him the results of my trip. He was glad to hear it, and again he told me not to take up arms, and to lead a peaceful life.[30]

The statement (which is not provided in its entirety here) ends with "This is a true statement and I give my cross thereto." Star Blanket's "X" is at the bottom of the passage, along with the words "Witness Joseph Z. La Roque."

While reviewing other documents in the J.Z. LaRocque Papers, I encountered additional contextual information about the Star Blanket narrative. In a typed essay entitled "Thoughts, Fancies, and Facts," J.Z. LaRocque reminisces about a chance encounter with an individual directly involved in his father's arrest.

> Apparently odd things will happen in a life time. When I was a Field Officer for the Department of Natural Resources, I was up good and early one morning and proceeded to the Sioux Bridge in the Qu'Appelle Valley to check duck hunters. There were several Regina sportsmen there. I will mention a few[:] Sir Frederick Haultain, his brother Wilmot, former Chief Justice W.W. Martin, his late brother Dr. Martin and some prominent men from the surrounding country. The last man I checked was William Charles Maguire of 1928 McIntyre St. Regina. He told me he had come to Winnipeg in 1882 and was a cavalryman in the Riel Rebellion. That he had been an employee of the Massey-Harris Company for nearly fifty years.
>
> He asked me when I came West and I told him I was always in Saskatchewan, born on the valley flats at Lebret. He went on describing when Col. O'Brien of Toronto during one night, picked 200 strong men, including himself, to go on patrol to Lebret, then known as "La Mission Qu'Appelle" to arrest

Antoine LaRocque. They arrived there from Fort Qu'Appelle and pushed a gun in every window. Col. O'Brien with other officers and an interpreter went in and arrested my father. My mother told me when I became age of reason, that father had a revolver under his pillow and he was going to shoot but mother pleaded with him not to … I asked Mr. Maguire if he didn't see a craddle [sic], as may be no officer would be checking him this morning. He seemed a nice man and jokingly I told him, it was my turn to use the law on him.

At the same time the formidable Cree Chief Star Blanket of File Hills Reserve, was also arrested and he and LaRocque were incarcerated for nine days in the Regina guard room but for lack of evidence for seditious acts both were liberated without trial.

In the Mary Weekes' Book, entitled "The Last Buffalo Hunter" on page 185 are published pure fabrication about Antoine LaRocque, that Norbert Welsh had lent money to LaRocque to pay a fine over the 1885 rebellion. It's a pitty [sic] for such a well known author as Mary Weekes is, didn't make searches in the R.C.M.P. records and find out the truth, and avoid printing erroneous statements against a dead man. This same man Norbert Welsh makes derogatory remarks against the character of Antoine LaRocque in pages 112–13 and the falsehoods he had printed against this man on page 185, what he says about him in pages 112–3 must also be falsehood.

However, in about 1915, Norbert Welsh was guest at my house where the arrest was made in 1885, along with Chief Star Blanket, and my brother John LaRocque, both of whom had been official interpreters for the Indian Department, and thoroughly understood the Cree language. We also had another guest the late Mr. John Hawkes, author and Saskatchewan Legistive [sic] Librarian. Mr. Hawkes thro these interpreters, point blank, asked Chief Star Blank [sic], who persuaded him not to go on the war path in 1885: He replied: "My brother 'Chie-ca-nay' the Cree name of my father, meaning "Humming bird". Now why didn't Norbert Welsh deny the Chief as in Mary Weekes' book, he claims he persuaded him not to go on the war path. Not forgetting to mention we all had liquid refreshments but the Chief refused to take any. Also my good wife served a tasty meal to the remarkable gathering. Mr. Hawkes took several notes, and included them in his Book "People I have Met". The Late John Hawkes' Books can be found in the Regina Public Library.[31]

There are intriguing elements in the account above that embody several of the diagnostic characteristics of vernacular history as discussed by Lyle Dick. Perhaps the most obvious characteristic of this story is that it is written largely in the first person – a literary convention that is typically frowned upon by most historians because it does not reflect the "scholarly detachment" that provides an aura of credibility to historical writing. J.Z. LaRocque the narrator is *not* removed from the account; instead, he is featured as a direct participant in the story – first as the wildlife officer meeting William Charles Maguire, and later as the baby in the crib during his account of his father's arrest by Col. O'Brien's men. It is also quite clear that the author demonstrates what professional historians might consider an unseemly, even "passionate involvement" with his subject of study, to paraphrase the words of Lyle Dick. There are numerous folksy asides in the account, as well as direct criticisms of another community member from Lebret, and the professional writer who previously published a book containing that person's inaccurate statements about the LaRocque family. As a rule, most writers (and their publishers) are careful to avoid such statements, particularly if they are discussing living people, as these remarks could be considered libellous if published. Professional historians by definition generally confine themselves to discussing events of the distant past where the parties are usually deceased. But vernacular historians, who are recounting their own eyewitness experiences (or those of a family or community member), do not consider their writing from a legal point of view. It is *their* truth, as they understand it to be.

However, there is some effort on the part of J.Z. LaRocque to provide corroborating evidence for the statements in his accounts, by his listing of other individuals who could be consulted to verify the presented facts. Indeed, the process of establishing the veracity of Antoine LaRocque's experiences during his arrest began, first of all, with having Chief Star Blanket provide his own eyewitness testimony of both his and Antoine LaRocque's arrest by the authorities. Moreover, John Hawkes's actual presence

3.7 John Hawkes, Saskatchewan Legislative Librarian. Provincial Archives of Saskatchewan.

in J.Z. LaRocque's home to witness Star Blanket's deposition was, in itself, a method of substantiating the validity of the eyewitness evidence provided by Star Blanket, in accordance with Indigenous protocols for establishing the veracity of evidence. Archivist Mary Ann Pylypchuk has argued:

> The formalized telling of oral histories, the display of artifacts, singing of songs, and the staging of ceremonies in the presence of others is considered a form of evidence and establishes the legitimacy of evidence. It also establishes its spiritual power.[32]

The subsequent publication of the account in *The Story of Saskatchewan and Its People* was a further step toward establishing the veracity of the information in a "fixed," that is, published format. It is surprising that this revisionist account was featured in a provincial history at all, since it was only forty years since the end of the Northwest Rebellion, and emotions regarding the event still ran high in Saskatchewan and elsewhere. However,

J.Z. LaRocque was a staunch Liberal and one of the early members of the party in Saskatchewan. John Hawkes, the author of *The Story of Saskatchewan and Its People*, was the legislative librarian in the Liberal government of Charles Avery Dunning during the period 1922–26. Star Blanket's story was possibly included as a personal favour to Joseph LaRocque, though it should be noted once again that the account is not featured prominently in the part of the collection devoted to the Northwest Rebellion.

A third version of this story was published as an illustrated article in *Liberty* magazine in 1955, during the fiftieth anniversary of Saskatchewan's creation as a province.[33] This particular iteration of the account, entitled "I Saw Saskatchewan's Bloody Rebellion," amply illustrates yet another characteristic of vernacular writing, that being the tendency of a vernacular account to change over time according to the nature of the audience, and the chronological and situational context of the story's presentation.

In this telling of the tale, which features the byline "A *Liberty* Salute on Sask.'s 50th Birthday," LaRocque begins the account with a brief introduction to the topic of the Northwest Rebellion and his father's arrest. Then he introduces himself to the reader with a prologue that establishes the contemporary context for the publication of the article.

> This year, the province celebrates its Golden Jubilee. It will be 50 and I'll be 74. I'm Joseph Zephrian [sic] La Rocque, a Saskatchewan half-breed. I was a year old before the tent city of Regina was born. And I was 24 when Sir Wilfrid Laurier came to Regina to give Canada a new province. I'm happy to have grown up with Saskatchewan.
>
> To celebrate its birthday, a Jubilee Pageant, Passion Play, parades, art exhibitions, folk dances and sport programs will be held this year. One feature, on September 4, will be the re-enacting of the inauguration ceremonies over which Canadian prime minister Laurier presided. Five of Saskatchewan's seven premiers will attend the ceremony for the province which, though rich in agricultural produce, is now second only to Alberta in oil production.
>
> With a population of nearly 900,000, my Saskatchewan has, in five years, increased its spending on the search for oil from $2,000,000 to $60 million. Some three-quarters of my province

is covered in timber; it has, in fact, more untouched forestland than any province east of British Columbia.

The University of Saskatchewan boasts the country's second largest – Chalk River, Ont. Is the biggest – atomic research center. And the first cobalt bomb, for cancer treatment, was built at the university.[34]

Following this rather boosterish description of modern-day Saskatchewan, LaRocque proceeds with the retelling of his story. In this 1950s account, he repeats virtually all of the salient details contained in the previous iterations, but there are cosmetic additions to the story, no doubt suggested by the co-author identified in the first page of the article, Robert Tyre, a journalist and former public relations specialist in the office of CCF Premier Tommy Douglas.[35] In this version, there are scenic descriptions that may or may not be actual memories, but provide colour and immediacy to the story. And there are a few additional details that are new and unique, such as the following anecdote:

> When Laurier came to Regina to help launch the new Province, I attended the ceremony. The big day was September 4, 1905.
>
> I joined the solid mass of humanity that overflowed from Victoria Park. When Sir Wilfrid read the proclamation that made Saskatchewan a province, I forced my way through the crowd to him.
>
> I reached for his hand and shook it mightily, saying, "The LaRocques thank you very much, sir."[36]

This final (?) telling of the LaRocque family's experiences in 1885 is the most "literary" version of the various accounts that exist. The plot elements – the introduction of the LaRocque family and the outbreak of the Saskatchewan rebellion (exposition); the arrest and jailing of Antoine LaRocque as a rebel (rising action); the failed lawsuit and confiscation of the family's land (rising action); the providential meeting with Wilfrid Laurier (rising action); and the restitution of the family property by Prime Minister Wilfrid Laurier (climax) – follow a time-tested pattern for plot development. It also provides a satisfactory "denouement" to the various versions of the LaRocque story, in that the narrator, Joseph LaRocque, has lived to a ripe old age and had the opportunity to watch his descendants – and his province – prosper.

The conclusion of the story also serves to illustrate another, rather puzzling aspect of vernacular scholarship – that being the tendency of some vernacular writers (particularly minority writers) to internalize the cultural values of the dominant society that has sought to marginalize them.

In the 1955 *Liberty* article, LaRocque espouses his Canadian patriotism and his pride in his modern homeland while telling the story of how the Canadian government illegally incarcerated his father and the territorial government of Saskatchewan confiscated the family landholdings. Although this may seem hypocritical or even naive, it is important to remember that the dispossession and marginalization that characterized the vast majority of Indigenous experiences with Euro-Canadians were also variable in their impact. The transition of Western Canada from a frontier to a settled society was a racialized and gendered experience, to be sure. But it was also an undertaking that was influenced by class. Educated and affluent Métis had the social and economic resources to make the lifestyle adjustments essential for adapting to the new order of things. As a result, certain Métis families were able to achieve a "happy ending" for themselves – and craft it into history.

Conclusion: Vernacular history as "usable past"

Joseph LaRocque was a member of the Saskatchewan Liberal Party, a founding member of the Métis Society of Saskatchewan, and an active vernacular historian during his lifetime. For J.Z. Larocque, preserving and sharing local history served several functions. First of all, it enabled LaRocque, on behalf of himself and his less literate Métis kin, to preserve the remaining oral accounts of local Métis history before they were forgotten. His sharing of reminiscences in public talks and local newspaper columns allowed him to supplement, and occasionally challenge, the dominant historical and sociopolitical narrative being promulgated in Western Canada – a triumphant nationalist narrative that tended to portray Indigenous people as a defeated minority doomed to poverty due to their inability to adapt to modern society. His initial step was to write alternative accounts of the Northwest Rebellion of 1885 that incorporated his own family experiences and those of other Indigenous people, with the intention of directly challenging, and correcting, perceived inaccuracies and omissions in the "official" historical accounts of the event. His recollections, which were an entertaining mix of historical fact and community anecdote, were also intended to be didactic in tone, stressing the solid moral and community values of the Métis people as a means of challenging the anti-Native biases of some of his non-Native reading audience.[37]

In addition to his vernacular writing, J.Z. LaRocque set out to establish a public persona as an educated, knowledgeable individual regarding Aboriginal historical and contemporary issues, which enabled him to find decent employment and achieve his own political goals within both the Métis Society of Saskatchewan and the Saskatchewan Liberal Party. He accomplished these goals by cashing in his Métis scrip to further his formal education in Winnipeg, using his scrip money to take business training and to purchase a Remington typewriter, which he used to good effect for the rest of his life.

A third important goal was to preserve the Métis past, through his collaboration and friendship with various members of historical societies, with museum curators, and with archivists in Saskatchewan and Manitoba. He generously shared documents and artifacts with these individuals, even when organizations such as the Saskatchewan Museum betrayed his trust by not returning items they had borrowed.[38]

Vernacular histories are an important, and little utilized, source of fresh and original historical information. These accounts, produced by non-professional historians, were often discounted by professional scholars in previous decades due to elitism, ethnocentrism (some might say racism), and a misplaced aesthetic which equated passion and connectedness to the subject matter with historical inaccuracy.

Métis-written histories, like those of other Indigenous peoples, are largely unknown and unstudied by scholars. It is time that these materials were circulated to a larger audience and incorporated into the broader historical record of the Canadian West.

Notes

1. I would like to acknowledge the financial support of the Social Sciences and Humanities Research Council Insight Grants Program for my research project entitled "The J.Z. LaRocque Papers: Métis History and Politics in Southern Saskatchewan, 1886–1945." I would also like to thank the late Lucy LaRocque, and her surviving family members, for granting me permission to work with this collection of papers. Finally, I would like to thank the anonymous reviewers, and Bill Waiser, for their helpful comments on earlier drafts of this chapter.

    There is considerable debate over whether the Métis uprisings in 1869–70, and in 1885, should be called " resistances" or " rebellions." It is currently the policy and practice of the Gabriel Dumont Institute, and many other Indigenous and non-Indigenous collectives, to call *both* conflicts "resistances." I have chosen to refer to the 1869–70 conflict as a "resistance" and the 1885 uprising a "rebellion." The District of Assiniboia, which incorporated most of what is commonly known as the Red River Settlement, was in a period of jurisdictional limbo during the final six months of 1869. The region finally joined Canada as the province of Manitoba in 1870 after considerable negotiations with the Métis following the resistance of local residents to the attempted transfer. As of 1882, the North-West Territories consisted of the territories of Alberta, Saskatchewan, Assiniboia, and Athabasca, which comprised most of what are now the provinces of Alberta and Saskatchewan. At this time, Manitoba and the North-West Territories were firmly under Canadian jurisdiction. Indeed, the ability of the Canadian government to try Louis Riel for treason in 1885 was based, in part, on the fact that the North-West Territories were part of Canada. See "North-West Territories, 1870–1905," in *The Canadian Encyclopedia* (online), http://www.thecanadianencyclopedia.ca/en/article/north-west-territories-1870-1905/ (accessed 22 June 2016).

2. A massive, and growing, bibliography on Louis Riel, has accumulated over the years. For readers wanting a thematic introduction to the primary and secondary literature on Riel to 1980, see Lewis H. Thomas, "Louis Riel (1844–85)," in *Dictionary of Canadian Biography*, vol. 11, University of Toronto/Université Laval, 2003–, http://www.biographi.ca/en/bio/riel_louis_1844_85_11E.html (accessed 4 August 2016). A more recent publication which deals directly with societal perceptions of Riel (and his mental state) is Albert Braz, *The False Traitor: Louis Riel in Canadian Culture* (Toronto: University of Toronto Press, 2003).

3. See Peter S. Li, "Visible Minorities in Canadian Society: Challenges of Racial Diversity," in *Social Differentiation, Patterns and Processes*, ed. Danielle Juteau Lee (Toronto: University of Toronto Press, 2003), 120.

4. After the Riel conflicts of 1885, the Canadian government revised the Indian Act to confine treaty First Nations people in Western Canada to their respective reserves via the implementation of a "pass system." Under this system, it was illegal for a treaty Native to leave the reserve without an official pass, signed and dated by the Indian agent, that stated the person's business off the reserve, where they were going, and when they were supposed to return. This system was in place for over sixty years.

5. A detailed analysis of how Métis identity has been portrayed in literature – by non-Métis and Métis alike – is provided in Darren R. Prefontaine, Lean Dorion, Patrick Young, and Sherry Farrell Racette, "Métis Identity," at the Gabriel Dumont Institute, *The Virtual Museum of Métis History and Culture*, http://www.metismuseum.ca/media/db/00726 (accessed 12 May 2015).

6   The phrase "respectable Métis" was a term used by nineteenth- and twentieth-century writers to describe those individuals and families who had made a successful transition to farming or business after the demise of the buffalo and fur trade economy. It became formally entrenched in government terminology during the Ewing Commission hearings of the 1930s. See Gerhard J. Ens and Joe Sawchuk, *From New Peoples to New Nations: Aspects of Métis History and Identity from the Eighteenth to Twenty-first Centuries* (Toronto: University of Toronto Press, 2015), 280. For a nineteenth-century example of the term in use, see Isaac Cowie, *The Company of Adventurers* (Toronto: W. Briggs, 1914), 464, where he describes hosting a ball at Fort Qu'Appelle in honor of "Messrs Kavanagh and Kelly, two soldiers retired from the U.S. Army at Fort Totten, Devil's Lake, Dakota. They had married charming daughters of a respectable Métis named Klyne."

7   In fact, those Métis communities that existed in remote regions to the north and west persisted independently for a period of time after 1885. These isolated settlements continued to practice a traditional subsistence round of hunting, trapping, gathering, transport of goods, and itinerant labour despite the restrictions from federal hunting and trapping regulations for non-treaty Natives. However, the introduction of the Natural Resources Transfer Agreement in 1930, which assigned the administration of land and wildlife to provincial control, resulted in considerable hardship for those Métis who could not afford licences and were prosecuted for hunting illegally. See Nicole O'Byrne, "Challenging the Liberal Order Framework: Natural Resources and Métis Policy in Alberta and Saskatchewan (1930–1948)" (PhD diss., University of Victoria, 2014).

8   An excellent historiographical essay encapsulating this period of Métis scholarship is J.R. Miller's "From Riel to the Métis," *Canadian Historical Review* 69, no. 1 (1988): 1–20.

9   Of the different initiatives, perhaps the most prominent and long-lasting is the Gabriel Dumont Institute of Native Studies and Applied Research, founded in 1980 with the goals of preserving, respecting, promoting, and enhancing Aboriginal culture. Today this multi-faceted organization continues to preserve and make available a vast quantity of historical and cultural information on its website. The institute is also heavily involved in Aboriginal teacher training, adult education, and student funding. See the Gabriel Dumont Institute, https://gdins.org/about/overview/history/ (accessed 12 May 2015). During the same period, Nicholas Vrooman, in his role as State Folklorist of North Dakota, recorded, compiled, and annotated a selection of Plains Chippewa/Métis music on the Turtle Mountain Chippewa Reservation, which was first released by Smithsonian/Folkways Records on vinyl in 1984, and continues to be available. See Smithsonian/Folkways "Liner Notes – *Plains Chippewa/Métis Music From Turtle Mountain*" http://media.smithsonianfolkways.org/liner_notes/smithsonian_folkways/SFW40411.pdf (accessed 12 May 2015).

10 One Métis vernacular writer active in Alberta, for example, was Marie Rose Delorme Smith, who wrote several newspaper articles, as well as poetry, and fiction, based on her life during the early days of settlement prior to 1905. See Doris Jeanne Mackinnon, *The Identities of Marie Rose Delorme Smith: Portrait of a Métis Woman, 1861–1960* (Regina: University of Regina Press, 2012).

11 Lyle Dick, "Vernacular Currents in Western Canadian Historiography: The Passion and Prose of Katherine Hughes, F.G. Roe, and Roy Ito," in *The West and Beyond: New Perspectives on an Imagined Region*, ed. Alvin Finkel, Sarah Carter, and Peter Fortna (Edmonton: Athabasca University Press, 2010), 13–46.

12 Ibid., 14.

13 Ibid., 18.
14 Ibid.
15 Ibid., 15.
16 Ibid., 15–16.
17 Ibid., 15.
18 Lyle Dick, "Red River's Vernacular Historians," *Manitoba History* 71 (Winter 2013): 3.
19 Ibid., 5–6.
20 See David A. Stewart, "The First Half Century: A Sketch of the Early Years of the Historical and Scientific Society of Manitoba." Originally published in *Manitoba Pageant*, 24, no. 3 (Spring 1979), http://www.mhs.mb.ca/docs/pageant/24/firsthalfcentury.shtml (accessed 15 May 2015).
21 Margaret Conrad, "A Brief Survey of Canadian Historiography," in, *New Possibilities for the Past: Shaping History Education in Canada*, ed. Penney Clark (Vancouver: University of British Columbia Press, 2011), 33–54.
22 For a detailed analysis of early Canadian intellectuals and their influence, see Doug Owram, *The Government Generation: Canadian Intellectuals and the State, 1900–1945* (Toronto: University of Toronto Press, 1986).
23 See J.M. Bumsted, "Trying to Describe the Buffalo: An Historiographical Essay on the Red River Settlement," in *Thomas Scott's Body: And Other Essays on Early Manitoba History* (Winnipeg: University of Manitoba Press, 2000), 25. See also Michel Verrette, "Trémaudan, Auguste-Henri De," in *Dictionary of Canadian Biography*, vol. 15, University of Toronto/Université Laval, 2003–, http://www.biographi.ca/en/bio/tremaudan_auguste_henri_de_15E.html (accessed 16 April 2015); and A.H. de Trémaudan, *Histoire de la Nation Métisse dans L'Ouest canadien* (Montreal: Albert Lévesque 1936), in English translation by Elizabeth Maguet, *Hold High Your Heads* (Winnipeg: Pemmican, 1982).
24 It is not known at this time whether any of these conservation essays have been published, though there are a number of copies of his historical articles in draft form and, as published newspaper clippings, in his papers. See J.Z. LaRocque Papers (hereinafter JZLP). Private collection.
25 Examples of primary and secondary sources examined, unsuccessfully, for information on J.Z. LaRocque's role in the Saskatchewan Liberal Party and his friendship with James G. Gardiner include F 65 – James G. Gardiner Fonds (finding aid), Saskatchewan Archives Board, http://sab.minisisinc.com/sabmin/scripts/mwimain.dll/246/1/2/525732?RECORD&DATABASE=DESCRIPTION_WEB (accessed 28 May 2015). See also David E. Smith, *Prairie Liberalism: The Liberal Party in Saskatchewan, 1905–71* (Toronto: University of Toronto Press, 1975); David E. Smith and Norman Ward, *Jimmy Gardiner: Relentless Liberal* (Toronto: University of Toronto Press, 1990); and Nathanial A. Benson, *None of It Came Easy: The Story of James Garfield Gardiner* (Toronto: Burns and MacEachern, 1955).
26 See J.L. LaRocque to Hon. W.J. Patterson, Premier, 24 June 1939, JZLP. The version of this letter that is presented here is edited for length, and the excerpt provided here contains the information dealing specifically with his father's 1885 arrest. For further information on lawyer T.W. Jackson and his subsequent career, see John Palmerston

Robertson, *A Political Manual of the Province of Manitoba and the North-west Territories* (Winnipeg: Call Printing, 1887), 109.

27 See "Star Blanket," in Christian Thompson, ed., *Saskatchewan First Nations: Lives Past and Present* (Regina: Canadian Plains Research Center, 2004), 125–27; and John Tobias, "AHCHUCHWAHAUHHATOHAPIT (Ahchacoosacootacoopits, Star Blanket)" in *Dictionary of Canadian Biography*, vol. 14, University of Toronto/Université Laval, 2003–, http://www.biographi.ca/en/bio/ahchuchwahauhhatohapit_14E.html (accessed 24 February 2016).

28 See John Hawkes, *The Story of Saskatchewan and Its People*, 3 vols. (Regina: S.J. Clarke, 1924). Copies of this account are also featured in the S.D. Hanson Fonds, University of Saskatchewan Archives, and the Indigenous Studies Portal, University of Saskatchewan, http://iportal.usask.ca/index.php?sid=538872931&id=21255&t=details (accessed 24 February 2016).

29 Ibid., vol. 1, 163–67.

30 Ibid.

31 "Thoughts, Fancies and Facts," by J.Z. LaRocque. In D-1 (Media), JZLP.

32 See Mary Ann Pylypchuk, "The Value of Aboriginal Records as Legal Evidence in Canada: An Examination of Sources," *Archivaria* 32 (Summer 1991): 54.

33 See Joseph LaRocque (as told to Robert Tyre), "I Saw Saskatchewan's Bloody Rebellion," *Liberty*, July 1955, 23 and 51.

34 Ibid., 23.

35 Robert Tyre authored a number of histories, including the biography *Douglas in Saskatchewan: The Story of a Socialist Experiment* (Vancouver: Mitchell Press,1962). See E. Laurie Barron, *Walking in Indian Moccasins: The Native Policies of Tommy Douglas and the CCF* (Vancouver: University of British Columbia Press 1997), xv.

36 Joseph LaRocque, "I Saw Saskatchewan's Bloody Rebellion," 51.

37 LaRocque's historical writings appeared in several Saskatchewan newspapers, including the Regina *Leader-Post*, the Melville *Advance*, the Saskatoon *Star-Phoenix*, and the Yorkton *Enterprise*. He also gave speeches at various local and regional functions. See JZLP, Series D – Publications and/or Media Activities, Series E – Historical Activities and Contributions, and Series F-2 – Speeches.

38 In the J.Z. LaRocque Papers, there is a file devoted to information and correspondence related to the Saskatchewan Historical Society. This file not only documents specific artifacts and documents provided to the society by J.Z. LaRocque but also features carbon copies of correspondence from LaRocque to the society politely, but firmly, requesting the return of family artifacts provided on loan to the Saskatchewan Museum. See JZLP.

4

Colonizer or Compatriot?: A Reassessment of the Reverend John McDougall

Will Pratt

The Reverend John McDougall's historical reputation budded in the somewhat hagiographic and self-justifying histories of fellow Methodists and pioneers in the early twentieth century. It grew to maturity in the popular histories of the Canadian West. And it suffered great damage by the frosts of the 1980s with the incorporation of First Nations testimony and criticism of post-colonial theory.[1] From a historiographical perspective, McDougall, the once stalwart pioneer-missionary, friend, and compatriot to the Cree and Stoney Nakoda tribes, has been transformed into the image of self-interested colonizer and harbinger of the Canadian Dominion's imperial death-march across the West.

However, the analysis and collapse of these historiographical "binaries" allows for a more complex reconstruction of the historical Native–Newcomer relationship. As Keith Smith suggests, "Not everyone in settler society acted simply as local agents of colonialism, either consciously or unconsciously. [...] Colonialism in Western Canada was far more complicated than a simple Manichean duality despite the forces that harmonized to make it appear to be an uncomplicated binary."[2] A nuanced and dynamic perspective of John McDougall moves beyond post-colonial caricature and suggests a well-intentioned missionary whose worldview is, nevertheless, best situated in the colonial context. While McDougall may not have been the selfless "friend of the Indian" that early church history and autobiographical works promoted, his lobbying against Indian Department parsimony and for fair dealings with First Nations suggests that there is a grain of truth in earlier hagiographic harvests. As the twentieth century dawned on Canada's Prairie West, McDougall's "oldtimer" pioneer identity saw him increasingly emphasize his allegiances and sympathies with the Stoney Nakoda people, and question emerging Dominion government Indigenous policies.

"Dynamic paradox" may be the best way to sum up the Reverend John McDougall's attitudes toward First Nations assimilation and government policy. In the 1870s, when he arrived in what was to become the hamlet of Morleyville on the Bow River, he wrote in the binaries of the colonial gaze, contrasting Native "savages" with civilized Christianity. Yet, shortly after the 1877 creation of the Stoney Indian Reserve astride the Bow River in the foothills of the Rocky Mountains, McDougall's attitude towards the Stoney Nakoda, who were increasingly subject to Indian Department and North West Mounted Police surveillance, was clearly one of sympathy.[3] McDougall's goals of religious and cultural assimilation, in the face of his paradoxical accommodation for the seasonal round of Stoney hunting patterns, is observed in everything from treaty payments to visitation rights at the residential school. As historian Courtney Mason has recently observed, the McDougalls "did express a genuine concern for the welfare of the Nakoda communities within which they worked and lived," yet they also pushed for a civilizing and assimilative mission with all its accompanying pressures and problems.[4] While reinforcing the binaries of colonial discourse in his writings, McDougall navigated what Myra Rutherdale called the "contested terrain of shifting identities" by accommodating traditional Stoney cultural patterns.[5] Indian reserve economics and First Nations culture are recurrent themes in an examination of the Reverend's role in establishing the Stoney reserve around the Morleyville mission, his advocacy for government resources, and his increased protest of Department of Indian Affairs (DIA) laws and policies.

John McDougall was raised in the mission schools surrounding his father's Methodist postings on the Upper Canadian frontier. He briefly studied at Victoria College, Cobourg, Canada West, but left there in 1860 to join his father George McDougall at the Rossville mission near Norway House, Rupert's Land.[6] By 1862, when the family moved farther

4.1 The Reverend John McDougall. Glenbow Archives, S-222-24.

west to what would become the Victoria Settlement, John spoke Ojibwa and Cree. As a young missionary's son in the 1860s, he worked as an interpreter and teacher; he was officially received on a trial basis by the church and sent to Pigeon Lake along with his First Nations wife Abigail Steinhauer. Ordained in 1872 at the first missionary conference held in the West, McDougall briefly returned to Ontario where he married Elizabeth Boyd (Abigail having passed away in 1871 after bearing three daughters during the marriage). In 1873, the mission at Morleyville was established and John was selected as its minister. This would be the family's base for a generation, and upon the death of George McDougall on a buffalo hunt in 1876, John would take over the commissioner role of the Methodists' Saskatchewan District. Upon his 1906 retirement, McDougall would take government commissions to investigate both Doukhobor and First Nations grievances regarding land claims in British Columbia.

Treaty signatory: Gathering disciples in the Bow River watershed

McDougall's role at the signing of Treaties 6 and 7 was once portrayed as that of intermediary between Indigenous people and newcomers. This interpretation has not survived the incorporation of First Nations voices into the historical record. Former Stoney Nakoda Chief John Snow's history of the Stoney tribe, and more directly the edited volume featuring Indigenous elders, *The True Spirit and Original Intent of Treaty 7* (1996), question both McDougall's motivation and skill as translator. The details of why the Stoneys signed to Treaty 7, despite the traditional hunting grounds of at least one of the bands being located north of the Red Deer River, are unclear, but McDougall's wish to consolidate them at Morleyville must have played a role.[7] The primary function of the 1877 treaty from the perspective of federal authority is evident in the text of the document itself:

> The Blackfeet, Blood, Piegan, Sarcee, Stony [sic] and other Indians inhabiting the District hereinafter more fully described and defined, do hereby cede, release, surrender, and yield up to the Government of Canada for her Majesty the Queen and her successors forever, all their rights, titles, and privileges whatsoever to the lands included with the following limits.[8]

Yet oral tradition maintains that the Stoneys were unaware of the land surrender and felt they were entering into a traditional alliance with the government. John McDougall's questionable ability as translator, his own self-interest in gathering the Stoneys around his new mission, and Stoney misunderstanding of what was being agreed upon are central to new perspectives on Treaty 7 which have incorporated the voices of First Nations elders.[9]

The placement of the reserve astride an Indigenous communications hub, where montane trails crossed the route westward into what would soon be called the Kicking Horse Pass, meant that several options were available to the Stoneys for their hunting expeditions. Late nineteenth-century Morleyville was situated at the convergence of a number of Indigenous trail systems at the site of a shallow ford across the Bow River. David Thompson reported using what he called the "Wolf Trail" (which would become the route from Fort Edmonton to Morleyville) in his earlier travels.[10] The ability to hunt the game of the Rocky Mountains meant that the extinction of the buffalo was not as catastrophic for the Stoneys as for other plains tribes.[11] Hugh Dempsey notes that the foothills bands adopted plains customs but hunted elk, deer, and moose. The ability of the Stoneys to hunt, and the bio-region's unsuitability for agriculture, frustrated the Indian Department's hope for their transition to sedentary agriculture, a cornerstone of the project of assimilation in the prairie West.[12] In the early years of the reserve, the district superintendent wrote, "from its proximity to the mountains, and from the character of the soil, I have grave doubts regarding the general success of agriculture here, the soil being light, sandy loam, on a bed of gravel (the knolls being entirely gravel)."[13] These environmental realities resulted in a compromise surrounding treaty payments in the early years of the reserve, as the annual payment was postponed until the Stoneys returned from the hunt.[14] John McDougall's pragmatic approach recognized the need to accept Stoney cultural and subsistence patterns for the success of the colonial project of assimilation. He realized that pushing too hard to deny the hunt to Stoneys would cause them to resist his evangelizing mission.[15]

Government agent or Indigenous advocate: Navigating the reserve economy

An alternate title for this paper, in keeping with the spirit of false dichotomy, might have been "Government Agent or Indigenous Advocate." At several points during his life, McDougall acted as an emissary for the government. He announced the arrival of the North West Mounted Police in the Treaty 7 area, and his role in treaty negotiations has already been examined. During the 1885 Riel resistance he was asked to visit First Nations camps to reassure them. Yet Reverend McDougall also lobbied the government for more resources and fair treatment of the Stoneys. The more cynical might claim that such advocacy was the result of a small-time chieftain defending powers over his own fiefdom, but McDougall's motivations in these cases are worthy of greater examination.[16]

In the early 1880s, the first indications of conflict between the Indian Department and the Methodist mission arose in a dispute over contract labour relating to the market for railway lumber. Indian Agent Cecil Denny ordered the Stoneys to stop cutting and selling lumber on the reserve. McDougall had employed them to cut railroad ties for Denny, reportedly paying them only "a little grub" for their work.[17] The Stoneys also complained that they were obliged to trade with McDougall what little money they had. It would not be the last time that the missionary would be accused of profiting from his authoritative position.[18] In 1887, Reverend John Shaw, assistant secretary to the Methodist Church Missionary Department, warned McDougall that the Indian Department had complained of missionaries trading with Indigenous people, and that "there may be cases in which, for the sake of the Indians, the missionary may consider it his duty to put employment in their way, but unless the reasons for this be very strong and very clear, it is not desirable that either missionaries or teachers should engage in trade."[19]

From the 1870s, a series of debates in the Dominion House of Commons led to restrictions on First Nations integration into the economy.[20] In 1885, these efforts culminated in the permit system, which required approval from the Indian Department agent or farm instructor before selling any goods off the reserve. While McDougall profited from his position as local authority, he could also act as a lobbyist for Indigenous expansion beyond constricted reserve economies. In 1886, Deputy Superintendent of Indian Affairs Lawrence Vankoughnet wrote McDougall to chastise him for writing criticisms against the department in the Toronto *Globe*.[21] Vankoughnet reminded McDougall of the work-for-rations policy and that the Stoneys were not to market their lumber, as the timber should be maintained for future generations. McDougall had claimed in the *Globe* that certain government employees were of immoral character. Vankoughnet's letter apparently made little difference, as he had to write McDougall again at the end of the year to note his disapproval of a critical pamphlet the Reverend had published.[22]

Another instance of McDougall chiding the government came in the late 1890s concerning Stoney anxieties over the issuing of government cattle brands. He reported that the Stoneys had already developed personal brands, and that despite this, the government branded their cattle with the government "ID" (for Indian Department) while they were away on the hunt. In McDougall's words, "they were righteously incensed, and as many of these cattle were not from the Government, the Indians began to kill and eat their cattle, and this accounts for the smallness of the number of cattle when [the farming instructor, P.L.] Grasse came to Morley."[23]

The Indian Act's revision in 1876 stifled First Nations' abilities to shape the economic realities on the reserves. In 1894, on McDougall's instigation, the Stoneys from the Morley, Peace Hills, Saddle Lake, and Stoney Plain reserves signed a petition for more control of their agriculture and ranching assets.[24] The Indian Department reply to the petition reflected its resistance to conceiving Indigenous people as anything but wards of the state. The department stated that it did not believe that the Stoneys were ready to deal yet with the "white men," and that they lacked "business acumen."[25] The Stoneys asked for partial handling of their cattle, more say on how they were sold, and a third of the profits from their sale. The department conceded to their request to charge money for grinding flour at their mills, but not to distributing the money to band members at the time of the annuity payment, claiming that such dispersal of the profits would mean they would be "frittered away."[26] Such attitudes show that the system designed to assimilate Indigenous peoples into Euro-Canadian society was seriously flawed. Since they had no say in the use of the profits of their labour, there was little motivation to adopt the agricultural methods the department pressed for.

With the appointment of Farming Instructor P.L. Grasse in 1891, tensions between the Indian Department and the McDougall Mission flared once again. There was a pronounced personality conflict between Reverend John McDougall and Farming Instructor Grasse, the latter being described by investigators of later Stoney grievances as "wanting in tact."[27] Grasse claimed that the clash began with McDougall asking the department to issue the McDougall Orphanage's beef ration to merchants to pay that institution's debts. The result was the cancellation of the beef ration to the orphanage, as the grant that it had received was supposed to include all operating costs. Grasse accused McDougall of not operating the orphanage on some days, paying his land lease from the bands in "lump jawed beef," and preaching against Grasse and the department. Grasse claimed that McDougall "[could] not get over the days when he was sole ruler in the camp."²⁸ McDougall fought back with a list of accusations which claimed that Grasse neglected the sick, withdrew rations for two months and gave them unfairly, did not sympathize with the Stoneys, swore, and drank. As late as 1896 the feud continued over the poor quality of beef fed at the McDougall Orphanage.²⁹ McDougall defended himself in a letter to his ecclesiastical superior, Reverend Sutherland of Toronto, claiming Grasse had denied the individuality central to the work of the missionary, and encouraged Nakoda dependency.³⁰ McDougall's animosity toward the government did not end at letters to his superiors. He published articles in eastern newspapers and distributed his own pamphlets condemning the administration of the Indian Department.³¹

With the expansion of Rocky Mountains National Park in 1887, and more restrictive game laws of 1895, McDougall again became involved in government controversy.³² Complaints had been lodged specifically against the Stoneys for trespassing and shooting prairie chicken and partridge. McDougall allegedly called a meeting and told the Stoneys to hunt when they pleased, as the game laws made exception for those who were in "actual" or "immediate want."³³ McDougall's compromise with the Stoney Nakoda, recognizing the hunt central to their well-being and accepting their absence from the reserve and neglect of agriculture to pursue it, came to characterize his mode of operations at Morley.

Compromise, coercion, and education

Despite today's condemnation of the form and method of government- and church-administered Indigenous education, in the late nineteenth century some Western Canadian First Nations felt that schools would allow their children to survive under the rapidly changing conditions they were experiencing.³⁴ Education promised in Treaty 7 set the precedent for the establishment of the McDougall Orphanage (which was a part-residential and part-seasonal boarding school) as well as a day school on the reserve. By January 1877, the Morley mission had both day and Sabbath schools, the former boasting thirty pupils.³⁵ Reverend McDougall reported that the day school was doing well and noted the need to "get the natives [to] break off from their wanderings and live more at the mission."³⁶ By 1880, the day school held twenty-three boys and twenty-two girls. Attendance was said to increase in winter, when parents left for the hunt.[37] The district superintendent for Treaty 7 noted that children only attended school when their parents were out hunting. The acceptance of the Stoney hunt would long dictate the rhythms and possibilities of education in Morley.

There may have been a role for the orphanage on the reserve caused by high parental mortality, but it seems that motivations related to education and child care were factors for placing children at the McDougall Orphanage. The ease with which children were recruited in the early years of the institution suggests that this was the case.[38] Colonial powers of coercion were weak in the days when Indigenous peoples far outnumbered Euro-Canadians.[39] This situation suggests that Morley was different than elsewhere in Western Canada, where "from the beginning, school officials complained about the problems involved in recruiting students."[40] Why children would not be placed with extended family is unclear.[41] The degree of demographic disruption in the mid-nineteenth century may have meant that some children had little in the way of family networks left intact. Whether or not the orphanage served a community purpose does not, however, erase its intended role of assimilation. A report for the year of 1882 noted that school progress on the reserve was slow and "the only way to really teach the Indian children is to separate them altogether from their parents, as these will never force the children to attend school if they wish to shirk."[42]

The increasing conflict at the McDougall Orphanage in the years surrounding Reverend John McDougall's retirement in 1906 suggests that the cultural compromise forged in the late nineteenth century was destroyed. With a change in principals from John Niddrie (a close colleague of McDougall's) to C.B. Oakley in 1903, ideas of accommodation were abandoned. The Indian agent and Royal North West Mounted Police increasingly used coercion to return truants to the school.[43] In 1905, Superintendent David Laird wrote to Oakley that the difficulty in managing the many requests for time off stemmed from Niddrie's previous lenience. Laird stated that "if an Indian takes away his child without leave, you can go to a magistrate ... and get a warrant to bring the pupil back."[44] Evidence exists of increasing use of school corporal punishment and harsh treatment coinciding with Principal Niddrie's departure and McDougall's own frequent absence from the reserve.

Vanishing "Indians" and oldtimers: McDougall's changing attitude toward assimilation

While Reverend John McDougall's legacy focuses on his promotion of Indigenous culture as a "friend of the Indian," in reality, this role was adopted later in life. The Reverend's speeches in the 1880s reveal more racial discourse castigating Indigenous culture as savage, base, ignorant, superstitious, blind, and helpless.[45] They mirrored the common colonial discourse of the time, which created a dichotomy between civilized and savage that justified evangelizing and assimilating efforts.[46] Historian Ernest Nix, writing for the *Dictionary of Canadian Biography*, expressed McDougall's attitude toward Indigenous peoples in what was then Rupert's Land:

> Well aware of the destruction which advancing settlement had inflicted on the native people of Upper Canada, they hoped that the Indians of the region would gather around the mission and enjoy some measure of isolation from white society for a generation in which they could adjust to the coming changes. Their only chance in the new west seemed to lie in their conversion to Christianity and eventual adoption of European cultural values. It was the solution favoured by social activists generally, who believed it would enable native people to participate in the future as full citizens.[47]

In a speech given in 1886, McDougall attacked the "tomtom," body paint, feathers, incantations, and the Sun Dance as pagan worship.[48] A reporter noted that McDougall "condemned most strongly the pow wow, and urged, on all people, to discourage this among the Indians, as it served to keep alive and bring up their heathen worship and idolatrous practices." McDougall had claimed that under his guidance, the Stoneys had turned from making drums, and that these were not to be allowed on the reserve. In the late 1870s and 1880s, then, John accepted the notion of the "vanishing Indian." He wrote in his 1878–79 annual report to the Missionary Society:

> There are about twenty-five thousand Indians in the North-West; the greater part, as yet, untouched by either Christianity or civilization. Shall they remain so? They *cannot*. They will either be saved by the action of the Church of God or ruined by the advance of frontier civilization.[49]

McDougall saw the orphanage working for the eternal salvation for his pupils: "What we want is to civilize and Christianize a people who have all the native material for progress. Left to themselves, or to indifferent Government management, they will retrograde – they will perish."[50] Nix notes that McDougall "refused to believe that the role of Indians was to die out. He considered himself their friend and worked to prepare them, in the way he thought best, for the inevitable changes he saw coming."[51] Taking three Indigenous representatives to Ontario in 1886, McDougall noted that "the degradation of the past was melting away, giving place to those Christian characteristics which go to make a strong national and social manhood."[52] The display of converted Indigenous peoples was common to a colonial discourse which sought to reinforce the dichotomy of civilized and savage.[53] That Chiefs Pakan, Samson, and Bigstoney, who travelled with McDougall to Ontario, spoke in both Cree and English and wore a mixture of Euro-Canadian and traditional attire suggested that their lived realities were more ambiguous. As far back as 1887, Stoney pupils at the McDougall Orphanage displayed their knitting and sewing at an exhibition in Calgary.[54] Such displays were likely to show the effects of assimilation, in this case, with girls showing off a Euro-Canadian seamstress custom they were able to learn.

McDougall's earlier attitudes toward the suppression of Indigenous culture and religion began to fade in the 1890s and became nearly reversed by the twentieth century. After 1885 the Indian Act was amended to prevent First Nations from travelling to other reserves and to practise the Sun Dance.[55] Together with the pass system, which required that First Nations be given permission from an Indian agent before leaving the reserve, government policy sought to suppress First Nations culture and mobility.[56] McDougall "annoyed" the Indian Department by writing to the *Winnipeg Free Press* in support of government tolerance toward the Sun Dance, expressly contradicting this assimilation policy.[57] The church was also

4.2 John McDougall and Indigenous participants at the Calgary Fairgrounds. Glenbow Archives, NA-5329-14,

perturbed by his continued support of the display of traditional clothes and dance at various exhibitions. In 1895, the *Christian Guardian* carried a bitter exchange between McDougall and Egerton Ryerson Young where the former defended the subtleties of Indigenous culture from its dismissal as mere savagery. McDougall also reinforced his own status as a true westerner against the accusations of the mere "tenderfoot" Young.[58]

The display of Stoney culture at Banff Indian Days and the Calgary Exhibition and Stampede was also a contentious point advanced by McDougall.[59] In 1908 he was the secretary for the Committee of the Dominion Exhibition, writing to Indian agents in hopes of encouraging First Nations participation in the parade. These were to represent the old West, along with their use of dog travois, and hunting and war costumes. At the first Calgary Stampede in 1912, the *Calgary Eye Opener* wrote, "The famous missionary John McDougall will, of course, handle the Indians for the occasion."[60] Now McDougall was encouraging Indigenous culture and associating himself with a bygone and imagined West. In the year before his death in 1917, he wrote in the *Christian Guardian* to defend First Nations against accusations of savagery and vengefulness while criticising the greed of Canadian society. He wrote, "A material civilization will produce more unforgiveness, and desire for revenge, and cultivate a grosser savagery than was ever to be found among a purely aboriginal people."[61]

John Chantler McDougall was neither a caricature of an evil colonialist nor a selfless champion of Indigenous rights. In her master's thesis, Sarah Carter noted the complexity of the Reverend's publications:

> An ambivalence of thought is most conspicuous in John McDougall's books. A sense of uncertainty and unease about the superiority of the civilization that he urged the Indians to adopt is clearly detectable in McDougall's writing. [...] It is perhaps in this ambivalence of thought that the root of a natural need for a quiet conscience may be found; McDougall felt a need to appease his doubts and anxieties and did this through his writing.[62]

He was also not a static character. His early efforts to repress Stoney culture were reversed in later years with his support for the continuation of the Sun Dance. As a member of a select group of pioneers in the Calgary area, McDougall saw his own way of life being eroded by the rapid changes in Canadian society. McDougall had long associated himself in writings as part of the dying West, even adopting a pseudo-Indigenous identity at times.[63] In 1873, when McDougall arrived in Morleyville, his source of imported material supplies was over three hundred miles away on an ox and cart trail to Fort Benton, Montana. In the early twentieth century, at the time of his retirement, McDougall could take the CPR to Calgary, ride a streetcar across town, and drive Stephen Avenue in an automobile. McDougall's friction against the government could be interpreted as simply the pragmatic protest of a local authority who knew that federal policy would not work. Yet McDougall expressed a genuine desire to ameliorate the Stoneys' quality of life during the rising tide of settlement and government intrusion. McDougall's worldview shifted away from his early acceptance of the strict colonial dichotomy of savagery and civilization, toward a more celebratory understanding of First Nations culture.

Notes

1. Early writings include John Maclean, *McDougall of Alberta: A Life of Rev. John Mc-Dougall, D.D., Pathfinder of Empire and Prophet of the Plains* (Toronto: Ryerson, 1927); a writer in one church publication claimed, "John McDougall, who labours to-day in Morley, is one of the grandest, most self-sacrificing heroes the world has ever seen": M.W.E., "The Heroine of Morleyville: A True Story of North-West Missions," *The Methodist Magazine*, January 1890. The beginning of the post-colonial critique can be traced to Sarah Carter, "Man's Mission of Subjugation: The Publications of John Maclean, John McDougall and Egerton R. Young, Nineteenth-Century Methodist Missionaries in Western Canada" (master's thesis, University of Saskatchewan, 1980); it is explicitly expressed in Sarah Carter, Walter Hildebrandt, and Dorothy First Rider, *The True Spirit and Original Intent of Treaty 7* (Montreal: McGill-Queen's University Press, 1996).

2. Keith Smith, *Liberalism, Surveillance, and Resistance: Indigenous Communities in Western Canada, 1877–1927* (Edmonton: Athabasca University Press, 2009), 20–21.

3. Ibid., 234.

4. Courtney Mason, *Spirits of the Rockies: Reasserting an Indigenous Presence in Banff National Park* (Toronto: University of Toronto Press, 2014), 26.

5. Myra Rutherdale, *Women and the White Man's God: Gender and Race in the Canadian Mission Field* (Vancouver: University of British Columbia Press, 2002), 152.

6. Ernest Nix, "McDougall, John Chantler," *Dictionary of Canadian Biography*, vol. 14, University of Toronto/Université Laval. 2003–,http://www.biographi.ca/en/bio/mcdougall_john_chantler_14E.html.

7. Hugh Dempsey, *Indian Tribes of Alberta*, repr. and rev. ed. (Calgary: Glenbow-Alberta Institute, [1979] 1988), 44; the most recent treatments are offered by Dempsey, *The Great Blackfoot Treaties* (Calgary: Heritage House, 2015), 87–88; and Carter, Hildebrandt, and First Rider, *The True Spirit and Original Intent of Treaty 7*, 22, 140.

8. Sessional Paper No. 10, *Sessional Papers of the Dominion of Canada* (Ottawa: 1878), p. xliv, available at Early Canadiana Online (hereafter ECO), http://eco.canadiana.ca (accessed 20 February 2011).

9. Carter, Hildebrandt, and First Rider, *The True Spirit and Original Intent of Treaty 7*.

10. Jean L. Johnson, ed., *Big Hill Country* (Cochrane, AB: Cochrane and Area Historical Society, 1977), 73; the route would later be called the McDougall Trail. The Indigenous trail has also been referred to as the "Old North Trail." MacLean, *McDougall of Alberta*, 76; Dempsey, *Indian Tribes of Alberta*, 44.

11. All Treaty 7 tribal populations declined from 1871 to 1917, except the Stoney-Nakodas': Smith, *Liberalism, Surveillance, and Resistance*, 42.

12. Sarah Carter, *Lost Harvests: Prairie Indian Reserve Farmers and Government Policy* (Montreal: McGill-Queen's University Press, 1990).

13. The report offers one of the few criticisms of the land as good cattle country. Norman Macleod suggested that the land was poor winter pasture due to the effect of brush and timber drawing cattle in during the winter where there is no grass. Macleod to Dewdney, "Report of the Department of Indian Affairs for the Year Ended 31st December, 1881," Sessional Paper No. 6, *Sessional Papers of the Dominion of Canada*: 5, Fourth session of the Fourth Parliament, 1882 (Ottawa: MacLean, Roger, 1882), xxviii, ECO, http://eco.canadiana.ca (accessed 20 February 2011).

14 Ibid.; in 1887, a survey of the reserve was postponed until the three chiefs returned from the hunt. Sessional Paper No. 14, *Sessional Papers of the Dominion of Canada*: 12, Second Session of the Sixth Parliament, Session 1888 (Ottawa: A. Senecal, 1888), ECO, http://eco.canadiana.ca (accessed 18 February 2011).

15 Hugh Dempsey, "One Hundred Years of Treaty Seven," in *One Century Later: Western Canadian Reserve Indians Since Treaty 7*, ed. Ian Getty and Donald B. Smith (Vancouver: University of British Columbia Press, 1978), 26.

16 John Larner described the McDougall influence on the Treaty 7 process as satisfying McDougall's wish to create "a duchy on the upper Bow." As cited in Smith, *Liberalism, Surveillance, and Resistance*, 155.

17 The position of the reserve on the Canadian Pacific Railway, as it approached the Kicking Horse Pass, gave the reserve a market for lumber, although the Indian Department's desire to conserve the timber lands of the reserve meant that access to such income would be regulated. Assistant Indian Commissioner Hayter Reed in June 1884 allowed the sale of deadwood but prohibited the cutting the new growth. Hayter Reed, "Report of Inspector T.P. Wadsworth on the Stony Reserve at Morley," 17 June 1884, Department of Indian Affairs, RG 10, Black Series, vol. 3680, file 12,349, Library and Archives Canada (hereafter LAC).

18 On 21 January 1884, Dewdney advised Ottawa, "I would not advise that any supplies be left in charge of the Rev. Mr McDougall at Morleyville": "Correspondence Stemming from Inspector Wadsworth's Annual Report On the Stony Indians at Morleyville," 1883, Stony Agency, Department of Indian Affairs, RG 10, vol. 3637, file 6882, reel C10112, LAC; in 1891 McDougall's request for a grazing lease on the reserve was denied by the department due to conflict of interest. Carter, Hildebrandt, and First Rider, *The True Spirit and Original Intent of Treaty 7*, 268.

19 Shaw to McDougall, "Correspondence. – January 4–December 21, 1887," McDougall Family Fonds (hereafter MFF), M729-44, 11 October 1887, Glenbow Archives (hereafter GA).

20 Smith, *Liberalism, Surveillance, and Resistance*, 99.

21 Vankoughnet-McDougall Correspondence, 5 July 1886, M-729-41, Series 2c, MFF, GA.

22 Vankoughnet-McDougall Correspondence, 27 Dec 1886, M-729-43, Series 2c, MFF, GA.

23 "Correspondence regarding charges brought against Rev. John McDougall by farmer, Mr. P.L. Grasse," 1896–97, p. 168, Department of Indian Affairs, RG 10, vol. 3966, file 151,384, reel 10, LAC.

24 "Petition from the Indians that they should be allowed full control of their own grain, cattle and timber and to charge settlers a toll for gristing at their mills," 1894, Department of Indian Affairs, RG 10, vol. 3917, file 116,493, LAC.

25 Ibid.

26 Ibid.

27 "Report of Unpleasantness Between Farmer Grasse and the Authorities of the Methodist Church," 1892, Department of Indian Affairs, RG 10, vol. 3881, file 94,262, reel C10156, LAC.

28 Ibid., P.L. Grasse to Hayter Reed, 31 May 1892; Lump Jaw, or Lumpy Jaw, is a bacterial infection caused by lacerations in the mouths of cattle.

29 "Correspondence regarding charges brought against Rev. John McDougall by farmer, Mr. P.L. Grasse," 1896-97, Department of Indian Affairs, RG 10, vol. 3966, file 151,384, reel 10168, LAC.

30 John McDougall, *Pathfinding on Plain and Prairie* (Toronto: William Briggs, 1895), 70, as cited in Sarah Carter, "The Missionaries' Indian: Publications of John McDougall, John Mclean, and Egerton Ryerson Young," *Prairie Forum*, 9, no. 1 (1984): 33.

31 Vankoughnet–McDougall Correspondence, 1886, M-729-43, Series 2c, MFF, GA. In the 30 June 1886 Toronto *Globe*, McDougall claimed "the Indian is being defrauded by the government": Vankoughnet–McDougall Correspondence, 1886, M-729-41, Series 2c, MFF, GA.

32 As of 1 January 1895, Canadian game laws would apply to the Stoney bands on the reserve, restricting their hunting during certain times of the year. "Correspondence regarding the application of the Game Laws to Stony [sic] Indians forbidding them to hunt or trap within the limits of the Rocky Mountain Park," 1893–95, Department of Indian Affairs, RG 10, vol. 3796, file 47,441-2, LAC; as early as 1884, on Ontario reserves, similar restrictions by game wardens were being implemented: Robin Brownlie, *A Fatherly Eye: Indian Agents, Government Power, and Aboriginal Resistance in Ontario, 1918-1939* (Don Mills, ON: Oxford University Press, 2003), 87–88; Theodore Binnema and Melanie Niemi, "'Let the Line Be Drawn Now': Wilderness, Conservation, and the Exclusion of Aboriginal People from Banff National Park in Canada," *Environmental History* 11, no. 4 (2006): 724–50.

33 The game laws ultimately succeeded in keeping the Stoneys on their reserves for the greater period of the year. McDougall to Sutherland, 28 January 1897, "Correspondence regarding charges brought against Rev. John McDougall by farmer, Mr. P.L. Grasse," 1896-97, Department of Indian Affairs, RG 10, vol. 3966, file 151,384, reel 10168, LAC.

34 Jennifer Lorretta Jane Pettit, "'To Christianize and Civilize': Native Industrial Schools in Canada" (PhD diss., University of Calgary, 1998), 91; Carter, Hildebrandt, and First Rider, *The True Spirit and Original Intent of Treaty 7*, 122.

35 McDougall to Dr. Wood, "John C. McDougall's Letterbook, 1876–1877," early 1877, M-729-37, MFF, GA.

36 Ibid.

37 "Report of the Department of Indian Affairs for the Year Ended 31st December, 1881," Sessional Paper No. 6, *Sessional Papers of the Dominion of Canada*: 5, Fourth Session of the Fourth Parliament, Session 1882 (Ottawa: MacLean, Roger, 1882), xxix and 42, ECO, http://eco.canadiana.ca (accessed 20 February 2011).

38 In 1886, Inspector McGibbon noted that "the parents on this reserve are most anxious to have their children educated." McGibbon Report, 23 August 1886, "Report of the Department of Indian Affairs for the Year Ended 31st December, 1886." Sessional Paper No. 6, *Sessional Papers of the Dominion of Canada*: 5, First Session of the Sixth Parliament, Session 1887 (Ottawa: MacLean, Roger, 1887), 149, ECO, http://eco.canadiana.ca (accessed 20 February 2010).

39 Carter notes that refusal of baptism and excommunication were weak measures of coercion against polygamy. Sarah A. Carter, "Creating 'Semi-Widows' and 'Supernumerary Wives': Prohibiting Polygamy in Prairie Canada's Aboriginal Communities to 1900," in *Contact Zones: Aboriginal and Settler Women in Canada's Colonial Past*, ed. Katie Pickles and Myra Rutherdale (Vancouver: University of British Columbia Press, 2005), 137.

40 Pettit, "To Christianize and Civilize," 144.

41 Chief John Snow argues that records indicate that children in the institution were not orphans and that extended family support made orphanages unnecessary. Chief John Snow, *These Mountains Are our Sacred Places: The Story of the Stoney People* (Toronto: Fitzhenry & Whiteside, 2005), 27.

42 "Report of the Department of Indian Affairs for the Year Ended 31st December, 1882," Sessional Paper No. 5, *Sessional Papers of the Dominion of Canada*: 4, First Session of the Fifth Parliament, Session 1883 (Ottawa: MacLean, Roger, 1883), 176, ECO, http://eco.canadiana.ca (accessed 18 February 2011).

43 The Department of Indian Affairs' regulations of 1894, which fell short of requiring compulsory attendance, appear to have become more interventionist by the end of the decade. John S. Milloy, *A National Crime: The Canadian Government and the Residential School System, 1879 to 1986* (Winnipeg: University of Manitoba Press, 1999), 70; in 1894, under Deputy Superintendent Hayter Reed, the Indian Act was modified to regulate Indigenous school attendance. Brian Titley, *A Narrow Vision: Duncan Campbell Scott and the Administration of Indian Affairs in Canada* (Vancouver: University of British Columbia Press, 1986), 15; in 1894, fines of $2 were intended to make parents compel attendance. Snow, *These Mountains Are our Sacred Spaces*, 249. Commissioner Edgar Dewdney's reforms in 1883 hoped to provide for future compulsory attendance. Brian Titley, *The Frontier World of Edgar Dewdney* (Vancouver: University of British Columbia Press, 1999), 56.

44 Laird to Principal, 16 November 1905, Incoming Correspondence, McDougall Orphanage and Home Fonds, M-1380, Folder 3, GA.

45 McDougall was said to admire the "frontier skills" of the Plains tribes, though he thought of them as beneath him. Carter, Hildebrandt, and First Rider, *True Spirit and Intent of Treaty 7*, 52.

46 Rutherdale, *Women and the White Man's God*, 34–35; the opposite ideal in this dichotomy hoped Aboriginals would became more practical, industrious, useful, intelligent, and self-supporting. John Milloy, *A National Crime*, 25; post-colonial studies suggest that a "cultural schizophrenia" may have resulted from those caught in the middle of this racially constructed duality. Bill Ashcroft, *Post-Colonial Studies: The Key Concepts* (New York: Routledge, 2000), 24; Cree elder John Tootoosis noted that the graduate of the residential school "is hanging in the middle of two cultures." Katherine Pettipas, *Severing the Ties that Bind: Government Repression of Indigenous Religious Cultures on the Prairies* (Winnipeg: University of Manitoba Press, 1994), 81–82.

47 Nix, "McDougall, John Chantler."

48 Possibly published in the *Calgary Herald*. "The Western Indians: What the Gospel and the Missionaries Have Done," 1886, M-729-66, MFF, GA; missionary "fundraising lecture tours and published reports" contributed to the public discourse of Indians as savages: Pettipas, *Severing the Ties that Bind*, 101; Carter, Hildebrandt, and First Rider, *True Spirit and Intent of Treaty 7*, 157.

49 "Fifty-first annual report of the Missionary Society of the Methodist Church of Canada from June 1878 to June 1879," Toronto, Methodist Conference Printing Office, 1879, CIHM no. 00934-1874-75, p. xv.

50 "The Western Indians: What the Gospel and the Missionaries Have Done," 1886, M-729-66, MFF, GA.

51 Nix, "McDougall, John Chantler."
52 MacLean, *McDougall of Alberta*, 161–62.
53 Rutherdale, *Women and the White Man's God*, 120.
54 "Report of the Department of Indian Affairs for the Year Ended 31st December 1887," Sessional Paper No. 15, *Sessional Papers of the Dominion of Canada*: 13, Second Session of the Sixth Parliament, Session 1888 (Ottawa: Maclean, 1888), ECO, lvii , http://eco.canadiana.ca (accessed February 2011).
55 James R Miller, *Skyscrapers Hide the Heavens: A History of Indian-White Relations in Canada* (Toronto: University of Toronto Press, 1991), 192–93.
56 Smith notes that the pass system had no basis in law and was feebly enforced: *Liberalism, Surveillance, and Resistance*, 60–71.
57 Nix, "McDougall, John Chantler."
58 Carter, "Man's Mission of Subjugation," 26.
59 See Jonathan Clapperton, "Naturalizing Race Relations: Conservation, Colonialism, and Spectacle at the Banff Indian Days," *Canadian Historical Review* 94, no. 3 (2013): 349–79; Mason, *Spirits of the Rockies*; Laurie Meijer Drees, "'Indians' Bygone Past': The Banff Indian Days, 1902–1945," *Past Imperfect* 2 (1993): 7–28.
60 *Calgary Eye Opener*, 7 September 1912, as cited in Carter, "Man's Mission of Subjugation," 155.
61 John McDougall, "The Aborigine Not So Bad," *Christian Guardian*, 27 September 1916. Thanks to Don Smith for sharing this article.
62 Carter, "Man's Mission of Subjugation," 9.
63 McDougall referred to himself in 1898 as "Nine-tenths Indian": *Pathfinding on Plain and Prairie*, 61.

5

Exploring the "Thirteenth" Reason for Suffrage: Enfranchising "Mothers of the British Race" on the Canadian Prairies

Mallory Allyson Richard

In the 9 November 1910 issue of the *Grain Growers' Guide*, the editor of its "Around the Fireside" women's feature published a list of "Twelve Reasons for Supporting Women's Suffrage." The *Guide* was a weekly publication for farmers on the Canadian Prairies that was founded in 1908 and had reached a circulation of nearly 30,000 before World War I.[1] It was written in English for an Anglophone readership and was an important source of information and advice related to farming and farm life in Western Canada. It also served as a forum for passionate political debate and championed social and political change. It was in that spirit that, in 1910, Isobel Graham included a list entitled "Twelve Reasons for Supporting Women's Suffrage" in the women's pages. Wedged between advice columns and humour pieces, the list suggested reasons why readers should join the movement advocating for women's enfranchisement:

1. Because we believe in government by the people, and the people include both men and women.
2. Because women pay taxes, and taxation and representation should go together.
3. Because women must obey the laws and should take their part in making them.

4. Because men and women look at things from a different standpoint and so cannot represent each other's views.
5. Because the vote would improve the economic position of women.
6. Because the vote would tend to establish an equal standard of morality for men and women.
7. Because questions affecting the home are constantly dealt with by parliament.
8. Because the experience of women would be valuable to the state.
9. Because women already have the vote for local elections.
10. Because thousands of hard-working women demand it.
11. Because the enfranchisement of the people is a liberal principle and should include women.
12. Because it is just.[2]

Today the franchise is recognized as a fundamental right, something to which every Canadian citizen is entitled on the basis of their inherent dignity and humanity, and this may prompt a tendency to indicate the importance of the eleventh and twelfth reasons over the others in the present day. In 1910, however, it was more common for the franchise to be viewed as a privilege, and all women and men needed to prove themselves worthy of it. While some of the *Guide*'s twelve reasons serve to justify women's receipt of the vote by measuring women's contributions in, for example, the taxes they paid, advocates of women's suffrage also argued for the franchise by measuring their contributions relative to those of ethnocultural and Indigenous groups. In effect, the implied and unspoken "thirteenth" point in support of women's enfranchisement was that women were at least as deserving of the vote as some enfranchised males, and were *more* deserving than their fellow disfranchised Canadians.

In 1910, some women in Canada could vote in municipal elections, but all were denied the vote at the provincial and federal levels. All Asian

Canadians and status Indians were disfranchised, as were people serving time in prisons or mental institutions. Thus some women, including Asian-Canadian and First Nations women with Indian status, faced multiple barriers to enfranchisement because they were disqualified from voting on the basis of both their race and gender. The movement for women's enfranchisement in Canada was, at this time, led by white, British-Canadian women and focused on the gender-based restrictions on the franchise. This held true on the Prairies as well: the best-known champions and organizations promoting women's suffrage in Manitoba, Saskatchewan, and Alberta were British-Canadian women, and their perspectives were well represented in the pages of the *Grain Growers' Guide*. Nellie McClung, the best-known champion of women's suffrage in Canada, was particularly loyal to the British Empire and used *In Times Like These,* her "1915 suffrage manifesto," to praise the qualities of British-Canadian women relative to European immigrants and non-white Canadians.[3]

Veronica Strong-Boag has written that suffrage movements cut across class lines, uniting middle- and working-class women with a common cause.[4] She is correct that movements for women's enfranchisement overcame certain social and economic barriers, but it did not overcome all of them. While a common argument in favour of women's suffrage on the Prairies was that women deserved the vote because they were dedicated workers, the articulation of this reasoning by several prominent British Canadian advocates of women's suffrage made it clear they were not suggesting *all* women deserved to vote because *all* women were hard workers. In fact, some British Canadians who called for women's suffrage did so by arguing that white women were more deserving of the vote and more likely to use it responsibly than non-white Canadians, recent immigrants, or out-of-work transients.

These comparisons, along with other arguments for and against women's suffrage, were offered in the *Guide* by its columnists and its readers. Their commentaries, which effectively became discussions as they responded to one another's ideas, serve as a rich source for explaining how the idea of women's suffrage spread and was justified within the prairie region. Manitoba, Saskatchewan, and Alberta also had in common certain suffragist champions and organizations whose speaking tours, conventions, and publications brought the movement – and then the franchise – to each province. They were the first three provinces in

Canada to remove gender restrictions on the franchise, beginning in 1916 with Manitoba and then Alberta and ending in 1917 with Saskatchewan. While these regional commonalities make it possible to study how British-Canadian women compared themselves to already-enfranchised and disfranchised male Canadians to improve their standing, they bear similarities to the promotion of women's suffrage elsewhere in Canada. It was common for women in one region to borrow strategies, arguments, and literature from women who had used them effectively elsewhere. They also responded to similar impediments expressed against the vote for women, such as the need to assuage fears that agitation for the vote betrayed Christian and British-Canadian values (though the latter was not a significant concern in Quebec). Finally, the racism and nativism evident in this aspect of the women's suffrage movement on the Prairies likewise extended to other regions.

Debating entitlement

At the turn of the twentieth century, the belief that women and men were inherently unequal was so widespread that for many Canadians, the idea of women seeking the same rights and opportunities as men was appalling. In such a climate, challenging the status quo exposed women to scorn. What made the franchise worth fighting for? Certainly the vote carried the potential to have a say in how government was formed and what legislation it passed, but its power was also symbolic. As Ian McKay has pointed out, the franchise was previously reserved for those individuals who were "self-possessed – whose body and soul [were theirs] alone" and who realized the liberal ideals of personal liberty and independence which, McKay argues, were part of the hegemonic classical liberal model that persisted in Canada until the 1940s.[5] According to McKay, women, Asian Canadians, and First Nations Canadians were viewed as incapable of meeting this standard and were therefore denied the rights and responsibilities that came with it. McKay's assertion that liberal values informed prevailing notions of the franchise during this period is supported by Canadian political debate.

At least as early as 1885 and continuing for decades thereafter, men (and legislators in particular, the very people with whom the authority to extend the franchise rested) commonly discussed women's entitlement to vote by comparing them to racial and ethnic minority groups in terms of their merits and potential as engaged political subjects. Such comparisons were made in the House of Commons in 1885, when Sir John A. Macdonald presented a bill to consolidate the legislation governing the franchise so it would be solely under federal control. When it was introduced, the future Electoral Franchise Act included a clause that would extend the federal franchise to unmarried women and widows. Married women would still be ineligible to vote, but the legislation was nonetheless significant for proposing to lift, however incompletely, some of the restrictions on women voting. Macdonald had introduced bills to centralize the franchise while also extending the vote to some women in 1883 and 1884, but both times the bills failed to pass and the enfranchisement of women was not debated at any length.[6] Macdonald's bill survived to be passed in 1885, but without the clause that would allow women to vote. It had been dropped from the bill, though not before Members of Parliament weighed in on whether they felt women deserved the franchise.

Several members expressed their opinions on women's suffrage by comparing the perceived merits of white women (the only women whose enfranchisement seems to have been seriously considered) to the respective merits of Chinese Canadians and First Nations Canadians, whose entitlement to vote was also being decided. George Landerkin, the Liberal member representing the riding of Grey South in Ontario, opposed Macdonald's proposal to give the vote only to women who did not have husbands on the basis that it would enfranchise "an unmarried female, who may be Chinese, or a squaw, or any other person naturalized," but deny the vote to "the mothers of this country," whom he described as "the most deserving class of people that are found in the Dominion."[7] John Milton Platt, a Liberal representing Prince Edward, Ontario, argued that Macdonald's reluctance to enfranchise all British-Canadian women was inappropriate because they paid more taxes and purchased more taxable goods than status Indians who received government annuities. It was, according to Platt, "a monstrous proposition that we should, in the same parliament, refuse the same franchise to the women of this country and give it to the low and filthy Indians of the reserves."[8] Malcolm Colin Cameron, the Liberal representing the Ontario riding of Huron West, spoke debasingly of non-white women. But, rather than comparing women in terms of who deserved the vote, he described the propriety of their values according to whom he viewed as wanting the franchise. "I have no doubt," Cameron declared, "it will be of some consequence to some people of that Province [British Columbia], for instance the Chinese, that their women should be allowed to vote. I am, however, quite satisfied that the great mass of respectable women ... are not desirous to exercise the franchise."[9]

It is noteworthy that both Landerkin and Platt used the term "of this country" to recognize the membership and contributions of white women only. Indigenous and Asian women, in their eyes, resided in Canada without enjoying the same degree of connection or belonging. Other Members of Parliament rounded out the emerging hierarchy of potential voters by comparing Chinese immigrants to status Indians – sometimes favourably, describing the former as responsible and peace-loving, and sometimes not, contrasting their "foreignness" with a characterization of Indigenous people as "sons of the soil."[10] When the property and income qualifications – also enacted by the Electoral Franchise Act – were debated, the opposition members complained that the proposed qualifications would deny the vote to many members of the working class and young men who had recently served in the militia as part of the government's response to the Northwest Rebellion. Peter Mitchell, the Independent representing Northumberland, Ontario, observed during the debate that some Members of Parliament objected to universal manhood suffrage on the grounds that "universal suffrage would include paupers."[11] In this sense, women were placed in the same category as Chinese, First Nations, and unemployed men – people who were carefully scrutinized for their ability to contribute to Canada's development as a British nation – while also making it clear that there were sharply imposed limits on what they could expect in return.

While Richard Gwyn argues in his biography of John A. Macdonald that his support for women's suffrage was proof of his progressiveness,[12] among other historians "the suspicion remains that Macdonald had inserted the clause as a sacrificial lamb, never intending that it survive final reading of the bill."[13] Macdonald informed his fellow Members of Parliament that "I have always and am now in favour of" women's enfranchisement when he presented his bill to them, and yet the section extending the vote to property-holding single women and widows was removed from the final version of the bill without any particular protest on Macdonald's part.[14] Regardless of whether the gesture to enfranchise women was, indeed, an empty one, Macdonald had a profound impact on public discourse on women's suffrage simply by raising the issue in the House of Commons.

The attitudes voiced by Landerkin, Platt, and other Members of Parliament set the tone for how Canadians' entitlements to vote were conceived and measured. There was the occasional endorsement, such as the one made by Arthur H. Gillmor of Charlotte, New Brunswick, for an inclusive franchise made on the basis of inherent human equality,[15] but more often Canadians were treated as existing on a continuum of those worthy and unworthy of full citizenship. The franchise operated as the dividing line between the worthy and the unworthy, but there was understood to be a hierarchy even within those categories. The hierarchical location of women, Aboriginal Canadians, Chinese Canadians, and Black Canadians was debated in the House of Commons in 1885, but it was echoed and elaborated on in multiple settings thereafter.

Over two decades later, politicians continued to consider women's suffrage in relative terms, requiring a metaphorical yardstick of citizenship to evaluate the strength of their franchise claim. Janice Newton describes the argument employed by James Hawthornthwaite, a Socialist, when he introduced a bill for women's suffrage in 1906 in the Legislative Assembly of British Columbia, as suggesting women's enfranchisement was an insignificant issue compared to women's economic oppression, but that it was outrageous that recent immigrants from Southeast Asia could vote and women could not.[16] Hawthornthwaite insisted he "knew no greater civilizing force than the enfranchisement of their mothers, wives, and sisters."[17]

Thus, by the time prairie women were developing suffrage organizations and a relatively cohesive suffrage movement, there were precedents for debating the suitability of women's enfranchisement based on their contributions to the Dominion and for measuring those contributions through comparisons with different groups. The readiness to draw sweeping characterizations of different social and racial groups and to emphasize the inequality of their respective characteristics also surfaced in literature and education. J.S. Woodsworth's *Strangers Within Our Gates* was published in 1909, before the author had become a Member of Parliament. It drew on his experiences working as a Methodist minister and superintendent of the All Peoples' Mission in Winnipeg's North End, where many immigrants lived. He was assisted by A.R. Ford, who wrote for a local newspaper and contributed sections on Ruthenians, Poles, and Doukhobors. *Strangers Within Our Gates* attempted to humanize the incoming waves of immigrants by describing their traits and their potential to assimilate into British-Canadian society. The book's success in this regard has since been questioned by historians because of its preoccupation with the purported weaknesses of each categorically defined nationality of immigrant, and the organization of its chapters, which effectively ranks immigrants from most desirable (British and American immigrants) to least (Asians and Blacks and, interestingly, Aboriginal people, who were hardly immigrants but were viewed by Woodsworth and his British-Canadian audience as being strangers all the same). These comparisons were drawn in education as well. As Amy von Heyking notes in *Creating Citizens: History and Identity in Alberta's Schools, 1905 to 1980*, students were specifically asked to compare people of different races and ethnicities "with the expectation that the virtues of Anglo-Saxons would be stressed [in students' responses]. The 1911 Standard VII history examination directed students to 'Point out the excellences and defects of the Greek character. Contrast with the national character of the Hebrews, Romans and Anglo-Saxons.'"[18]

Calling for an extension of privilege

The women's suffrage movement in Western Canada can be traced back to the 1890s, when a group of Icelandic women organized a suffrage association. The cause was subsequently picked up by the Women's Christian Temperance Union, which viewed women's enfranchisement as strengthening their bid for prohibiting the sale and consumption of alcohol, which it hoped in turn would reduce rates of domestic abuse and poverty. Additional organizations with women's suffrage as their primary aim formed later, and included the Political Equality League, the Manitoba Equal Franchise Club, the Manitoba Suffrage League, the Provincial Equal Suffrage Board of Saskatchewan, and the Equal Franchise League of Edmonton.[19] The goals of these organizations were supported by female and male members of the Grain Growers' Associations in Manitoba and Saskatchewan and the United Farmers of Alberta.

Prairie advocates of women's suffrage, like their counterparts elsewhere in Canada, were tasked with educating the public on women's suffrage and convincing legislators that women wanted (or, better yet, demanded) the vote. They extolled the benefits of women's suffrage and dispelled myths about its risks at conventions, agricultural fairs, mock parliaments, and public debates, and through pamphlets, newspapers, and the *Grain Growers' Guide*. It was not, however, just male voters and lawmakers who needed to be convinced that women should have the vote. As Francis Marion Beynon noted in her column in *The Grain Growers' Guide*, public education would most importantly convince women that enfranchisement was desirable.[20]

Many women were hostile toward the concept of voting. As *Guide* reader Minnie Kieler observed when sending the Country Homemakers' section editor a letter and a poem in 1913, "Some women seem to think that if they had the vote and mixed in politics, that they would lose their womanliness and modesty."[21] This fear was founded in the belief that participation in politics was incompatible with a commitment to one's family. In a period when women's employment prospects were severely restricted and the home was the epicentre of women's accepted roles and activities, the prospect of losing their "womanliness" threatened to undermine their influence in that one area where they were acknowledged to have a central role. If perhaps not as often as women in Quebec, women on the Prairies were consistently told by opponents of women's suffrage that if they wished to participate in activities outside of their designated sphere, they could best achieve their aims by exerting subtle influence within the home. This line of thinking preserved men's power as decision makers within the family. Such a division was not practical for single women or families where both partners were members of the paid labour force, but many middle-class women would need to be brought around to believing political engagement could be an extension of – and not detrimental to – their status as wives and mothers.

Meanwhile, women's suffrage had to gain the support of male voters and lawmakers. For them, the franchise was a privilege and, as with male privilege more generally during this period, there were legal and attitudinal barriers to its extension. Few advocates of women's suffrage took issue with the then-prevalent notion that the franchise was a privilege by calling for universal suffrage. Even when women stated that they should be enfranchised, "because it is just," their definition of justice was sufficiently vague as to not contradict dominant notions. Those advocates who saw the franchise as a right to which all citizens were entitled were among the minority. Francis Marion Beynon left Winnipeg for New York during World War I when she was punished socially and professionally for her pacifism and opposition to the government's plan to disfranchise immigrants from enemy countries.[22] For the most part, however, arguments that advocated extending the privilege of enfranchisement to women demonstrated that female suffragists accepted the dominant society's conceptions of the franchise and intended to use their votes, once obtained, in a manner that contributed to – without significantly challenging – British Canadian society and values.

A range of arguments was employed by Western Canadian advocates of women's suffrage. Some were founded on women's inherent equality, others drew on proof of women's hard work, and some relied on the promise of changes that could be effected by women's votes. Rose Turrell used examples of each in her 1910 letter to the *Guide* when outlining her reasons for supporting women's suffrage:

> Because a big section of our women demand it, and must have it … Because it is proven that women can fill any position (physical strength excepted) that man can hold, so the time-worn, thread-bare theory that a female brain is inferior to a male's is put out of date and relegated to a place in a museum as a curiosity of the density of man … [and because it is necessary to] the extinction of the White Slave traffic, … to reform the divorce laws, … to adjust the wage scales, … [and] to put down child labor [*sic*].[23]

Turrell concluded her letter by reassuring readers that she was not a "man-hater." Certainly for some Canadians at the time, speaking in favour of women's suffrage was tantamount to criticizing or betraying men. Turrell and other white women who were anxious for the vote, however, mitigated the threat they were considered to pose to the country that enfranchised men were credited with building. They managed this by positioning themselves as "mothers of the British race" who stood side-by-side with enfranchised Canadian men as partners in settling and developing the country and strengthening the Empire.

Partners in empire building

As mothers of the British race, white women had a responsibility to apply to all of society their maternal instincts for nurturing and protecting their families.[24] The franchise, by allowing them to have a say in legislation that was passed, would allow them to do that. Mrs. A.V. Thomas espoused this view in a speech to the Springhill Grain Growers in Manitoba, declaring, "The race cannot get any higher than its women" and that women therefore had both social and political responsibilities to elevate it.[25] This characterization of white women cast political engagement as a necessary extension, rather than an unseemly contradiction, of women's socially accepted roles as wives and mothers. Embracing their power to protect the future of the British race meant raising their children to share its language and values and using politics and charitable activity to extend these to their fellow Canadians, who were portrayed as unfortunate or ignorant in comparison. It was a form of maternal feminism that gave them licence to agitate for the franchise in a way that was understood to be compatible with their British-Canadian values and Christian faith. Reconciling their activism and faith was particularly significant in convincing prairie women that the franchise was both desirable and socially acceptable, as opponents of women's suffrage often cited Bible passages declaring man's dominion over women to justify their inequality at the polls.[26]

The rhetoric about women having a crucial role to play in protecting the future of the British Empire and its people also seems to have been intended for enfranchised males, in hopes of gaining their support. Stella Richardson wrote to the *Grain Growers' Guide* to say that she knew men who opposed women's suffrage on the basis that "foreign women would also have the power to vote" and their allegedly shaky grasp of the English language would make them ignorant of political issues and therefore unable to make reasoned political decisions.[27] In 1915 the United Farmers of Alberta and its women's auxiliary discussed the topic of an "educational qualification for woman suffrage" at their joint meeting for just this reason.[28] It was not, however, only female immigrants who were accused of being unworthy of the franchise. Nellie McClung referred to enfranchised male immigrants as "the corruptible foreign vote" swayed to vote by "political heelers, well paid for the job, well armed with whiskey, cigars, and money."[29] McClung did claim to have sympathy for "the poor fellow who sells his vote," though, and instead reserved her ire for the corrupt politicians who attempted to buy the votes of recent immigrants as well as the immoral drinkers who influenced them since, according to McClung, "around the bar they get their ideals of citizenship."[30] Her criticism is consistent with McKay's assertion that during this period the franchise was reserved for those considered capable of making sound judgments that honoured liberal values and the greater good, and was seldom entrusted to people whose appreciation of those concepts was held in suspicion.

McClung's emphasis on foreign voters can partly be explained by the fact that many racialized Canadians were already disfranchised, so it was hard to point to evidence that women were more capable of voting than they were. Members of the "Asiatic or Mongol race" were prohibited from voting in federal elections and provincially in British Columbia. Indigenous men could only vote if they did not have, or had forfeited, their Indian status, and very few who had status felt that the benefits of enfranchisement outweighed the cost. Although women of all ethnicities were in the same position as Asian and First Nations men in being barred from full participation in the democratic process, some advocates of women's suffrage sought to discourage any association between disfranchised men and white women. In the pages of the *Grain Growers' Guide*, the Chinese were regularly referred to in relation to their dependence on opium. A political cartoon published in a 1914 edition of the guide, intended to incite sympathy for the respectable white woman, showed her excluded from a line forming at a polling station that included stereotypical representations of a male transient, an Asian man, and a status Indian man being led to the polls by a well-dressed white man.[31]

Nativism surfaced in the writing of McClung and fellow suffrage activist Emily Murphy, both ardent maternal feminists who used their writing to warn about the potential threat Asian immigrants posed to British Canadian society and values. Murphy implicated the Chinese, in her 1922 book *The Black Candle*, as playing an insidious role in spreading opium addiction, with its destructive effects on the white race.[32] Indeed, a group's perceived compatibility with British-Canadian society and values was commonly the lens through which Murphy assessed their value in her writing. In 1910, she described the diverse American and European immigrants in Winnipeg as foreign but "rapidly becoming irreproachably

5.1 "Everybody Votes but Mother," 1. *Grain Grower's Guide,* 1 July 1914, courtesy of Peel Library, University of Alberta.

Canadian."[33] She expressed a less optimistic view of First Nations people. McClung observed while writing in *Janey Canuck in the West*:

> One hardly knows whether to take an Indian as a problem, a nuisance, or a possibility. He may be considered from a picturesque, philanthropic or pestiferous standpoint, according to your tastes or opportunities.... Regarding his future, we may give ourselves little uneasiness. This question is solving itself. A few years hence there will be no Indians. They will exist for posterity only in waxwork figures and in a few scant pages of history.[34]

As Devereux notes, Nellie McClung used her fiction (including some works published after gender restrictions on voting were lifted on the Prairies) to convey parables and messages about Asian Canadians and First Nations Canadians that emphasized their "otherness" relative to her British-Canadian and European immigrant characters and, by extension, the differences between Asian Canadians and Indigenous Canadians and her white audience. Racial difference was seen as creating an insurmountable barrier between British-Canadian women and the Chinese, Japanese, Indian, and First Nations Canadians who shared their position of exclusion from the franchise. Racial distinctions were also made between British

Canadians and European newcomers who were not members of the "British race," although they were seen as having desirable qualities in common with British Canadians and as having the potential to assimilate with the dominant society.

Women also traded on their contributions to settlement and development of the Prairies to criticize the enfranchisement of men who were supported by the state rather than contributing to it. These included men in prisons and insane asylums, and the out-of-work men who travelled from one community to another in search of employment or relief. In 1913, the *Grain Growers' Guide* republished a political cartoon from *Life* magazine which provided a biting commentary on the enfranchisement of transients by hyperbolizing their filth and apparent indifference and offsetting it with the caption "Woman is not fit for the ballot."[35] Nellie McClung cited the scourge of the transient voter as one of the reasons women's suffrage was necessary to protect the interests of families in Western Canada. She argued this in *In Times Like These*:

> It is said that [women] would all vote with their husbands, and that the married man's vote would thereby be doubled. We believe it is eminently right and proper that husband and wife should vote the same way, and in that case no one would be able to tell if the wife were voting with the husband or the husband voting with the wife. Neither would it matter. If giving the franchise to women did nothing more than double the married man's vote it would do a splendid thing for the country, for the married man is the best voter we have; generally speaking, he is a man of family and property – surely if we can depend on anyone we can depend on him, and if by giving his wife a vote we can double his – we have done something to offset the irresponsible transient man who has no interest in the community.[36]

A reader named Norma used her letter to the *Grain Growers' Guide* to try to convince other women that the franchise, as a dividing line that differentiated between contributing and non-contributing citizens, was forcing women to keep poor company. "Do you want to stay classed with minors, idiots, lunatics and criminals?," she asked the *Guide*'s female readers.[37] Catherine Cleverdon wrote in her history of women's enfranchisement in Canada that prairie women had an easier time convincing provincial governments that they deserved the vote on account of the hard work they put into establishing homesteads. Accepting the idea that the franchise was a privilege and calling attention to their significant contributions to Western Canadian settlement allowed women to argue that they did not belong among the disfranchised.

Provincial and federal milestones

The petitions, public events, media campaigns, conventions, meetings with politicians, and the other work of suffrage activism began to pay off in January 1916, when Manitoba passed legislation allowing women to vote in provincial elections for the first time. Saskatchewan followed suit in March, followed by Alberta a month later.[38] Then, in 1917, in anticipation of a crucial federal election on which the fate of Canada's conscription policy would rest, Prime Minister Robert Borden extended the vote to women serving in the military and women who had a husband, father, or brother in the military. At the same time, he stripped the vote of enemy aliens – recent immigrants whose country of origin was a wartime enemy of Canada – and conscientious objectors – Canadians whose religious convictions prohibited them from bearing arms against or committing acts of violence toward fellow human beings. The distinctions white women drew between themselves and Canadians whose assimilability they questioned were becoming reflected in provincial and federal franchise legislation.

After all, by voicing criticisms of enfranchised and disfranchised men that called into question their entitlement to vote, white women on the Prairies had not been enthusiastically endorsing universal suffrage. Rather, for the most part, they were reaffirming popular notions about the franchise being a privilege rather than a right, and weighing in on whether they felt various segments of the population had earned that privilege. While all advocates of women's suffrage made the case that women's intelligence, hard work, and contributions to Canadian society were proof that they deserved to be enfranchised, some sought to further underscore this point by comparing women's contributions to those of marginalized men. They reinforced the social and racial inequality by praising British-Canadian men for their reasoned and responsible political participation while criticizing recent immigrant voters and men who had no vote at all. They were, as Martin Banton and Gurnam Singh have put it, members of a marginalized group who had themselves succumbed to oppressive ideologies, seeking "to identify a position within the strata [of society] that is superior to as many other groups as possible."[39]

White prairie women invoked arguments for their comparative superiority while calling for the franchise because many sincerely believed them, and because these arguments had the potential to convince British-Canadian men and women that white women deserved the franchise. This hierarchy had already been accepted by politicians and public figures, and reinforced women's roles as protectors of the British race. It may also have been sheer pragmatism that led some white prairie women to advance their claim to the franchise by arguing their superiority to marginalized and racialized Canadians. Attitudes in Western Canada – where women had worked so hard for the vote, Asian Canadians' efforts to gain the franchise had proven unsuccessful thus far, and voters in some provinces still had to meet property qualifications – made it clear that the franchise was still viewed as a privilege and that there was strong resistance to universal adult suffrage. It was enough of a challenge for some women to achieve an expansion of the franchise; a redefinition of its entire role in Canadian society may have been too radical.

Admirably, some women did call for universal suffrage. Francis Marion Beynon was the women's editor for the *Grain Growers' Guide* from 1912 to 1917 and was an active member of the Political Equality League. Her advocacy for women's suffrage was rooted in her firm belief in women's equality, which she voiced most prominently in her novel, *Aleta Day*, and which was considered more radical than the maternal feminism of women such as McClung who were more accepting of distinct gender roles. The distinction between these two perspectives was especially evident during World War I when Canadians naturalized after 1902 were stripped of their right to vote in the general election of 1917. "The franchise can never be considered a reward for service rendered," Mary McCallum argued in the *Grain Growers' Guide* in September 1917. "The franchise is and always shall be a sacred right, and one with which no government may tamper."[40] Another *Guide* writer agreed. When Prime Minister Robert Borden's Wartime Elections Act disfranchised Canadians with enemy alien or conscientious objector status, but extended the vote to women with immediate male relatives in the military,[41] s/he informed the *Guide*'s readers that "those citizens of alien birth or extraction who will be disfranchised will pay their taxes in the same manner and to the same extent as before and will exercise all the duties and privileges of citizens except the franchise. Those women who will not receive the franchise will have the same obligations and duties to the state as will their sisters who will be permitted to cast a vote."[42]

However, other women, most notably Nellie McClung, had supported the Wartime Elections Act. McClung had met with Borden earlier in 1917 and used the opportunity to urge him to deny the vote to immigrants with enemy alien status. Francis Marion Beynon was quick to point out in her column in the *Grain Growers' Guide* that McClung had not been speaking for Beynon when she made that request to Borden, but some of Beynon's readers wrote letters in support of McClung. In the end, Canadians with enemy alien or conscientious objector status were unable to vote in the 1917 general election, which returned Borden to power while the political backlash he faced from Canadians focused more on the issue of conscription than enfranchisement.

Conclusion

Devereux has noted that maternal feminists, such as those who advocated women's suffrage on the Prairies at the turn of the twentieth century, are often "seen to be capitulating to patriarchal gender ideology, investing blindly and unquestioningly in the rhetoric of race, empire and reproduction."[43] I agree that many white women on the Prairies invested in that rhetoric, but it was hardly done blindly. Rather, these women shied away from a radical reconsideration of rights and citizenship by focusing on expanding the franchise just enough for themselves to enjoy it. This is an important consideration, given how the historical legacy of Nellie McClung and other maternal feminists is so hotly debated and how important the recognition of privilege is to dismantling persisting barriers to equality. As Devereux points out, women such as McClung are commemorated today as national heroes for their work to remove gender restrictions on the franchise.[44] That these same women fought for privilege, in the form of a legal authority and a set of assumptions about their character and abilities, makes their contemporary memory and commemoration significant in its potential to reflect – positively or negatively – on contemporary values and our commitment to equality.

Reaffirming the nativist views of the dominant society as they were espoused in the House of Commons and elsewhere enabled white women (especially British-Canadian women) to demonstrate that, if enfranchised, they were unlikely to upset the status quo in ways that might further erode white male power and privilege. It is, after all, significant that prairie women were quick to praise their male supporters in their bids for enfranchisement and claim to have the power to double mens' voting power, while criticizing both the voting behaviour of those marginalized males fortunate enough to be enfranchised and the social and economic contributions of disfranchised men.

The women's suffrage movement on the Canadian Prairies unfolded during a period of major growth and expansion in that region. The advocates of women's suffrage were in a position to influence the future directions for social and political movements in Western Canada and beyond. And they succeeded in doing this in two distinct ways. First, they promoted women's rights, not only by lobbying for women's enfranchisement but also by convincing women of the necessity of enfranchisement because it would offer them the political power to demand and win legislation that would improve working conditions in factories, protect children, and provide dowers and mothers' allowances to women.[45] Second, they applied their activism, wherever possible, within the constraints of the dominant society's norms and values. Thus, while white women were demanding the vote, they were using the language of the dominant society to do so, leaving many of its core values and assumptions uncontested. Although arguments for women's suffrage that insisted on women's inherent equality with enfranchised men and "no taxation without representation" would have facilitated subsequent bids for enfranchisement by marginalized groups, the most prevalent arguments among advocates of women's suffrage accepted and echoed the dominant society's belief that the franchise was a privilege to which not everyone was entitled.

Those arguments paid off for white women in Manitoba, Saskatchewan, and Alberta. And while their hard work proved that the dominant society could be convinced to extend the vote to previously disfranchised communities and demographics, it also reinforced ideas about race and class that were responsible for the continued disfranchisement of Chinese Canadians until 1946, Indo-Canadians until 1946, Japanese Canadians until 1947, Inuit Canadians until 1950, Indigenous Canadians with First Nations status until 1960, and prison inmates until 2000 (2002 for inmates serving sentences of two years or more).[46]

One final aspect of the legacy of prairie women's suffrage activism continues to be felt. White women lobbying for enfranchisement spent years arguing that they deserved the vote more than their fellow disfranchised Canadians (such as Chinese Canadians and First Nations Canadians) and even some enfranchised males (specifically recent European immigrants and unemployed transients). When the legislated gender barriers to the provincial franchise were lifted in Manitoba, Saskatchewan, Alberta, and then federally, each victory was celebrated as winning the vote for women. They still are.[47] However, since removing gender-based restrictions on the franchise still left thousands of prairie women unable to vote, mostly due to race-based restrictions, to describe 1916 as the year Manitoban, Saskatchewanian, and Albertan women "got the vote" is to accept and perpetuate the early twentieth-century argument that suffrage was extended to all the women who mattered. It is now, in effect, compulsory to at least acknowledge the racism of the maternal feminists of early twentieth-century Canada. Accounts of women's enfranchisement likewise temper their praise for McClung, Murphy, and their peers with an admission that their victories were incomplete.[48] But the marginalized women and men who remained disfranchised are so often portrayed as left behind that it obscures white women's role in distinguishing between themselves and members of disfranchised racial minorities to an extent that ensured they would not be enfranchised together, or at the same time.

The maternal feminists advocating for the enfranchisement of British-Canadian women were hardly alone in defending social and racial inequality in Canada, and were not the only ones responsible for continuing to defend the franchise as a privilege. But in order to fully appreciate the agency and influence of prairie advocates of women's suffrage, it is necessary to consider both their power to effect legislative change and to defend the status quo.

Notes

1. Paul F. Sharp, *The Agrarian Revolt in Western Canada* (Winnipeg: Hignell, 1997), 27.
2. "Twelve Reasons for Supporting Women's Suffrage," *Grain Growers' Guide*, 9 November 1910, 36.
3. Cecily Devereux, *Growing a Race: Nellie L. McClung and the Fiction of Eugenic Feminism* (Montreal: McGill-Queen's University Press, 2006), 4.
4. Veronica Strong-Boag, *The New Day Recalled: Lives of Girls and Women in English Canada, 1919-1939* (Toronto: Copp Clark Pitman, 1993), 189.
5. Ian McKay, "The Liberal Order Framework: A Prospectus for a Reconnaissance of Canadian History," *Canadian Historical Review* 81, no. 4 (November 2000): 623-25.
6. Catherine L. Cleverdon, *The Woman Suffrage Movement in Canada* (Toronto: University of Toronto Press, 1974), 105.
7. George Landerkin, quoted in *Official Report of the Debates of the House of Commons of the Dominion of Canada*, 21 April 1885, 18 (Ottawa: MacLean Roger, 1886), 1356.
8. J.M. Platt, quoted in *House of Commons Debates*, ibid.,1 May 1885, 1526.
9. Malcolm Cameron, quoted in *House of Commons Debates,* ibid., 16 April 1885, 1142.
10. Veronica Strong-Boag, "'The Citizenship Debates': The 1885 Franchise Act," in. *Contesting Canadian Citizenship: Historical Readings*, ed. Robert Adamoski, Dorothy Chunn, and Robert Menzies (Toronto: University of Toronto Press, 2002), 88.
11. Peter Mitchell, quoted in *House of Commons Debates*, 18 May 1885, 19 (Ottawa: MacLean Roger, 1886), 1945.
12. Richard Gwyn, *Nation Maker - Sir John A. Macdonald: His Life, Our Times, Volume 2: 1867-1891* (Toronto: Random House Canada, 2011), 520.
13. Elections Canada, *A History of the Vote in Canada* (Ottawa: Office of the Chief Electoral Officer, 2007), 49.
14. John A. Macdonald, quoted in *House of Commons Debates*, 16 April 1885, 18 (Ottawa: MacLean Roger, 1886), 1134; Cleverdon, *The Woman Suffrage Movement in Canada*, 107-8.
15. Arthur H. Gillmor, quoted in *House of Commons Debates*, 4 May 1885, 19 (Ottawa: McLean Roger, 1886).
16. Janice Newton, *The Feminist Challenge to the Canadian Left, 1900-1918* (Montreal: McGill-Queen's University Press, 1995), 141.
17. *Western Clarion,* 10 February 1906, 1, quoted in Newton, *The Feminist Challenge to the Canadian Left*, 141.
18. Amy von Heyking, *Creating Citizens: History and Identity in Alberta's Schools, 1905 to 1980* (Calgary: University of Calgary Press, 2006), 25.
19. Cleverdon, *The Woman Suffrage Movement in Canada*, 46-69.
20. Francis Marion Beynon, "Working for an Unpopular Cause," *Grain Growers' Guide*, 27 August 1913, 9.
21. Minnie F. Kieler, "A Poem to Motherhood," *Grain Growers' Guide*, 11 June 1913, 9.
22. Gordon Goldsborough, "Memorable Manitobans: Francis Marion Beynon (1884-1951)," *Manitoba Historical Society*, http://www.mhs.mb.ca/docs/people/beynon_fm.shtml (accessed 15 February 2016).
23. Rose Turrell, "Her Reasons," *Grain Growers' Guide*, 21 December 1910, 37.

24 Devereux, *Growing a Race*, 22–23.
25 Mrs. A.V. Thomas, "Manitoba Section," *Grain Growers' Guide*, 4 June 1913, 14.
26 Cleverdon, *The Woman Suffrage Movement in Canada*, 6.
27 Stella Richardson, "Concerning Manitoba Women," *Grain Growers' Guide*, 26 January 1916, 27.
28 S.M. Gunn, "A Half Year's Program," *Grain Grower's Guide*, 30 June 1915, 19.
29 Nellie McClung, *In Times Like These* (Toronto: University of Toronto Press, 1972), 54.
30 McClung, *In Times Like These*, 54.
31 "Everyone Votes But Mother," *Grain Growers' Guide*, 1 July 1914, 14.
32 Emily Murphy, *The Black Candle* (Toronto: Thomas Allen, 1922).
33 Emily Murphy, *Janey Canuck in the West* (Toronto: McClelland and Stewart, 1975), 11.
34 Murphy, *Janey Canuck in the West*, 76–77.
35 "Woman Is Not Fit for the Ballot," *Grain Growers' Guide*, 12 November 1913, 10.
36 McClung, *In Times Like These*, 49.
37 Norma, "Does Not Wonder at Militancy," *Grain Growers' Guide*, 29 January 1913, 10.
38 Cleverdon, *The Woman Suffrage Movement in Canada*, 65, 73, 82.
39 Martin Banton and Gurnam Singh, "'Race,' Disability and Oppression," in *Disabling Barriers, Enabling Environments*, 2nd ed.,, ed. John Swain, Sally French, Colin Barnes, and Carol Thomas (London: Sage, 2000), 113.
40 Mary P. McCallum, "The New Franchise Bill," *Grain Growers' Guide*, 19 September 1917, 9.
41 Those disfranchised included Germans, Austrians, Hungarians, Ukrainians, Mennonites, Hutterites, Doukhobors, and Quakers.
42 "The War Election Franchise," *Grain Growers' Guide*, 19 September 1917, 5.
43 Devereux, *Growing a Race*, 25.
44 Ibid., 11–12.
45 All of these examples were, in fact, effected in Alberta after women's enfranchisement in that province: Cleverdon, *The Woman Suffrage Movement in Canada*, 73.
46 Elections Canada, *A History of the Vote in Canada*, 98.
47 See, for example, Cleverdon, *The Woman Suffrage Movement in Canada*; Charlotte Gray, *Nellie McClung* (Toronto: Penguin Canada, 2008); Elections Canada, *A History of the Vote in Canada*; Canadian Human Rights Commission, "Women's Rights," *Human Rights in Canada: A Historical Perspective*, http://www.chrc-ccdp.ca/historical-perspective/en/browseSubjects/womenRights.asp (accessed 26 September 2016).
48 See, for example, Megan Cécile Radford, "How Canadian Newspaper Women Won the Vote," *Walrus*, July/August 2011, http://walrusmagazine.com/articles/2011.07-dalton-camp-award-how-canadian-newspaperwomen-*won*-the-vote/ (accessed 12 August 2012); Canadian Human Rights Commission, "Women's Rights."

6

"Develop a Great Imperial Race": Emmeline Pankhurst, Emily Murphy, and Their Promotion of "Race Betterment" in Western Canada in the 1920s

Sarah Carter

Emmeline Pankhurst visited Canada for the fifth time in 1919, initially for a lecture tour, but in the summer of 1920 she decided to stay permanently, settling first in Victoria, British Columbia. She stayed for only four years, but during the time Pankhurst made Canada her home, she tirelessly criss-crossed the country, lecturing in major cities and remote locations at theatres, Chautauquas, factories, colleges, churches, and private homes. Her main topic was the virtue and supremacy of the British Empire; and the duties and responsibilities of the British women of the Empire as the "guardians of the race."[1] She emphasized how enfranchised women ought to turn their attention toward "race betterment."[2] The "disease" of Bolshevism was another central theme of her speaking engagements, but increasingly the perils of venereal disease, the "feeble minded," and the "foreigner," combined with her dedication to the British Empire, took centre stage, particularly after she found employment with the Canadian National Council for Combating Venereal Disease (CNCCVD). In Canada, Pankhurst's belief in eugenics came to fruition and crystallized.[3]

Pankhurst was particularly active in Western Canada. In the summer of 1922, for example, she spoke in sixty-three different western towns, beginning her tour at Admiral, Saskatchewan, and ending at The Pas, Manitoba.[4] In one month alone she spoke at Fort William, Saltcoats, Regina, Prince Albert, North Battleford, Saskatoon, Swift Current, Weyburn, Wynyard, Yorkton, Calgary, Lethbridge, and Medicine Hat.[5] She often shared the podium with prominent Alberta reformer, writer, and magistrate Emily Murphy, with whom she became well acquainted. They influenced each other; their convictions about the virtues of the British Empire and "racial" purity gained strength together. Murphy's ideas provided support for Pankhurst's work with the CNCCVD, and Pankhurst's endorsement of these ideas added credibility and legitimacy to Murphy's views, fully articulated by the mid-1920s, that the "feeble-minded" should be sterilized. Their ideas and causes intertwined, and increasingly focused on paths to "racial" betterment within Canada and the British Empire. In their articulations of who belonged and who did not in the Canadian nation, they helped to frame and bolster the "grammars of difference" that distinguished the powerful and privileged from the inferior.[6] Pankhurst and Murphy helped to craft a Canadian manifestation of "Britishness" and "Otherness," of inclusion and exclusion, as the vision for the nation.[7]

Over 2,800 people were sterilized in Alberta between 1929 and 1972 under the authority of the province's 1928 Sexual Sterilization Act.[8] Alberta and British Columbia were the only two Canadian provinces who enacted such legislation, and Alberta was much more devoted to the cause, sterilizing about ten times as many people as in BC. In seeking answers why the eugenics movement was institutionalized and pursued so rigorously in Alberta, the support of highly influential women reformers Emily Murphy and Nellie McClung is often mentioned, although Murphy is seen as much more prominent and instrumental.[9] As legal historian John McLaren wrote, Murphy "played an important role in creating a climate of opinion in which this eugenicist initiative became possible."[10] That Murphy's eugenicist ideas began to seriously take root in Alberta during Pankhurst's Canadian interlude, when the latter lectured with Murphy throughout the province, strikes me as significant. Another goal of this chapter is to bring the extent of Pankhurst's engagement with Canada and the ideas that she espoused from 1920 to 1924 to the attention of historians of feminism.[11]

Pankhurst appears fleetingly in many books and articles about the first wave of feminism in Canada, and photographs of her with Nellie McClung, Emily Murphy, and other prominent Canadian women activists are often included, but with little commentary or analysis. References to Pankhurst in Canada tend to disappear completely in the post–World War I era.[12] But I suggest that it was in the early 1920s that Pankhurst had an even greater impact on the Canadian scene that has not been appreciated or comprehended, and not because of her stand on suffrage.

Emmeline Pankhurst (1858–1928) was sixty-two when she arrived in Canada in 1920, and she needed money to support her three adopted "war" daughters. Originally from Manchester (born Emmeline Goulden), she and her husband, lawyer Richard Pankhurst (who died in 1898), were socialists, supporters of women's suffrage, and of the far-left Independent Labour Party (ILP). Their daughters Christabel, Sylvia, and Adela also became prominent activists. Impatient with the slow pace of progress on the issue of women's suffrage in the ILP, in 1903 the Pankhursts founded the Women's Social and Political Union (WSPU), which grew rapidly, having 3,000 branches by 1907. Mass marches, demonstrations, and poster campaigns were the initial strategies.[13] There was a gradual shift toward more direct and militant action with acts of violence and arson. The height of the militancy was 1913–14. When suffragettes were arrested, they protested with hunger, thirst, and sleep strikes. Emmeline Pankhurst was imprisoned in London's Holloway jail a dozen times and was severely weakened by hunger strikes.

When war broke out in 1914, however, Emmeline Pankhurst, recuperating from her tenth hunger strike, embraced patriotism and suspended all suffrage activities. She declared support for the government that had denied women the vote. She reasoned that the defeat of Germany trumped all other causes, and there was no point in continuing the campaign for the vote as there might be no country to vote in if Germany won the war.[14] Her daughter Christabel agreed with her, but Sylvia opposed the war, and many other former allies and associates were horrified with Emmeline's militarism and imperialism.[15] During the war Emmeline became an ardent, passionate imperialist.

Both her recent biographers June Purvis and Paula Bartley argue that her wartime jingoism was in keeping with her firmly held beliefs from childhood – her allegiance to Britain was combined with a love of France, where she had lived as a young woman. To her the war was fought for humanity and in defence of democracy, liberty, and civilization. One of her wartime activities was leading a campaign to adopt babies born to single women whose partners were in the armed forces. She adopted three "war babies" herself. Pankhurst also travelled to Russia in 1917, a journey sponsored by the British government as it was hoped she could persuade the country to stay in the war. She was there for several months including during the October Revolution. Her horror of communism and Bolshevism was then firmly established.

Pankhurst lectured in Canada during the war in 1916 and 1918, drawing capacity audiences; she was an electrifying, dramatic public speaker. In 1916 Pankhurst asked Alberta feminist and writer Nellie McClung to arrange two public appearances in Edmonton. It was there that Pankhurst met Emily Murphy (1868–1933), also known as the author "Janey Canuck." Pankhurst's first Edmonton lecture, to an immense crowd at McDougall Methodist Church, was the same day that Murphy's appointment as a police magistrate was announced, and they shared the front page of the *Evening Bulletin*.[16] Murphy, the first female magistrate in Canada and in the British Empire, presided over a court where female offenders were tried by a woman in the presence of other women.

Murphy, née Ferguson, was from a prosperous Ontario family prominent in the legal community and with strong ties to the Conservative party. She moved west with her husband, an Anglican cleric, first to Winnipeg, then rural Manitoba and in 1907, to Edmonton. Although Murphy was not a lawyer herself, she was devoted to women's rights, and in particular the legal protection of women and children. She believed that magistrates could improve the lives of the people who came before them, and referred to her role as that of "magistrate-physician," a person who would not only diagnose the patient and prescribe a course of treatment but would also follow up to ensure that the prescription was working and the cure achieved.[17] John McLaren has argued that as a magistrate Murphy could demonstrate compassion and empathy, but that there were limits to her understanding and patience. McLaren found in Murphy's magistrate's notebooks that "references to the ethnic origins of some of those whom she sentenced suggest an association in her mind between delinquency and insanity and certain minority and immigrant groups."[18] She increasingly came to believe that a high proportion of offenders were "feeble-minded or mentally defective."[19] By the mid-1920s Murphy became an outspoken advocate of sterilization of the "unfit."

Murphy and Pankhurst had much in common by 1916, but Murphy had been a devoted and outspoken British imperialist for more years.[20] In a 1914 lecture on "citizenship" in Victoria, BC, Murphy told the members of the Canadian Women's Club and Alexandra Club that "not only should we be loyal citizens to Canada, but to the United Empire."[21] She was also concerned with the assimilation of the "foreigner" in Canada and told the Victoria club women that "one of the chief duties of Canadians as patriots was the work of educating into useful and loyal citizens the foreign people who come to this Western country in such great numbers. The task of welding this rude conglomerate mass into a disciplined and coherent whole seemed a well-nigh titanic one. To neglect these people was a dangerous error." Murphy believed in the superiority of the northern, Nordic "race." In her view, the solution to the "problem" of the "foreigner" was "that Canada was a northern country. The climatic discipline of the north was bound to produce qualities of dominance, just as its productivity made for opulence." Murphy was convinced that "the best peoples of the world have come out of the north, and the longer they are away from the boreal regions in such proportion do they degenerate."[22]

There is a photograph of Pankhurst's 1916 meeting with Murphy, McClung, and members of the Edmonton Equal Franchise League, fresh from their victory with the provincial vote two months earlier. It was an exuberant moment for supporters of women's suffrage in Alberta, and the presence of Pankhurst added great prestige to the occasion. It was not until 1918 in Britain that women over the age of thirty, and subject to property qualifications, acquired the vote, and it was not until 1928 that British women received the vote on the same terms as men. As "Janey Canuck," Murphy wrote an article, "Emmeline Pankhurst in the North," an account of the 1916 visit to Edmonton in which she expressed her adulation, writing that "in the years to come, some keen-eyed, well-balanced historian ... will say 'To this City, from all parts of the world, came many notable authors, artists, actors and workers in sociology, but, among them all, none stood out with such exceeding luster of [sic] that woman whose flaming spirit has touched to the quick the civilized world ... Emmeline Pankhurst.'"[23] Murphy admired Pankhurst's "indominitable [sic] will,"

6.1 The 13 June 1916 meeting of the Edmonton Equal Franchise League at Nellie McClung's Edmonton home included a reception in honour of Emmeline Pankhurst. Pankhurst gave two lectures in the city to overflowing crowds. Emily Murphy's appointment as police magistrate was announced the same day. Pankhurst is seen in the front row wearing a white blouse, with flowers. She wears her "Holloway Brooch," presented to suffragettes who had undergone imprisonment. On her left is Emily Murphy, and on her right is Nellie McClung. The child is Mark McClung. Image B-06786. Courtesy of the Royal British Columbia Museum and Archives.

and her "unconquerable spirit," yet was "amazed" to find a "soft-voiced, gentle-mannered, reposeful little lady."

There were only subtle hints in 1916 of the "out and out imperialist" Pankhurst had become by the time of her second wartime lecture tour to Canada in 1918, when she praised the British Empire as an equalizer that would promote gender equality in all countries, freeing women who "were in subjection of the most abject kind, without rights of any kind."[24] In 1919 Pankhurst went to North America again, speaking on the dangers of Bolshevism to declining audiences in the United States. But in Canada in November 1919 she was much more appreciated, and here her imperialistic fervour took flight. In Vancouver she talked to a packed theatre on the virtues of the British Empire, its "duty and responsibility to the rest of the world."[25] She called for co-operation among the people of the British Empire against the monster of Bolshevism. Pankhurst concluded: "The danger is a real one and the enemy insidious and we must all guard against it. As members of a great and mighty Empire we have a great trust, and our duty and responsibility to the Empire is all the greater."[26]

In the summer of 1920 Pankhurst completed a lucrative Chautauqua tour of Western Canada, where it was estimated that she addressed 70,000 people.[27] Pankhurst claimed in August of that year that she had seen "more of Western Canada ... than many Western Canadians themselves and state[d] that she [was] very interested to have met representatives of practically every type which goes to make up Canada."[28] Her visits were recalled as major highlights in the local histories of small prairie towns.[29] As her biographer June Purvis writes, the warm reception Pankhurst received in Canada seemed to revitalize her, and as biographer Paula Bartley notes of the same time period, although Pankhurst was a "political embarrassment" in postwar Britain, she commanded enormous respect and admiration in Canada.[30] Her themes in her lectures at this point were the need for loyal support of the Empire and how women should use their newly won citizenship to advance "the feeling of loyalty and faithfulness to the Mother Country."[31] Women, meaning white women of British ancestry, had to make sacrifices for the salvation of the British Empire.[32]

After her exhausting summer, she decided to stay in Canada. Pankhurst found Victoria particularly welcoming and to her taste. She first settled in the James Bay Hotel in August 1920 with her three adopted daughters. She told Ethel M. Chapman, for *Maclean's Magazine*, that she chose Victoria as "it is the nearest thing we have to a bit of old England – with its cluster of gardened, tennis-courted, restful English-looking homes set close to the sea." Chapman wrote that Pankhurst wanted Canada to be her home because "she believes that it offers a future for her children."[33]

It was in Victoria, in the fall of 1920, that Pankhurst met Dr. Gordon Bates, who had formed the Canadian National Council for Combating Venereal Diseases, an organization devoted to a public campaign of education and treatment. The organization was about more than venereal disease, as it also served as a metaphor for other ills of society – it was linked to racial and national health and to the vitality and strength of the Empire. But the organization lacked a speaker who could "appeal to the people's conscience and breathe life and the ardour of a moral crusade into a collection of statistics."[34] Pankhurst needed the income, and venereal disease was a subject "dear to her heart," as she had experience with the tragic effects of the disease through her work as a registrar of births and deaths in Manchester. In 1913 her daughter Christabel had published a book called *The Great Scourge and How to End It*, in which she urged all women to refuse marriage and motherhood until men gave up the licentiousness that was the root cause of venereal disease. Biographer Paula Bartley argues that Pankhurst had long been interested in issues of "feeble-mindedness, race and venereal disease" and the relationship between these and white slavery and prostitution.[35] Bartley notes that as a poor law guardian in Manchester, Pankhurst had worked closely with Mary Dendy, a noted eugenicist, and that by the late 1890s she was advocating increased powers of detention for "feeble-minded" children. Neither biographer considers Pankhurst's friendship with Murphy as an important influence on her eugenic thought.

Eugenics, the "science" of selective human breeding, sought to combat "race deterioration" and improve the fabric of the nation and Empire by encouraging the best stock to reproduce. Eugenics was supported and promoted by scientists, legislators, judges, and feminist reformers in the early decades of the twentieth century.[36] Eugenics played a formative role in feminist movements in Britain, Canada, and the United States[37] Some British feminists were particularly enthusiastic proponents of eugenics. As Ann Taylor Allen has argued, "eugenic theory was a basic and formative, not an incidental, part of feminist positions on the vitally important themes of motherhood, reproduction, and the state."[38] Feminists "did not simply manipulate eugenic theory, but critiqued, expanded and promoted it."[39] In the interwar period, British feminists renounced the "anti-male" militancy of the prewar era, and called for co-operation between men and women in the task of "enlightened" reproduction.[40] A "eugenic feminism" also emerged in the United States whose supporters argued that "the eugenic decline of the race could be prevented only if women were granted greater political, social, sexual, and economic equality."[41]

In the most comprehensive study of "eugenic feminism" in Canada, Cecily Devereux focuses on Nellie McClung. Although McClung was never as outspoken an advocate of eugenics as Murphy, Devereux argues that "eugenical thinking informs every aspect of her [McClung's] feminism and social reform, her fiction, and her vision 'of a better world.'"[42] Devereux found that eugenics ideas were widely shared, that feminists of that time were concerned about the family and the mother as the centre of that unit, and that they advocated the control of reproduction to strengthen the family and better the nation and the "race." Devereux argues that for McClung, controlling reproduction – the basis of eugenics – was crucial to

> liberating women, improving social conditions, protecting what seemed to her to be weaker or needier members of society, and maintaining national economic strength in what was imagined, if never actually realized, as a community organized around principles of 'common good.' Eugenics was not for her and her contemporaries a 'bad' measure adopted for a 'good' end but a spectrum of 'solutions' to perceived problems in the national community. It would ultimately include sexual sterilization in Alberta and British Columbia. Its central premises were birth control, sexual education for men and women, instruction and support for mothers, and the empowerment of women to implement these premises.[43]

McClung's feminism, like Murphy's, was "a discourse of imperialism and a technology of empire."[44] Little of this was new to Emmeline Pankhurst when she arrived in post–World War I Canada, but these themes did not as yet dominate her public addresses. It was Emmeline's Canadian interlude, and particularly her association with Emily Murphy, that transformed Pankhurst into an avid supporter of eugenics, and I argue that Pankhurst gave credibility and legitimacy to eugenic thought in Western Canada. For both women their imperialism intersected with their belief in eugenics; Britain led the world and could only continue to do so if the "race" remained pure and proliferated in the face of threats from Asians and others.

During her first Canadian tour for the CNCCVD in 1921, Pankhurst spoke all across the West, including Winnipeg, Portage la Prairie, Brandon, Regina, Medicine Hat, Lethbridge, Calgary, and Edmonton.[45] In Alberta she toured with Emily Murphy.[46] They travelled by train, conversing for many hours. Murphy learned to play solitaire from Pankhurst.[47] They shared the podium and the headlines in the newspapers, and they echoed each other's thoughts and points. Their arrival was eagerly anticipated. In the Medicine Hat newspaper, it was declared that their town would "have the pleasure of hearing two world class speakers."[48] But Pankhurst was the main attraction, as "there is little doubt that Mrs. Emmeline Pankhurst was the greatest single personal influence in the achievement of the vote of women in England." It was noted, however, that the once "militant suffragette" had done "quiet, persistent, earnest work for the nation during the war."

The title of Pankhurst's lecture throughout Alberta was "Social Hygiene and the World's Unrest," and there was great admiration for the "delicate yet forceful manner" with which this "earnest little woman … handled a difficult subject."[49] At Lethbridge on 11 May Pankhurst and Murphy were interviewed together and they both emphasized the dangers of unrestricted immigration to the future of Canada, pointing out the supposed link between venereal disease, the Russians, and Bolshevism. Pankhurst told the Lethbridge newspaper reporter that in Russia, where, she claimed, venereal diseases were rampant, there was the most Bolshevism: "It was their unbalanced minds that led to their destructive tendencies."[50] Murphy echoed this during her lecture that evening at the Majestic Theatre in Lethbridge, saying that "whole villages in Russia are infected. Yet these people are coming in ship loads to our shore. It is time Canada woke up." At Calgary two days later, Murphy said that in Canada "we are threatened with universal infection through immigration from Russia, which country is today seething with disease."[51] Murphy stressed that Canadians needed to "wake up" and "clean house." She spoke of her court, where a young girl was brought before her "whose mother sat there while the charges were being made against her child with a face that was about as intelligent as a dill pickle. I never saw such callousness or such stupidity. It wasn't that girl's fault that she had gone wrong. It was the fault of the ignorant mother." Murphy welcomed Alberta's planned "home for the feeble-minded" and added that "feeble-minded women composed one of the most difficult problems [with] which the government has to deal in stamping out venereal disease."[52] Pankhurst spoke in Calgary on what a "wonderful race we should have" if people were educated about social hygiene.

Adding further credibility to eugenics just at this time was the visit to Canada, including Alberta, of Caleb Saleeby, obstetrician, and sociologist.

He spoke in Toronto in May 1921 and the event received wide coverage. It was noted in the *Medicine Hat News* on the first page, under the headline "Racial Poisons Gain Grip Upon English Races," that Saleeby feared that venereal disease was "eating away at the virility of the English race."[53] Saleeby spoke in Calgary and Edmonton in June 1921 on the dangers of venereal disease and alcohol. Saleeby was concerned about the "physical degeneration" of the people of the British Isles, and saw great potential to avoid this in Canada, a theme that Pankhurst emphasized in her lectures. "Germs of precious stock to save the race are here," Saleeby told his Edmonton audience.[54] These were precisely the ideas that Pankhurst and Murphy had lectured on just a few weeks earlier. It is not known whether they met with Saleeby during his tour. Murphy was familiar with Saleeby's work, as she cited him in her 1922 book *The Black Candle*.[55]

When Pankhurst and Murphy lectured together in 1921, Murphy was working on *The Black Candle*, an exposé of the drug trade. Much of the book concerned the dangers posed by the "Chinaman" in Western Canada, their opium dens, and their alleged luring of young white women to the drug trade. If white women visited Chinese "chop-suey houses" they invariably found themselves peddling drugs, Murphy warned.[56] At the end of her chapter on opium, Murphy contended that "prolific Germans, with the equally prolific Russians, and the still more fertile yellow races, will wrest the leadership of the world from the British. Wise folk ought to think about these things for awhile."[57]

It was after the 1921 Alberta tour with Murphy that Pankhurst became more strident in her condemnation of Western Canada's diverse population, and she increasingly focused on the dangers of Chinese immigration. Anxieties and fears about the "foreigner" in Western Canada reached new heights during and just after the war. In this corner of the British Empire, "whiteness" alone could not be a marker of privilege. Rather, a unique brand of Canadian Britishness took shape, first in opposition to French Canada and the United States, and in the West it was shaped in opposition first to the Indigenous people and then the "foreigners" from eastern and southern Europe.[58] "Foreign" or "alien" women were particularly singled out for criticism. Winnipeg cleric Wellington Bridgman condemned "alien" women in his 1920 book, asking how women "of such low character and breeding should have been inflicted on this fair Dominion. ... There is not a cog of their primeval being that fits into the machinery of Canadian civilization."[59] Their children fell even lower into "vice and looseness of morals." Murphy's views, combined with the prevailing attitudes in Western Canada, which in BC in particular were characterized by hostility toward the Chinese, emboldened Pankhurst to speak more pointedly against non-British immigrants.

In September 1921, fresh from her prairie tour, Pankhurst lectured in BC, calling on Canadians to "think imperiously and work industriously," and saying that "immigrants of the British race are the best for the Dominion's development."[60] She said that excluding the "Oriental would mean that the white man would have to work harder and undertake uncongenial tasks," but from her own experience "the Southern States suffered by having an inferior race to work for the whites." Pankhurst emphasized that "unity of race" was necessary to the progress of a nation. Canada's highest development, she suggested, "would best be secured by bringing in men and women of the British race." To prolonged applause Pankhurst concluded that "how to build up Canada, make the people worthy of the country in which they lived, and develop a great imperial race, was a problem and a task requiring the brightest intellects and the highest energies of Canadians. To carry on the traditions of a race the first and the most splendid ever seen, was the task now committed to the Canadian people."

Pankhurst moved to Toronto in 1922 as she was appointed to the national staff of the CNCCVD as chief lecturer, but she continued to tirelessly lecture throughout the country for this organization, which changed its name to the Canadian Social Hygiene Council that year. In 1922 Pankhurst was once again in the West on the Chautauqua circuit, with her daughter Christabel, speaking at sixty-three towns and cities.[61] On this trip she began to articulate Murphy's ideas about the superiority of the northern "races," lecturing that the Scandinavians, the Icelanders, and Norwegians "among the Europeans ... make the best Canadian citizens, assimilating much more readily than some of the other races one finds on the prairies."[62] In 1923 Pankhurst spoke in over thirty towns, resorts, and lumber camps in northern Ontario.[63] Large crowds continued to gather.[64] In 1924 she toured the Maritimes. She increasingly emphasized the importance of marriage between healthy individuals as the prerequisite to a healthy race of children, again echoing the views of her friend Emily Murphy, and she complained that there was too much "sneering" at marriage.[65] She urged parents to "teach your children reverence for the marriage vow of men and women. Instill into their minds the belief in purity of body, mind and soul."[66]

By March 1924 Pankhurst was showing signs of physical and mental exhaustion. As biographer of the Pankhursts David Mitchell wrote, "For four and a half years she had imposed upon a frame already weakened by incredible exertions and ordeals a schedule calculated to sap the stamina of a woman half her age."[67] That same month the federal government and the Ontario government announced cuts to their grants to the Social Hygiene Council. Pankhurst was granted a leave of absence and the funds were never found to rehire her.[68]

Pankhurst's Canadian interlude was over. She first went on holiday to Bermuda, returning to England in 1925, after an absence of six years. She joined the Conservative Party and let her name stand as a parliamentary candidate for Whitechapel. Scholars have various explanations for why this former socialist became so conservative. Bartley wrote that "in effect, Emmeline was in an ideological vacuum," as she had left Liberalism and socialism far behind.[69] There was only one viable party left. Her friendships with prominent Conservatives Stanley Baldwin and Nancy Astor are also considered to have been important. June Purvis has provided the most comprehensive account of Pankhurst's post–World War I years to her death, arguing that her transformation into a Tory was not sudden, that even before the war she had become disenchanted with the Labour Party and trade unions who did not support women workers. Purvis argues that suffrage remained her goal even during the war; it was in abeyance but not abandoned. At the outbreak of war Pankhurst agreed to support Lloyd George, who had thwarted her suffrage campaigns, with the tacit understanding that the price would be postwar support for enfranchising women. According to one of Pankhurst's loyal supporters, their slogan during the war was "We have buried the hatchet, but we know where to find it."[70]

Pankhurst's friendship with Emily Murphy has not been included in any of the analysis thus far. Pankhurst emerged from Canada closely allied with Murphy's causes, opinions, and politics. While the seeds of many of these may have been planted much earlier, they began to take root and grow during Pankhurst's Canadian interlude when she was associated with Murphy. Murphy supported the Conservatives, and had always objected to a separate women's party.[71] As Pankhurst herself explained, "My war experience and my experience on the other side of the Atlantic have changed my views considerably. I am now an imperialist."[72] On 14 June 1928, Pankhurst died of septicemia in London at the age of sixty-nine, before she was able to run for the Whitechapel seat. She died before the great triumph of her friend Emily Murphy, who in 1929, along with Nellie McClung and three other Alberta women (The Famous Five), successfully challenged the exclusion of women from Canada's Senate, winning the "Persons" case, a pivotal moment in the struggle for women's rights. Murphy helped to raise funds from Canada for the Pankhurst Memorial in Westminster.

In Alberta, support for the involuntary sterilization of the "feeble-minded" grew following the Pankhurst and Murphy lectures. In 1922 at the convention of the United Farmers of Alberta (the UFA, then in power in Alberta), resolutions were passed urging the government to bring in legislation allowing the segregation of "feeble-minded" adults during their reproductive years, and calling for a study of the merits of forced sterilization.[73] At their 1925 convention, the UFA passed a resolution recommending the sterilization of mentally deficient people. The United Farm Women of Alberta joined the chorus and encouraged the government to pursue a policy of "racial betterment through the weeding out of undesirable strains."[74] In her public lectures and newspaper articles after Pankhurst left Canada, Murphy continued the crusade, warning that the "feeble-minded" reproduced at an alarming rate, urging the sterilization of all patients of marriageable age who were to be discharged from the Ponoka Asylum, and continuing to stress that the majority of the patients were foreign-born.[75] Alberta's UFA government passed the Sexual Sterilization Act in 1928.[76] Murphy continued to publish articles on sterilization until just before her death in 1933. For example, in 1932 as "Janey Canuck," she published "Should the Unfit Wed?," in which the answer was yes, but only if they agreed to "confine their unfitness to themselves" and were sterilized.[77]

Criticized and discredited in Britain following World War I, Pankhurst found herself adored, praised, and acclaimed, particularly in Western Canada. She spoke to capacity audiences and was warmly received in countless cities and towns across the nation during her Canadian interlude. While she arrived with beliefs about the virtues of the British Empire and the need for "racial" betterment, these flourished and proliferated in the Canadian setting because of her warm reception, her work with the CNCCVD, and her association with Emily Murphy. Together, Pankhurst and Murphy helped to articulate and bring important credibility to the unique brand of Britishness taking shape in Western Canada, while drawing stark dichotomies between inclusions and exclusions that justified the sterilization legislation aimed at creating an imperial "race."

Notes

1. June Purvis, *Emmeline Pankhurst: A Biography* (London: Routledge, 2002), 319. Purvis quotes from a *Victoria Daily Times* article describing Pankhurst's 27 November 1920 lecture, where she "brought all the oratorial [sic] fire and enthusiasm with which she gained the admiration of both supporter and opponent during her long and strenuous campaign for women's suffrage ... the gospel of Imperialism could have no better disciple than this clever woman."
2. Paula Bartley, *Emmeline Pankhurst* (London: Routledge, 2002), 216.
3. Ibid., 217.
4. *Victoria Daily Times*, 31 August 1922, 6.
5. Bartley, *Emmeline Pankhurst*, 214.
6. Ann Laura Stoler and Frederick Cooper, "Between Metropole and Colony: Rethinking a Research Agenda," in *Tensions of Empire: Colonial Cultures in a Bourgeois World*, ed. Frederick Cooper and Ann Laura Stoler (Berkeley: University of California Press, 1997), 3–4.
7. Sarah Carter, "Britishness, 'Foreignness,' Women and Land in Western Canada, 1890s–1920s," *Humanities Research* 13, no. 1 (2006): 43–60. See also the other articles in that journal issue from the conference "Britishness and Otherness: Locating Marginal White Identities in the Empire," Humanities Research Centre, Australian National University, Canberra, July 2004. See also Katie Pickles, *Female Imperialism and National Identity: Imperial Order Daughters of the Empire* (Manchester: Manchester University Press, 2002).
8. Jana Grekul, Harvey Krahn, and Dave Odynak, "Sterilizing the 'Feeble-minded': Eugenics in Alberta, Canada, 1929–1972," *Journal of Historical Sociology*, 17, no. 4 (December 2004): 358. See also Angus McLaren, *Our Own Master Race: Eugenics in Canada 1885–1945* (Toronto: McClelland and Stewart, 1990); Karen Stote, "An Act of Genocide: Eugenics, Indian Policy and the Sterilization of Aboriginal Women in Canada" (PhD diss., University of New Brunswick, April 2012).
9. Grekul, Krahn, and Odynak, "Sterilizing the 'Feeble-minded,'" 378.
10. John McLaren, "Maternal Feminism in Action – Emily Murphy, Police Magistrate," *Windsor Yearbook of Access to Justice* 8 (1988): 245.
11. Cecily Devereaux, *Growing a Race: Nellie L. McClung and the Fiction of Eugenic Feminism* (Montreal: McGill-Queen's University Press, 2005); Erika Dyck, *Facing Eugenics: Reproduction, Sterilization and the Politics of Choice* (Toronto: University of Toronto Press, 2013); Amy Samson, "Eugenics in the Community: The United Farm Women of Alberta. Public Health Nursing, Teaching, Social Work, and Sexual Sterilization in

Alberta, 1928–1972," (PhD diss., University of Saskatchewan, 2014); Amy Samson, "Eugenics in the Community: Gendered Professions and Eugenic Sterilization in Alberta, 1928–1972," *Canadian Bulletin of Medical History* 31, no. 1 (2014): 143–63; Sheila Rae Gibbons, "'The True [Political] Mothers of Today': Farm Women and the Organization of Eugenic Feminism in Alberta," (MA thesis, University of Saskatchewan, 2012); Sheila Rae Gibbons, "'Our Power to Remodel Civilization': The Development of Eugenic Feminism in Alberta 1909–1921," *Canadian Bulletin of Medical History* 31, no. 1 (2014): 123–42; Erin L. Moss, H.J. Stam, and Diane Kattevilder, "From Suffrage to Sterilization: Eugenics and the Women's Movement in 20th Century Alberta," *Canadian Psychology / Psychologie canadienne* 54, no. 2 (2013): 105–14; Janice Fiamengo, "Rediscovering our Foremothers Again: Racial Ideas of Canada's Early Feminists, 1885–1945," in *Rethinking Canada: The Promise of Women's History*, 5th ed., ed. Mona Gleason and Adele Perry (Don Mills, ON: Oxford University Press, 2006).

12 See, for example, Catherine Cleverdon, *The Woman Suffrage Movement in Canada* (Toronto: University of Toronto Press, 1974).

13 Margaret Walters, *Feminism: A Very Short Introduction* (Oxford: Oxford University Press, 2005), 78.

14 Ibid., 184.

15 Ibid., 184.

16 *Edmonton Evening Bulletin*, ()14 June 1916.

17 McLaren, "Maternal Feminism," 238.

18 Ibid., 242.

19 Ibid., 245.

20 Jennifer Henderson, *Settler Feminism and Race Making in Canada* (Toronto: University of Toronto Press, 2003), 159–208.

21 "Citizenship Talk by Janey Canuck," 13 March 1914 (n.p.), Emily Murphy clipping file #1, City of Edmonton Archives.

22 Quoted in Mariana Valverde, "'When the Mother of the Race Is Free': Race, Reproduction and Sexuality in First-Wave Feminism," in *Gender Conflicts*, ed. Franca Iacovetta and Mariana Valverde (Toronto: University of Toronto Press, 1992), 15.

23 This article appears never to have been published. Janey Canuck, "Emmeline Pankhurst in the North," draft typescript, box 1, file 39, Emily Murphy Papers, City of Edmonton Archives.

24 Quoted in Bartley, *Emmeline Pankhurst*, 205.

25 Purvis, *Emmeline Pankhurst: A Biography*, 319.

26 *Victoria Daily Times*, ()28 November 1919, 14.

27 Ibid., 18 August 1920, 6.

28 "Adopted Children Rejoin 'Mother,'" *Victoria Daily Colonist*, 19 August 1920, 8.

29 Wilkie Historical Society, *Wilkie, Saskatchewan, 1908–1988*, vol. 1 (Wilkie: Wilkie History Society, 1989), 661.

30 Bartley, *Emmeline Pankhurst*, 210 and Purvis, *Emmeline Pankhurst: A Biography*, 320.

31 Quoted in Purvis, *Emmeline Pankhurst: A Biography*, 322.

32 Ibid.

33 Ethel M. Chapman, "Mrs. Pankhurst – Canadian," *Maclean's Magazine*, 15 January 1922, 44.
34 David Mitchell, *The Fighting Pankhursts: A Study in Tenacity* (London: Jonathan Cape, 1967), 138.
35 Bartley, *Emmeline Pankhurst*, 50.
36 Mary Zeigler, "Eugenic Feminism: Mental Hygiene, the Women's Movement, and the Campaign for Eugenic Legal Reform, 1900–1935," *Harvard Journal of Law and Gender* 31, no. 1 (Winter 2008): 211.
37 See Ann Taylor Allen, "Feminism and Eugenics in Germany and Britain, 1900–1940: A Comparative Perspective," *German Studies Review* 23, no. 3 (October 2000): 477–505. See also Valverde, "'When the Mother of the Race is Free,'" 3–26.
38 Allen, "Feminism and Eugenics in Germany and Britain," 479.
39 Ibid.
40 Ibid., 489–90.
41 Zeigler, "Eugenic Feminism," 213.
42 Devereux, *Growing a Race*, 138.
43 Ibid., 12.
44 Ibid., 140.
45 *Victoria Daily Times*, 21 May 1921.
46 Ibid.
47 Bryne Hope Sanders, *Emily Murphy Crusader ("Janey Canuck")* (Toronto: Macmillan Canada, 1945), 129.
48 *Medicine Hat Weekly News*, 15 May 1921, 7.
49 *Calgary Daily Herald*, 14 May 1921, 7.
50 *Lethbridge Daily Herald*, 11 May 1921, 7.
51 *Calgary Daily Herald*, 14 May 1921, 12.
52 *Morning Albertan* (Calgary), 14 May 1921, 7.
53 *Medicine Hat Weekly News*, 19 May 1921, 1.
54 *Edmonton Bulletin*, 10 June 1921, 4.
55 Henderson, *Settler Feminism and Race Making in Canada*, 14.
56 Emily Murphy, *The Black Candle* (Toronto: Thomas Allen, 1922), 233.
57 Ibid., 47.
58 Carter, "Britishness," 56–57.
59 Wellington Bridgman, *Breaking Prairie Sod: The Story of a Preacher in the Eighties* (Toronto: Musson, 1920), 182.
60 *Victoria Daily Times*, 3 September 1921, 6.
61 *Toronto Star*, 15 September 1922, 18.
62 Ibid.
63 Ibid., 16 July 1923, 6.
64 Ibid., 14 September 1923, 7.
65 *The Globe*, 25 September 1923.
66 Quoted in Mitchell, *The Fighting Pankhursts*, 148.

67 Ibid.
68 Report of the general secretary to the annual general meeting of the Canadian Social Hygiene Council, 11 December, 1925, p. 2, vol. 10, file 23, Health League of Canada Fonds, Library and Archives Canada.
69 Bartley, *Emmeline Pankhurst*, 222.
70 Quoted in Carl Rollyson, "A Conservative Revolutionary: Emmeline Pankhurst, 1857–1928," *Virginia Quarterly Review* 79, no. 2 (Spring 2003): 333.
71 Robert J. Sharpe and Patricia I. McMahon, *The Persons Case: The Origins and Legacy of the Fight for Legal Personhood* (Toronto: University of Toronto Press, 2007), 189.
72 Quoted in Bartley, *Emmeline Pankhurst*, 221.
73 Grekul, Krahn, and Odynak, "Sterilizing the 'Feeble-minded,'" 362.
74 Quoted in ibid., 362.
75 "Birth Rate of Feeble Minded Causes Alarm," *Edmonton Bulletin*, 8 June 1926, Scrapbook 4, p. 137, Emily Murphy Papers, City of Edmonton Archives.
76 "The *Act* allowed for the sterilization of inmates of mental institutions if it could be shown that 'the patient might safely be discharged if the danger of the procreation with attendant risk of multiplication of evil by transmission of the disability to progeny were eliminated.'" A patient had to consent to the procedure unless deemed to be mentally incapable. Grekul, Krahn, and Odynak, "Sterilizing the 'Feeble-minded,'" 362–63.
77 Janey Canuck , "Should the Unfit Wed?," *Vancouver Sun*, 10 September 1932, Scrapbook 3, p. 87, Emily Murphy Papers, City of Edmonton Archives.

7

"The Country Was Looking Wonderful": Insights on 1930s Alberta from the Travel Diary of Mary Beatrice Rundle

Sterling Evans

In the late summer and fall of 1935, Mary Beatrice Rundle, a professional secretary, accompanied her boss (Sir Clement Anderson Montague Barlow), his wife (Lady Barlow), and a colleague (Mr. William Armour) to Canada as part of the Royal Commission on the Coal Industry in Alberta. She kept a running diary of the entire trip that lasted from August 24 to December 18, 1935 – nearly four months from beginning to end. She never missed a single day in adding an entry. Seventy-six of those days, or over two thirds of the trip, were spent in Alberta, where Rundle wrote the most detailed accounts of the things she saw and experienced. Thus, from her travel diary we have the chance of listening to her tell the story in her own voice, with her own nuances and inflections (and one can imagine, British accent), and we can gain important insights about Alberta in the 1930s.[1] However, as this chapter shows, Rundle's diary also reveals how much that she *missed* about Depression-era Canada and Alberta. What she sees, in many ways, is far different from what most other observers would notice, especially the growing unemployment and poverty in the cities, the drought conditions of the southern Alberta farm and ranch lands, and the general economic malaise of the time. Readers here can speculate on the privileged nature of her trip and how that separates her from larger social and economic realities.

The trip was necessary because the government of Alberta needed to conduct its second ten-year investigation and assessment of the coal mining industry, as dictated by provincial policy. It was Lieutenant Governor of Alberta William L. Walsh who, upon the advice of the provincial minister of trade and other officials, established the Royal Commission on the Coal Industry, which Social Credit Acting Premier Ernest Manning approved in September 1935. The need for the commission and its investigation was not merely for regular institutional data collection and reporting. As Canada's leading coal producer, especially in sub-bituminous and lignite coal, Alberta was enriched at the time with an estimated 1,717 square miles (4,447 square kilometres) or one million acres (404,685 hectares) of subsurface coal beds and seams, although not the entire amount was recoverable. But by 1935, markets for Alberta coal had dropped drastically and the industry was experiencing a variety of difficulties. The decline was striking, as the number of operating mines had dropped from 399 in 1924 to 276 ten years later. Output tonnage had dropped from a high of 7,336,330 tons in 1928 to 4,748,848 tons in 1934, a reduction in net worth of $23,532,414 in 1928 to half of that ($12,440,616) by 1934.[2] Thus, the provincial government was alarmed by the number of closed or abandoned mines and the precipitous decline in production and revenue.

The commission's goal was to investigate "the coal industry in Alberta, both in relation to the circumstances under which it is presently conducted and the possibilities of its future development." Matters under review included cost of production, transportation, distribution, and marketing of coal. Under consideration was "the capitalization, financial organization and cost of management" of the mines, especially to learn if any particular individuals were generating excessive expenses. Significantly, the commission was also charged with investigating "the wages and working conditions, living costs, and conditions of housing and general welfare of mine workers in and about the mines." Finally, there were matters of looking into "schemes" to increase demand and improved marketing for coal, coke, and their by-products.[3] The report recommended "schemes for better regulation of the industry," especially in terms of extending markets and "bringing production into relation of consumption." That Ontario had always been Alberta coal's largest market was of special interest to the commission, which investigated the market, subventions, and "possible further developments" for steam coal and other uses there. Manitoba, Saskatchewan, British Columbia, and the United States had always been active buyers of Alberta coal, markets that the commission likewise examined. A particular recommendation was the pushing of coal for more electrical generation in Canada. And the study of industry regulation, including organization of mining operations throughout the province, and comparing Alberta's regulations with that of other countries and provinces, made up over a third of the final report.[4]

Sir Clement Montague Barlow was the choice for commissioner because of his wide breadth of experience as a public servant in a variety of capacities and as a British government cabinet member. He had practised law early in his career, lectured in law at the London School of Economics, and entered public life when he was elected to the London County Council. He later served in a number of administrative positions in the British government, and was elected from a London riding as a Tory Member of Parliament in 1910. He was created a knight in the British Empire in 1918, a baronet in 1924, and was most well known as minister of labour in the Conservative Andrew Bonar Law and Stanley Baldwin governments in the early 1920s. Later, he devoted much of his time to travel: to India, central Africa, South America, Australia, and New Zealand on various kinds of commissions, including his service as Chairman for the Royal Commission on the Location of Industry in 1937. He married Miss D.L. Read (who then became Lady Barlow) in 1934 – just one year before the Royal Commission trip to Alberta. He died in 1951, at which time his baronetcy became extinct.[5]

But who was Mary Beatrice Rundle, this travelling secretary for Sir Montague Barlow, who left such a personal record of the commission's trip? Thanks to an *Edmonton Bulletin* society column (a regular feature entitled "The Social Round") about her visit to Alberta that appeared in the fall of 1935, and a letter that Rundle sent to the Provincial Archives of Alberta when she donated her travel diary in 1990, we have a biographical record from which to piece together this important part of her story. The anonymous columnist for the *Bulletin* had heard about the Royal Commission being in town to investigate the province's coal industry (and the paper had already reported on it and on Sir Montague Barlow and Lady Barlow), but he or she apparently also had heard about the travelling secretary Mary Rundle and how she would make for an interesting public interest article herself. The article began, "Private lives of private secretaries are not always just notebooks and pencils, and efficiency, plus – there's time for music, plays, travel, and all sorts of adventure," a very accurate picture of Rundle's trip that is corroborated in her travel diary. "Isn't a trip across the Atlantic, through the forests, and over the prairies of Canada something?," the article rhetorically asked.[6]

According to her letter and this interview, Rundle was the daughter of retired and recently widowed British Admiral Mark Rundle of Aylesbury, Buckinghamshire, England. He had "girdled the world time upon time" and was a decorated hero from his service in the Royal Navy during World War I.[7] Her mother had died "after a distressing disease" very soon before the trip, but Admiral Rundle, she wrote, "insisted that I should honour my undertaking and go to Canada." She was twenty-eight years old when she made the trip. When the Alberta government appointed Sir Montague Barlow to head the Royal Commission, he requested that he be permitted to bring along Rundle as his personal secretary and William Armour, "Technical Adviser to the Commision [sic]" and "an expert on coal mining." Rundle wrote that both she and Armour did the photography for the trip, and that she supplemented the travelogue with postcards, newspaper clippings, other documents, and hotel receipts. Rundle's diary would not only be a journal of the trip, but as she put it, "the record was kept in lieu of writing to family and friends, pages of carbon copy being posted home at intervals."[8] It was Rundle's first transatlantic trip, and her first journey to somewhere as remote-sounding for many Britons as Alberta in Western Canada.[9]

For Rundle this was a working business trip; however, the Royal Commission's business does not take a central role in Rundle's travel diary. She separated most of the business of the coal industry investigation from her own personal memoirs and correspondence that she sent home to family and friends. Nonetheless, there are moments that she captured in her diary that give readers a glimpse of the background details of the commission's work and its meetings. They had a total of twenty-four "sittings" (hearings) for which Rundle took the minutes: five in Edmonton and Drumheller; three in Calgary, Lethbridge, and Blairmore; two in Cadomin; and one each in Coalspur, Brazeau, and Saunders Creek.[10] And they undertook several field trips (that they called "probes") to the coal mining regions of

Alberta to investigate working conditions and document the technologies in use at each location. Rundle accompanied Sir Montague Barlow and William Armour to most, but not all, of the sites. They visited Tofield, the Drumheller area, Turner Valley, the Rabbit Hill District, the Lethbridge Collieries (controlled by CPR) and other mines in southern Alberta, and a couple of coal mines north of Edmonton. At each, they utilized two questionnaires, one for the "operators" (company management) and another for the workmen (miners). On September 25 at the Henderson Mine near Drumheller, Rundle described a bit about some of the new technology being used to extract coal. "They are using the long wall method here, which is new to this district," she wrote. "Everything is very mechanised; there are long rows of stalls, but only one pony kept now – for emergencies!" Surprisingly, she related how they did "part of our tour lying flat on a leather belt conveyor" when all of a sudden there was "a slight fall of roof stone." Sir Montague was injured by a falling rock, causing "quite a nasty scalp wound," and first aid and a doctor were rushed in.[11] Sometimes the commission met with leaders of the miners' unions. For additional background information on labour issues, Montague Barlow had consulted with officials at the International Labour Organization in Geneva, Switzerland, and with the office of US Secretary of Labour Francis Perkins in the Franklin Roosevelt government.[12]

Although indeed on a business trip, Rundle still had ample time for "delightful adventure" that she relished. She was particularly thrilled to see the Canadian Rockies, but she also enjoyed exploring the various cities she visited, and often commented on the more rural, agricultural sectors of Albertan society as well. Was Rundle's writing reflective of a growing genre of British women writers of the nineteenth and early twentieth centuries? Certainly she never achieved, nor tried to emulate, the fame of traveller and writer Isabella Bird – practically a household name in England in these years – who spent years exploring the world, especially Asia, the South Pacific, Australia, and the American West.[13] Bird wrote more in the style of natural history and adventure writers of that age, and Rundle was hardly as intrepid.

Nor did she venture much into politics or social criticism. The contributors of the volume *At Home and Abroad in the Empire: British Women Writers in the 1930s* suggest that common themes of modernism, colonialism, and critique of empire characterize many of the popular women writers' works from this period.[14] In her essay on Virginia Woolf, for example, Julia Briggs suggests that there was a sentiment of almost being ashamed of England, and rightfully so perhaps, given the brutal colonial experience in many parts of the world where the "sun never set." And Bonnie Kime Scott posits that similar intents characterized the letter writing of Rebecca West, especially as her construction of a public intelligence became visible in her letters home.[15] As she was not a novelist, or a published writer in any way (although she certainly had a flare for writing), it might be unfair to cast Rundle among this group. In many ways she could be the antithesis of a Woolf or a West; she was from a military household, was not at all critical of the British Empire, did not find fault with the British presence in the Dominion of Canada, and in fact relished the singing of "God Save the King" at all events. Even the final printed report, as it assuredly had to be, was directed to "George the Fifth, by the Grace of God, of Great Britain, Ireland and the British Dominions beyond the Seas, King, Defender of the Faith, Emperor of India."[16] Whether Rundle represented the Empire, then, or if she was a neutral player are questions that could be left to individual readers and literary critics. More important here is the way in which she responded to new stimuli around her in a foreign and faraway country, but one so heavily imbued with British history.

In 1930s grand style, Rundle journeyed from her home in London to Edmonton by first class rail and ship. Her route in England took her by train from London to Southampton, where she boarded the luxury steamer *Empress*. Reflective of the times, and certainly interesting in retrospect, was the point that she made of seeing German ships in the port, including the *Bremen* with "a natty little red aeroplane on board, complete with swastika" (August 24). The transatlantic trip to Quebec City took five days, and then after a few days spent each in Montreal, Ottawa, and Toronto, Rundle and her party took a boat from Port McNicoll, Ontario, to Fort William (now Thunder Bay), Ontario, and then by the Canadian Pacific Railway the rest of the way to Edmonton, with a few days' stay in Winnipeg en route. In Alberta, there were side trips to visit mine sites around the province, as well as time to do some sightseeing in the Canadian Rockies.

Rundle described each step of the way. And as she was a gifted writer, her diary entries read as most classical travel narratives do in beautiful and descriptive prose. They tend to be in the tradition of grand British diction, making careful use of selected words, consummate vocabulary, and precise and often glowing descriptions, as readers will note in some of the quotations from her diary in the following pages here.

Along this same light, Rundle made a variety of interesting observations comparing life in the Dominion of Canada to that in Great Britain. She liked Ottawa and the area around Parliament, the views of it from the Chateau Laurier, and especially the walks and roads around the Rideau Canal that she found "charming." "We have nothing like it in England for residential town planning," she noted. But as if she were writing today, she was amazed at the number of automobiles that people drove in Canada instead of walking, as was more customary in England. On Labour Day, while still in Toronto during the front part of the trip, Rundle proclaimed that "of course the traffic was quite dreadful!" She wrote on September 2, "I have never seen so many cars in one day in my life. There are few pedal cyclists & no pedestrians, and I only saw four motor cyclists all day. The most noticeable thing is the complete absences of signals – hand or mechanical. No-one seems to bother, except at busy crossroads." By September 22, now in Alberta, she was even more aggravated by Canadian motorists:

> The people of Edmonton have forgotten the use of their feet; all the way along the river, I met precisely two girls walking: All this within the City boundary and only a few yards from the main roads and houses by the hundred. It really is pathetic, and must have a serious effect on their health; I notice the inhabitants seem amazed that we walk to the Court House for the sittings of the Commission and it is actually in sight a couple of blocks away – not more than 5 minutes walk: Everyone has a car, and never dreams of walking, even a few yards.

While they were in Lethbridge, there was even less exercise by walking because the court house where they conducted meetings was across the street from their hotel. Thus on September 30 she wrote that because "we get less exercise than ever, I have taken a vow never to use the lift – we are only 2 floors up – and everyone else is following my example!" Later, on October 24, now back in Edmonton, she decided to walk the two miles back to the Hotel Macdonald after a luncheon on a "glorious afternoon" and was pleased that her host decided to join her, proclaiming that it was "delightful to find someone here who walks!" Rundle, Lord Montague

Barlow, Lady Barlow, and others in their party often took walks, even if it was just strolling up and down the queue at railroad depots, to get a little exercise when the weather allowed, and sometimes even when it did not. When the snow and wind came to Edmonton in October and November, there were days when Rundle could only stay out a few minutes, despite her desire to walk. But when the sun returned, cold or not, she was back at her routine. Armistice Sunday, November 10, was such a day, and after attending church services, she and others "went for a good long walk…. it was a glorious morning, but our ears froze!"

The Barlows and Rundle attended the Anglican church most of the Sundays of the four months they were in Canada (Lord Montague Barlow's father was a clergyman), missing only when they were in transit from one city to another, or when using the day to catch up from all the goings-on of the previous week. On Sunday, September 15, at the Pro-Cathedral of All Saints in Edmonton, Lord Montague Barlow even "read the lessons." Rundle mentioned that it was "Harvest Festival" Sunday; "We ploughed the fields and scattered." But being in Alberta in the 1930s, she noticed that church attendance was quite robust compared to that in England. For example, on that Armistice Sunday Rundle mentioned that she was glad they had gone early to the cathedral, getting seats in the lieutenant governor's pew next to the mayor of Edmonton, as by 11:00 "it was packed and people 'turned away,'" and noted that "they surely go to church in this country!" It was a "packed church, including a large detachment of Mounted Police in their scarlet uniforms; they really are the best turned-out lot I have ever seen." As noted above, she was always delighted to hear and partake in the singing of "God Save the King" at church services and elsewhere in Canada. In fact, on that particular Sunday, she wrote that the anthem had been sung "with more strength and unity of feeling than I have ever heard before." But she seemed bemused that the next day, Monday, November 11, was a day off for Armistice Day. "Another public holiday – any excuse is good enough in Canada!," she wrote.

Rundle likewise observed the difference between federal leadership elections in Canada and Great Britain. Her trip in 1935 corresponded with the end of the Tory government of R.B. Bennett and the election of a Liberal majority under William Lyon Mackenzie King. On Election Day (October 14) she noted Mackenzie King's "thumping majority at the expense of poor Mr. Bennett" (who had treated her so kindly in Ottawa earlier on the trip [see below]), and observed that "it was all very peaceful – very unlike election day at home." In Alberta, she witnessed an even more dramatic political turning point, as it was in 1935 that voters overwhelmingly abandoned the United Farmers of Alberta (in power since 1921) to elect the Social Credit Party under the leadership of evangelical radio preacher William "Bible Bill" Aberhart. She seemed a bit bemused, and somewhat concerned, with the "recent amazing elections" that favoured Aberhart, "who is to try out his Social Credit Scheme," she observed on August 31.[17] People were still talking about the "enthusiasm at the recent provincial election" and how that "was most unusual here [in Alberta]" with many residents who voted "who have never done so before" (September 14), and indeed Social Credit had won an absolute majority in 1935 with 54 per cent of the vote, picking up 53 of the 64 seats in the legislature, and as historian Alvin Finkel has written, "transforming the province's political landscape for generations to come." This election in Alberta, as Finkel has asserted, gained "international attention" as the "first electorate in the world to elect a government committed to social credit."[18]

Overall, however, Rundle was critical of the new Alberta government, thinking she had gotten "a very good idea" of the "rottenness of political life here," she wrote after having a luncheon on October 24. Another socio-political difference became more apparent to her in Alberta as well – that being the limited consumption of alcohol. While Albertans had rescinded their seven-year experiment with prohibition (1916–23) by plebiscite twelve years earlier, to Rundle it still seemed like a "dry land." Apparently most dinner parties she and the commission members attended refrained from serving preliminary cocktails. But on October 26, she seemed relieved to have a "nice dinner and drinks (for once in this dry land)" at Government House. Her father may have known of this curiosity about Alberta, having made sure to give her a big flask of brandy for the trip, which she occasionally tapped into.

Despite these minor points, Rundle was thrilled to be in Canada and ebulliently described the many beautiful sights that she saw on the trip around Quebec, Ontario, and especially Alberta. Like many people visiting the Prairies, she was struck by the light – "a brilliant light [that] made a never to be forgotten picture" (September 22). She marvelled in Edmonton a few days later how the "light in the woods across the [North Saskatchewan] river was lovely." Overall, the "country was looking wonderful" with "trees just beginning to turn," she observed on a day trip in mid-September to visit a strip mine near Tofield. At dusk in southeastern Alberta, she wrote about "the most beautiful sunset I have ever seen," and outside of Calgary, "a most gorgeous sunset, with satanic cloud formations over the Mountains" (September 26, 29). Similarly, she described Drumheller's setting near the Red Deer River Valley badlands as "set in a strange pocket of weird hills.… The formations are most peculiar, not to say sinister." The mines they needed to visit were at the end of "this weird valley," indeed a "valley of desolation" characterized by "weird rock formations" (September 25–27). Dinosaur Provincial Park in this badlands region would not be created for another twenty years, so she did not have the opportunity to visit, or comment upon, the paleontological resources of southeastern Alberta.[19]

But it was the Canadian Rockies that really captivated Rundle. Her "first thrilling sight" of the mountains was en route from Drumheller to Calgary on September 28, estimating that they were still 100 miles away. Even from her Calgary hotel window, the mountains were "superb." On October 2 she and her party ventured to Crowsnest Pass, observing the continental divide and the surrounding valley, all of which she found "very scenic" at the 4,300-foot (1,311-metre) elevation. Returning to Calgary, she was enthralled with the view of the Rockies with fresh snow, describing them as "a shining white glory from tip to toe – the most wonderful sight I have ever seen" (October 9). Later that month, they travelled to Banff National Park. October 11 was a "day of thrills! the beauty was quite indescribable," especially with the looming snow-capped peaks. Because of its eponymous name, she was especially taken with Mount Rundle, with its stunning view from the Vermilion Lakes. At one point (October 11), she bought "some postcards and a big photograph" of the mountain. That evening must have been beautiful: "We walked on the bridge over the River Bow – and behold it was a full moon, standing over Mt. Rundle, and the mountain and the moon were reflected in the river – one of the most lovely sights I have ever seen." She was delighted as well with Bow Falls, the various hot springs in the area, Lake Louise – and amused with the name of Kicking Horse Pass that they crossed en route, Lake Emerald ("a glorious spot, where the lake really is emerald green" [October 12]), and the wildlife. It was Rundle's first time to see elk, which she described on October 11 as "terrific thrills":

> It is the mating season, and they are supposed not to be safe, but we were all right in the car and stopped to watch them. There were about 8 females and calves on one side of the road, with a magnificent stag in charge, and a solitary female on the other; she was calling to a distant stag, which we could hear roaring in reply; she was not a bit frightened, and came within six or seven yards of the car.

At the end of her Alberta stay, and on the first leg of her trip home travelling from Edmonton to Calgary (November 24), she admitted her love for the mountains: "I had been so hoping for a last sight of the Rockies, and was not disappointed, for we watched the sun set behind them across 90 miles of snow – a very wonderful and never-to-be-forgotten picture."

At the same time, Rundle recognized that Alberta in the 1930s was not solely a Rocky Mountain scenic paradise. Drumheller, for her, was a "dreary little mining town" that was "smothered in coal dust" (September 23, 26). She was thankful that other coal-mining communities like Hardieville, Stafford, and Coalhurst were "favourable [in] comparison with awful Drumheller" (October 1). She tired quickly on the "tedious" train ride to Lethbridge. Her party had to fight "horribly dusty" roads along the Oldman River to tour the collieries there. Indeed, the "dust was frightful," to the degree that Rundle developed a sore throat on more than one occasion, and recognized the symptoms as "dust colds," as Albertans referred to them (but was relieved to find in local pharmacies her favourite Boots Iodized Lozenges from England, which provided considerable comfort). She recognized the hazards of mining life, and mentioned in her diary on October 2 that her party passed by "the sliding mountain" that "sent down ... crashing ruin" on the town of Frank in 1903. The rock slide, she noted, killed about 100 people and buried them and their homes 500 feet (152 metres) deep in debris, where they yet remain. "I hated the place," she admitted, "and felt scared each time we had to pass it." She also noted that the mountain was continuing to erode, causing people to worry about a "repeat performance before very long" – and again, "due to the mining operations underneath the mountain."[20]

And of course, Rundle alluded often to the weather – the "bitter" wind and cold for which Western Canada is famous. En route, Winnipeg as early as September 8 was already "bitterly cold and wet ... most unpleasant." For the most part, however, autumn of 1935 was mild. She noted in Lethbridge on September 30 that "the weather has been perfectly wonderful – brilliant sunshine every day, and delightfully warm and yet fresh. Everyone says they have never known such a good fall, so Canada is being kind to us." But winter came quickly. Coming from Great Britain, she had never before experienced the kind of frigid temperatures that Alberta can, and did, have that year. She described "a terrific wind that got up in the night" in Calgary on October 8, and the early fall snow that fell in Edmonton that day. The below-zero temperatures (still using Fahrenheit) later that month affected Lord Barlow's rheumatism, she remarked, and in November there were days that were so cold she could barely take her daily walk, quickly having to turn back to the hotel. But she also related how she knew she was not experiencing the depth of winter in Alberta. "Of course 10 degrees above is comparatively warm here," she wrote on October 28, "where for three solid weeks last winter the mercury never rose above 40 below." She also recognized that as cold as it was in Alberta, it seemed even colder upon her return through Ontario in December, as many Canadians would attest. On December 5 she posited that "it is very cold here; though the temperature is only about zero, it feels bitter, and we find it more trying than 20 below in dry Alberta."

Rundle observed the province's ranching business (including "hobby" ranches), noting those breeds of cattle she could identify, and farming, especially during the harvest, which seemed to interest her. "We watched them reaping barley with two teams of fine horses – four to each binder," she noted on September 18 near Tofield.[21] And of course there was discussion and description of coal mining, since that was the primary purpose of the trip. On September 18, for example, she described the strip mine they visited near Tofield – her first time to see such a mining operation. "It is an expanse of 200 acres," she began, with "a seam of coal 7' thick, and a depth of 8'.... All they have to do is to take off the surface dirt, and then scratch out the coal." More recent, of course, was the developing oil and gas industry in Alberta. The Royal Commission was not charged with investigating this aspect of resource extraction in the province, but Rundle made mention of it a couple of times, especially when her party travelled to Turner Valley on October 9. She witnessed the "host of derricks" and the "gas burning in huge flares." Oil had been discovered in Alberta in

1902, but not until 1914 in the Turner Valley area, and was going strong there when Rundle made her visit.[22] But the party never actually got to the town, as the muddy roads were just too impassable. "We simply had to crawl, and slithered about all over the place," she explained. After having gotten their car "completely stuck" in the deep mud, she and the others got out "and pushed the car fore and aft, like tugs at a liner, with the desired result," although they turned back there instead of trying to get on into town. Rundle did not seem too disappointed about missing Turner Valley, as "the smell even where we were was pretty strong!"

All of these things combined to make the seventy-six days she spent in Alberta a great experience for Rundle, and she grew quite fond of the province and its people. On November 22, the day before she and her party left to return to England, she wrote, "Our last day in friendly Edmonton – very sad." By mid-October she had ceased marking the mileage of the trip (mile 6,750 in Banff National Park), but since that point she would have possibly accumulated another 7,000 or so miles, making it nearly a 15,000-mile (over 24,000-kilometre) journey from beginning to end.

Rundle's travelogue not only provides accounts of the places and people she encountered along the way but also gives an insightful glimpse into the times – of life in Alberta and across Canada in the mid-1930s, especially the life of the upper classes. The first-class travel by steamship and rail was luxurious – emblematic of that golden era of elite travel – and was accompanied by exquisite meals and silver service. When travel was by automobile, she spoke of riding in Packards, Buicks, and Nashes. Meals and dining, such as the banquets with the British High Commission, the lieutenant governor, and Prime Minister Bennett in Ottawa, and the many luncheons, fashionable teas, and official dinners held en route, were often extravagant affairs. But Rundle observed that the events could be exhausting, and not always pleasant, as she noted on September 1 at a country club luncheon where she was forced to share a table with a "<u>very</u> dull" couple from Australia, and September 3 in Toronto, when one women's luncheon was "a most tedious affair!" There were even more events in Alberta, with members of Edmonton's and Calgary's high society and politicians, that often weighed heavily on her. In Edmonton, a tea with a group of "educationalists" was "not a very inspiring affair." Another tea on October 21 included conversation with an "objectionable English couple," and a dinner on November 17 became "a rather sleep-inducing evening."

Conversation at these events at times centred on the problems of the wealthy. At the October 3 luncheon in Crowsnest, Rundle noted that the community's nine-hole golf course was characterized with "browns" instead of greens since "they can't get grass to grow properly up there," and that the hostess complained "of the difficulty of getting 'help' – nothing but mainly not-too-clean miners' daughters." Sometimes she herself was frustrated with the maid service at the Hotel Macdonald. "The chief snag about this hotel," she mused on September 12, "is that the servants work on a rota system, and you never have the same maid or waiter more than once for some considerable time."

This kind of class-consciousness (sometimes tinged with racism) popped up here and there elsewhere in the journal. While still in Ontario and visiting Niagara Falls (September 2), she and her hosts went across to the US side, but on the way back into Canada she complained, "We had to go through immigration examination and were bullied by a horrible dago." Travelling from Crowsnest to Calgary (October 6), she described how "there was an enormous R.C.M.P. on the train, escorting a wretched little prisoner with a wooden leg; we all wondered what he had done, but didn't quite like to go and ask!"

At the same time, Rundle, and often Lady Barlow too, belied their upper-class ways and seemed to enjoy a more common Alberta lifestyle. They both often did their own sewing, darning, and ironing. They discovered a quick and inexpensive cafeteria in Edmonton (their first time to visit one) in which to eat, and became regular customers. They were good sports about having in-car picnics when on road trips throughout the province when there were just no restaurants available. Rundle even helped to push the car she was riding in out of deep mud when it got stuck on the way to Turner Valley. She befriended the staff at the Hotel Macdonald, to the degree that there were "almost tearful farewells" when their stay was over. She made sure to buy the telephone operator a gift of fine chocolates for all of her help with things related to communications for the Royal Commission. And she had befriended the elevator operators so much that on November 24 she wrote, "One of the lift boys said to me in tones of deepest gloom, 'You know, you may <u>never</u> come back again,' and although I protested, the gloom remained profound."

In so many ways, Rundle's travel diary gives strong hints on the role of women in the 1930s, and in this way can add a degree of gender analysis to the discussion here. Both she and Lady Barlow performed what could be considered "typical" women's household chores, including darning socks, ironing clothes, and sewing. She mentioned that she was glad that she had taken her knitting with her on long train and car trips to keep her busy. On September 12 she noted, "I have been darning stockings in Lady Barlow's room, while she ironed; a most domestic scene." She also frequented the lending library to get books, and occasionally went to the YWCA in Edmonton. And although it is doubtful that Rundle drove a car – she never did on this trip, at least (and if she had a licence in England, probably would not have appreciated the driving on the right-side of the road in North America), but a Miss Christie from Calgary, their host when in that part of the province and with whom Rundle had become a very close friend, drove them all over the Prairies and Rockies.[23] On that particularly muddy and slippery road ("a layer of mud over frozen ground") en route to Turner Valley on October 9, Rundle remarked, "Miss Christie is a marvelous driver, and we weren't a bit scared" – in the face of many stereotypes of women and women drivers, still a less common phenomenon in the 1930s.

Some of these stereotypes were based on fables and superstition. The most poignant example of this surfaced on September 20 when the party was investigating the Rabbit Hill mining district. But while Rundle was doing some photographing of the mine, she was discouraged from descending into it because of her gender. "Mr. Armour refuses to consider Lady Barlow or me going down a mine," she explained, "as the way it is considered very bad luck for a woman to do so; consequently we walk very delicately in the vicinity of coal." Nonetheless, a few days later (September 25) at a mine near Drumheller, she did descend. She said she was "diffident about going down" and "did not want to be a nuisance," but this time "everyone was insistent." Thus, "down I went, wearing a proper miner's cap and lamp, and enveloped in an enormous makintosh!" No bad luck seemed to have come to anyone there from this act. But, at the next stop on September 27 at the A.B.C. Mine, it was back to superstition dictating policy (and events?). Her story:

> I did _not_ go down this time. I should record that Mr. Armour thinks it frightfully bad luck for women to go down a mine, and was much against Miss Christie and I going down the other day. An accident is supposed to happen within 24 hours,

and sure enough, Sir Montague got a rock on his head, and the next morning Mr. Heeley, the local mines inspector, was badly kicked by a pit pony – one for each of us! So this time I sat in the car and knitted!

The anecdote is provided in her diary, we can suppose, more out of Rundle being bemused by the coincidence than by her actual belief in the cause and effect. Further, on October she made an important and telling point when discussing the coal mines at Crowsnest. She related what a workers' union representative told her about the history of the mines in that area: "He was most interesting … [and] he told me he thought the whole plan would have collapsed long ago if it had not been for the grim determination of the women." Readers of her diary could use a bit of expansion on this point, although that is where she dropped it. We can suppose, however, that the wives and women of the early mining camps there were the bedrock support for the men's work, made sure they were fed and clothed, perhaps helped with the finances and record keeping, and generally were community builders in supporting stores, schools, and churches in the area. Nonetheless, superstitions die slowly, as a similar incident earlier confirmed that not all of Albertans were living cosmopolitan lives quite yet. On September 15 Rundle reported that Edmonton was hosting a large convention of "men from all over the Dominion who suffered amputation as a result of the War [World War I]," and that it was "very sad to see them all." "They want us all to dine with them on Wednesday," she seemed excited to say, "but there is doubt if it is 'done' for ladies to accept!" The women in the party thus were not allowed to attend.

Rundle may also have been frustrated, bemused, or even miffed from time to time with these stereotypes about women, or at least about her, during this period. After an invigorating outing in Banff National Park on October 12, for example, she wrote that William Armour "said he could see I had a good time at Banff, and that I looked a 'different lassie.'" She responded in her diary, "Query; what on earth did I look like before?"

Her good nature and keen (and sometimes, sharp) sense of humour were evident in how she described a couple of comical things that happened to her at the Hotel Macdonald. First, on September 12 she mentioned that the night before she "could not find her pyjamas anywhere," necessitating a "frenzied search" in the morning that still "failed to discover them."

The next day she was relieved to declare the missing items found: "My pyjamas have returned to the fold, having gone down to the wash with the bed-linen." But the same night, an even more curious and humorous incident occurred: "I had a BEAST in my room last night, having foolishly left some window open at the top, where it is not screened. It chased me until 2:00 a.m., and left me utterly unnerved; I don't know what it was, but it was awful. Never again!" She even used her sense of humour to deal with the kind of bitter winter cold that she was unused to. On October 28, she related the following anecdote from her room at the Hotel Macdonald in Edmonton that illustrates her good nature on the subject:

> I woke up at 8:30 this morning to find it still snowing and bitterly cold. I hopped out of bed to turn on my radiator, and then huddled under the clothes in my woolly dressing gown for ten minutes to warm up. I did some work until about 12 and then ventured out, and it was <u>cold</u> – thermometer only 10 degrees above zero, and a bitter north wind blowing. I slithered along to the library and then bought some snow boots at the Hudson Bay, and then home as fast as I could, with a frozen face!

She stayed inside the rest of that day, "feeling very thankful that I had no engagements." Sarcastically, she then related the forecast for the next day: "'Cold; some snow and wind;' thoroughly cheerful."

Cultural points that pop up in Rundle's diary also reflect the 1930s in a variety of ways. Like many Canadians, she enjoyed shopping for things she needed at Hudson's Bay Company stores. Rundle was also fond of going to the movies, often writing about the films she had seen and the actors in them, sometimes very critically. She saw a couple of Shirley Temple movies on the trip, including *Baby Take a Bow* (that she thought "rather sickly") and *Curly Top*. Grace Moore's *Love Me Forever* was a "rotten film," but she liked *Barbary Coast*, as well as Will Rogers in *David Harum*, which was "excellent and most amusing." In Edmonton she and part of the Royal Commission group went to see the "colour film" *Becky Sharp*. And as any good student of British literature would point out, "It is of course based on 'Vanity Fair' and faithful to the book on the whole, though Thackery's [sic] share in it is not acknowledged at all." In Calgary she and others in the party "went to the pictures" to see George Carliss in *Cardinal Richelieu* – "not very good we thought."

Live theatre was also a very keen interest of Mary Rundle, especially given her experience with it during her time at Harrogate Girls' College in her youth, but there were few opportunities to see plays while on this trip to Alberta. One exception was the chance on October 26 to see a production of Eugene O'Neill's *Ah, Wilderness*, which Rundle asserted had "never been done by amateurs before." She gave a mixed critique, which also gives a glimpse of theatre production in Alberta in the 1930s: "It was excellently acted, but terribly long; we didn't get out till 12:45 a.m.! There were ghastly waits of about 20 minutes between each scene while the scenery was being shifted, during which I had to keep His Honour amused!"

She also enjoyed learning about historical events in Western Canada. For example, at a dinner in Edmonton on September 18 she ended up sitting next to Mayor J. Clarke, "who turned out to be 'Fighting Joe' from the Klondike." It ended up being "a most amusing dinner" in which she got to hear all about Dawson City and the Gold Rush of 1898. But apparently she was less interested in sporting events, as there is no record of her attending any football or hockey games while in Alberta. However, in Toronto (November 30), on the return trip home, she and members of her party went to see the Maple Leafs play the Montreal Canadiens. "We only stayed for two-thirds of the match," she admitted, "it was terrifically fast and very thrilling, and I should imagine one gets tremendously keen if one knows anything about the game."

A final cultural moment mentioned in Rundle's diary is also representative of this time period and worthy of mention here. On November 7 she noted that renowned evangelist Aimee Semple McPherson (a Canadian originally from Ontario, but based out of her Angelus Temple in Los Angeles since the 1920s) was in Edmonton for a revival meeting and was staying at the Hotel Macdonald. "Aimee Semple McPherson is here for a couple of days evangelizing, and is staying in the hotel," she wrote, "but so far I have not spotted the lady!" It would have been interesting had Rundle attended one of the evangelist's revivals (especially with her more staid Anglican perspective), as McPherson at this time was still in her rebuilding phase of the International Church of the Foursquare Gospel after her supposed death or kidnapping and miraculous re-appearance in the Arizona desert in 1926.[24] But according to Rundle, in Edmonton, "She seemed to have had a lot of heckling at her meeting here last night."

Although Rundle's travel diary represented life in the 1930s in a variety of ways, what is also significant is what might be considered *missing* about Canada and Alberta during this time. Most surprising is that there is no mention at all in Rundle's diary of the Great Depression, or how it was affecting Canadians, especially as 1935 was directly in the centre of the economic malaise. In fact, reading the diary, with its narrative of first-class travel and accommodations, and with description of new houses being constructed, and plenty of automobiles – many of them large, fancy models – motoring around the province, one might have no idea at all that times for a majority of the people were tough. Historian Hal Rothman has written about this phenomenon of tourists being presented with an artificial experience in Las Vegas, Nevada, in Santa Fe, New Mexico, and at ski resort towns in the Rocky Mountain West.[25] Although Alberta was not as touristy as those places, some of Rothman's conclusions apply here. Despite much of what Rundle witnessed, Albertans were, in fact, as Alvin Finkel has written, experiencing how the Great Depression had an "immense impact on the entire Canadian economy," and how it was "particularly disastrous for export-dependent provinces such as Alberta." A collapse in international grain markets hit Alberta farmers hard, and the mining industry suffered because of the lack of money available to buy Albertan coal or other minerals. Unemployment was high in the province, and federal authorities even deported some 2,500 immigrants. By 1935, an average of 14 per cent of the residents of Edmonton, Calgary, and Lethbridge were on relief. It was this kind of economic plight, as Finkel has explained, that "created the political space for radical political movements in Alberta," and gave the fundamentalist Aberhart and his Social Credit Party the chance to succeed.[26]

Only occasionally does Rundle mention that other dominant feature of the 1930s in the Prairies: drought. The lack of rain, causing the driest years since weather records had been kept in the region, combined with such natural disasters as wind and dust storms and grasshopper plagues, compelled historians to refer to the thirties as the worst decade in the history of the Prairie Provinces. As Gerald Friesen has explained, the dust storms began in 1931 and grew steadily worse by 1934 when "soil began to blow in mid-June, to destroy gardens and crops." The year 1935, when

Rundle visited, was only slightly better for farmers, but the next year was a "disaster [with the] coldest winter in history [and] the longest, hottest summer yet," with the winds causing "desert-like conditions."[27] One of the few times that Rundle alluded to what surely must have been these very visible conditions was on October 4 when she complained about her "dust cold" and how there was "no getting away from it; the dust from the roads hangs over the valley like a perpetual mist, as there has been no rain for weeks."

Likewise, First Nations people are basically absent in her account. This could perhaps be due to the few opportunities afforded her to see many Indigenous people, as most of her time was spent in downtown Edmonton. And the Royal Commission had no business on any First Nation reserves. At only one point, on October 9 when south of Calgary at the EP Ranch, does she mention this population: "Two full blooded Indians rode in while we were there, one on a lovely little brown pony, and the other on a stocky little grey beast. We tried to talk to them, but they were not very communicative." Given their location, it is most likely they were members of Treaty 7 nations, perhaps Nakoda (Stoney) First Nation, or Piikani (Peigan), Tsuu T'iina (Sarcee), Kainai (Blood), or possibly Siksika (Blackfoot Confederacy).[28] Rundle did not show any curiosity on the matter, but perhaps more than others in her British party, as she wanted to visit with the two whom she encountered here. First Nations across the Prairies in the 1930s were suffering tremendous economic and environmental hardships. The devastating drought had adversely affected farming and ranching on Treaty 7 lands (southern Alberta), without much attention from Ottawa, as the Bennett government focused primarily on business and economics during the Depression. The overall economy put a slump on prices for primary products (especially fish and furs) from First Nations lands, and, as historian Olive Dickason has written, put "Indian producers on welfare rolls." Dickason also pointed out that there were valid "fears that the Great Depression would drive hordes of whites into the bush" and onto reserve lands.[29]

Because Rundle was part of a commission investigating the coal mines in Alberta, however, she does mention the hard times experienced by miners and their families.[30] For example, on September 23, while touring the Drumheller area, Rundle noted that they went to look at the "housing conditions in Newcastle and Nacmine" and were "horrified at what we saw." She described how there were "hundreds of small shacks ... huddled together in large 'camps,'" that there was "no running water supply except from a communal tap in the middle of the camp, and no sanitation except what the people choose to arrange for themselves." Worse, she offered, "What the conditions must be like during the winter, I don't like to consider." "I believe the cold is very severe in this valley ... and in the summer they have dust storms." We are left to wonder, however, if these living conditions were standard for the industry or made worse because of the plight of the Depression. On September 25 they travelled to the Rosedale Mine, where miners were on strike (although she does not discuss the reasons for the job action), and where miners' quarters were leased to them by the company.[31] She did mention a strike in the works at the mine, and wrote that the workers' housing and conditions were deplorable there. The tour they were given suggested that the accommodations "were pretty comfortable and spotlessly kept," but, as she added, "we were only taken into carefully prepared and selected houses." They inspected the bathhouse there as well, but although Rundle took "feverish notes," she didn't allude in her diary to the conditions that they observed. There is barely any mention at all of any of the miners themselves, who in 1935 numbered nearly 10,000 in the province.[32]

The Alberta government, however, did in fact commission Sir Montague Barlow to investigate the working and housing conditions in the province's mining districts. Montague Barlow wrote that the commission "made personal examination of the provision made for the health and welfare of the mining community, including housing, sanitation, water supply, pithead baths, etc."[33] But the report on these matters was contradictory in some ways. Although Montague Barlow admitted that there had been "numerous complaints" by miners about their living conditions, especially regarding the "insufficient accommodation" of the wash-houses, he tended to side with management, arguing that management was "taking steps to improve" the conditions. In regard to housing, he admitted that the conditions were similar to those reported by the commission ten years earlier, but that some complaints now seemed "exaggerated," as he thought "houses were reasonably adequate," with running water, and with some having access to adjacent land for gardens. Sanitation standards, however, were not adequate. "There leaves much to be desired," he wrote, "especially in Drumheller." He noted that in many mining camps there were only "small outside privies" and "no provisions for the removal of waste." In conclusion, he advised that "a determined effort should be made to improve the housing and living conditions throughout the mining districts." When coal had been first discovered in some of those areas, the camps were "remote" and "meager," but now "efforts should be made to raise the general standard." He also noted that "non Anglo Saxon miners" in some mining communities lived in the "barest of shacks."[34]

Montague Barlow did not go into specific recommendations or make harsh demands of the coal companies or of the province regarding the remedy for these conditions. The same was true for his stance on wages and earnings, where he again appeared to side with management on the issue. He noted that few miners in Alberta's smaller pit mines were union members, and left it to the provincial minister of labour to "take steps" to deal with complaints about minimum wage earnings. For the times, with decreases in demand for coal, he maintained that there were overall too many coal miners in the province. The work was just too seasonal, as there was less demand for coal in the summer. Thus, Montague Barlow advised that the provincial minister work to regulate the situation, but did not give suggestions on how to do so.[35] Rundle did not engage in these kinds of political musings in her own writings, but did mention that some mines were soon to be closing, making no reference as to whether the closures were due to the Depression or if the coal seams had been spent.

All of these points reflect quite well the hard times of mining in Alberta in the 1930s. Despite coal being the province's "primary energy industry" in the beginning of the twentieth century, its decline had already started in the mid-1920s due to the postwar recession, high freight rates for shipping, stiff competition from coal mines in Germany, Great Britain, the United States, and Saskatchewan, and the advent of hydroelectric power in the Prairies. Likewise, discoveries of rich reserves of oil and natural gas in Alberta in the 1920s signalled even greater competition in the domestic energy market in Alberta and in the export market elsewhere in Canada, especially to Ontario, which had once been Alberta's biggest coal customer. Thus, production fell from a high of seven million tons in 1923 to less than half that amount by the 1930s.[36] By the time of the Depression, as historian Bradford Rennie has argued, coal mining in the province was "non-remunerative," with some operators making only a "hair-thin profit" and others actually losing money. So, although "no-one could have foreseen it, the old order of coal was passing; the industry teetered on the precipice of a long decline."[37] And decline it did. Despite a brief wartime boom during World War II, between 1948 and 1967 coal production dropped by 50 per cent, and by 80 per cent in value, when Japan was Alberta's only "viable export outlet" for coal.[38]

The decline that started was manifested in ways that hit the mining community hard in Alberta. Often the mines were only open a few days a week and only part of the year, wreaking havoc on household economies dependent on the mining wages. Worse, economic constraints caused operators to cut corners on safety, a situation that resulted in thousands of work-site accidents and injuries each year, and as Rennie stated, with "frighteningly common" fatalities.[39] All of these conditions created a scenario ripe for union activity in Albertan mining communities. In the 1910s and 1920s the One Big Union (OBU) was active throughout the province. The OBU promulgated a major strike in 1919 in Drumheller, where labour relations were "particularly hostile," an action that was partly in sympathy with the Winnipeg General Strike earlier that year.[40] Strikes, backed by the Mine Workers of Canada (after it broke away from the United Mine Workers of the United States), continued for the next two decades, "unruly and sometimes bloody," as Rennie described them, although Mary Rundle made no mention of violence at the job actions that took place during the commission's visits in 1935.[41]

Rundle's four-month work trip and adventure to Canada ended on December 18, 1935. She gave only scant attention in her travel diary to the final couple of weeks of travel in Quebec, the Maritimes, and the ship journey home to England. Hence, the journal seems to have a somewhat abrupt ending, but she devoted much of her time on the return trip in eastern Canada furiously typing up the final Royal Commission reports, which ended up being 110 pages. One can imagine that so much tedious work, as well as the fatigue of travel and living out of trunks, left her exhausted and not prepared to add too many details to her diary at the end of the trip. Her last entry is written with Britain getting nearer. "Had another bad night, but felt much better and got up at 11. Arranged about landing card, changing money, etc., and feel that England is almost in sight; indeed, by the chart we are nearly there. It is a beautiful day – sun and blue sky – but the incessant rolling goes on."

Mary Rundle's life largely returned to normal upon her arrival home. She continued working as a professional secretary, and two years later was back in the employ of Sir Montague Barlow for the Royal Commission on the Location of Industry located in the Treasury of Whitehall in London, one of the services for which Sir Montague Barlow became best known. However, two years later, duty called – this time to her country. In 1939 she left Sir Montague Barlow to join the Women's Royal Naval Service (WRNS), where she served for the next nine years and became a supervisor, the third-highest ranking possible for that organization.[42] Following military service she worked in London as a secretary to the managing director of the Metal Box Company until her retirement in the early 1960s. She lived the rest of her life in a cottage in Outgate on Lake Windermere in England's Lake District. She never married, a condition that most certainly allowed her to travel to Western Canada with the Barlows, to be a member of the WRNS for so long, and to pursue her career as a professional secretary. Thus, Rundle lived a long, full life, enjoying her centenary birthday party hosted in her honour at her Lake District home, and dying at age 103 on September 29, 2010.[43]

Notes

1. I would like to thank Elizabeth Jameson, commentator for the panel "Transnational Migrations and Political Networks" at the *Directions West* conference, for her insightful and helpful suggestions on an earlier draft of this chapter, and George Colpitts and the anonymous reviewers for their wise advice and suggestions in readying the conference paper for this volume.

    The travel diary is unpublished, but is in its original typewritten manuscript in the Provincial Archives of Alberta (hereafter PAA). "Trip Diary of Miss Mary Beatrice Rundle, Secretary to Sir Montague Barlow, former Minister of Labour in the United Kingdom, Heading the Royal Commission Appointed to Investigate the Coal Industry in Alberta, Aug. 24 to Dec. 18, 1935," PAA, 90.245.

2. Montague Barlow, *Report of the Royal Commission Respecting the Coal Industry of the Province of Alberta, 1935* (Edmonton: A. Shnitka, King's Printer, 1936), 7–9.

3. The act to establish the commission is Order-in-Council (O.C.) 1088/35, and is signed by both Lieutenant Governor W.L. Walsh and Acting Chairman (Premier) Ernest C. Manning: PAA, accession PR1990.0245.

4. Barlow, *Report of the Royal Commission*, 1–2, 4, 10.

5. Biographical information gathered from the obituary for Sir. A. Montague Barlow, "Life of Public Service," *The Times Picayune* (London), 1 June 1951.

6. "The Social Round," *Edmonton Bulletin*, 19 October 1935. Rundle included a copy of the article after page 36 of her travel diary, the copy from which this and the subsequent paragraphs are gleaned.

7. Ibid.

8   Mary Rundle to Keith Stotyn, Esq., Senior Archivist, Manuscripts, 6 May 1990, PAA, PR1990.0245. Information on Armour is from Barlow, *Report of the Royal Commission*, 4.
9   "The Social Round."
10 Montague Barlow, *Report of the Royal Commission*, 4.
11 All direct quotations are from "Trip Diary of Mary Beatrice Rundle," PAA, 90.245. To avoid citation repetition, for reference purposes each quotation in the body states the date the diary entry was made without needing to re-flag it in a footnote.
12 Montague Barlow, *Report of the Royal Commission*, 4, 6.
13 See Isabella Bird, *The Englishwoman in America* (London: John Murray, 1856), or Bird's arguably most famous work, *A Lady's Life in the Rocky Mountains* (1879; reprint, London: Virago, 1986). For analysis, see Robert Root, *Following Isabella: Travels in Colorado Then and Now* (Norman: University of Oklahoma Press, 2009).
14 Robin Hackett, Freda Hamer, and Gay Wachman, eds., *At Home and Abroad in the Empire: British Women Writers in the 1930s* (Newark, DE: University of Delaware Press, 2009).
15 See Julia Briggs, "'Almost Ashamed of England Being so English': Woolf and Ideas of Englishness," in *At Home and Abroad*, 97–118; and Bonnie Kime Scott, "Rebecca West: Construction of a Public Intelligence through Letters of the 1930s," in *At Home and Abroad*, 187–202. For further examples of this kind of British Empire critical writing see E.M. Forster, *Howards End* (1910; reprint, New York: Longman, 2010) and Forster's *A Passage to India* (1924; reprint, New York: Meiers, 1979).
16 Montague Barlow, *Report of the Royal Commission*, 3.
17 Some of the standard works on Aberhart and Social Credit include Alvin Finkel, *The Social Credit Phenomenon in Alberta* (Toronto: University Press of Toronto, 1989); Lewis H. Thomas, ed., *William Aberhart and Social Credit in Alberta* (Vancouver: Copp Clark, 1977); and John J. Barr, *The Dynasty: The Rise and Fall of Social Credit in Alberta* (Toronto: McClelland and Stewart, 1974). For a reassessment, see Alvin Finkel, "Alberta Social Credit Reappraised: The Radical Character of the Early Social Credit Movement," in *The Prairie West: Historical Readings*, ed. R. Douglas Francis and Howard Palmer (Edmonton: Pica Pica Press, 1992), 661–81; and Finkel, "1935: The Social Credit Revolution," in *Alberta Formed, Alberta* Transformed, ed. Michael Payne, Donald Wetherell, and Catharine Cavanaugh (Edmonton: University of Alberta Press, and Calgary: University of Calgary Press, 2006), 490–512.
18 Finkel, "1935," 491.
19 For more on this region, see Brian Noble and Glenn Rollans, *Alberta, The Badlands* (Toronto: Reidmore Books, 1981); Philip J. Currie and Eva B. Koppelhus, eds., *Dinosaur Provincial Park: A Spectacular Ancient Ecosystem Revealed* (Bloomington: Indiana University Press, 2005); Chuck Haney, *Badlands of the High Plains* (Helena, MT: Farcountry Press, 2001); and Sterling Evans, "Badlands and Bones: Towards a Conservation and Social History of Dinosaur Provincial Park, Alberta," in *Place and Replace*, ed. Leah Morton, Essylt Jones, and Adele Perry (Winnipeg: University of Manitoba Press, 2013), 250–70.
20 For more on the Frank landslide disaster, see Karen Buckley, *Danger, Death, and Disaster in the Crowsnest Pass Mines, 1902–1928* (Calgary: University of Calgary Press, 2004); Monica Field and David McIntire, *On the Edge of Destruction: Canada's Deadliest*

Rockslide (Crowsnest Pass, AB: Frank Slide Interpretive Centre, 2003); and Frank Anderson, *The Frank Slide Story* (Calgary: Frontier, 1979).

21 Most farmers in Alberta in the mid-1930s were still harvesting with binders, as combines were used only on the huge wheat ranches that were owned by large conglomerates located elsewhere. Thus, the scene of binders harvesting wheat and other grains, and the rows of stooks neatly organized in the fields to await threshing, became iconic symbols of rural Alberta and the Prairie Provinces in general. For more on the history of wheat farming in one particularly important place for the wheat industry, see Paul Voisey, *Vulcan: The Making of a Prairie Community* (Toronto: University of Toronto Press, 1988). For the history of such harvesting in the region, see Thomas D. Isern, *Bull Threshers and Bindlestiffs: Harvesting and Threshing on the North American Plains* (Lawrence: University Press of Kansas, 1990). On how the Prairie Provinces were connected to a larger North American complex because of the use of binders and the twine they required, see Sterling Evans, *Bound in Twine: The History and Ecology of the Henequen-Wheat Complex for Mexico and the American and Canadian Plains, 1880–1950* (College Station: Texas A&M University Press, 2007).

22 For a complete telling of this Turner Valley history, see David Finch, *Hell's Half Acre: Early Days in the Great Alberta Oil Patch* (Victoria: Heritage House, 2005); and Laura Golebiowski, "Oil Discovery in Turner Valley: Press Reactions," *Alberta History* 55, no. 3 (2007): 20–28. The really large Alberta oil reserves were not discovered until 1947, when the oil industry really developed, and it has remained an important part of the Albertan economy ever since. See Doug Owram, "1951: Oil's Magic Wand," in *Alberta Formed, Alberta Transformed*, vol. 2, 566–87.

23 British Columbia held out with left-hand side of the road driving until 1922, when provincial leaders opted to change the rules to right-hand driving, mainly in order to lure American tourists to BC during Prohibition. See Stephen L. Moore, "Refugees from Volstead: Cross-Boundary Tourism in the Northwest during Prohibition," in *The Borderlands of the American and Canadian Wests: Essays on Regional History of the Forty-Ninth Parallel*, ed. Sterling Evans (Lincoln: University of Nebraska Press, 2006), 248–49.

24 For further information, see Daniel Mark Epstein, *Sister Aimee: The Life of Aimee Semple McPherson* (New York: Harcourt Brace, 1994); Edith L. Blumhofer, *Aimee Semple McPherson: Everybody's Sister* (Grand Rapids, MI: W.B.. Eerdmans, 1993); and Thomas Lately, *Storming Heaven: The Lives and Turmoil of Minnie Kennedy and Aimee Semple McPherson* (New York: Morrow, 1970).

25 See, for example, Hal Rothman, *Devil's Bargains: Tourism in the Twentieth-Century American West* (Lawrence: University Press of Kansas, 2000); and *Neon Metropolis: How Las Vegas Started the Twenty-First Century* (New York: Routledge, 2003).

26 Finkel, "1935," 492–93; quotation is on 491.

27 Gerald Friesen, *The Canadian Prairies: A History* (Toronto: University of Toronto Press, 1987), 386–87. See also James H. Gray, *Men against the Desert* (Saskatoon: Western Producer Prairie Books, 1978); and David C. Jones, *Empire of Dust: Settling and Abandoning the Prairie Dry Belt* (Edmonton: University of Alberta Press, 1987).

28 On Treaty 7, see Treaty 7 Elders and Tribal Council with Sarah Carter, Walter Hildebrandt, and Dorothy First Rider, *The True Spirit and Original Intent of Treaty 7* (Montreal: McGill-Queen's University Press, 1996).

29 Olive Patricia Dickason, *Canada's First Nations: A History of Founding Peoples from Earliest Time*, 3rd ed. (Don Mills, ON: Oxford University Press, 2002), 309, 382.

30 For discussion of early coal mining in Western Canada, see D. B. Dowling, *Canada Department of Mines Geological Survey: The Coal Mines of Manitoba, Saskatchewan, Alberta and Eastern British Columbia* (Ottawa: Canada Department of Mines, 1909); and James White, *Power in Alberta: Water, Coal and Natural Gas* (Ottawa: Canada, Commission on Conservation, 1919). For a survey of mining operations in Alberta by the early 1960s, see John Duncan Campbell, *Catalogue of Coal Mines on the Alberta Plains (Research Council of Alberta Preliminary Report)* (Edmonton: Research Council of Alberta, 1964).

31 For more on labour history and strikes in Alberta, see Tom Monto, *Solidarity and Anger: History of the Alberta Labour Movement* (Edmonton: Crang, 1989); and sections on Alberta in Judy Fudge and Erick Tucker, *Labour before the Law: The Regulation of Workers' Collective Action in Canada, 1900–1948* (Toronto: Oxford University Press, 2001).

32 Number of workers is from Barlow, *Report of the Royal Commission*, 53. For further discussion, see Warren Caragata, *Alberta Labour: A Heritage Untold* (Toronto: Lorimer, 1979); and Tom Mitchell and James Naylor, "The Prairies: In the Eye of the Storm," in *The Workers' Revolt in Canada, 1917–1925*, ed. Craig Herron (Toronto: University of Toronto Press, 1998), 176–231.

33 Barlow, *Report of the Royal Commission*, 4.

34 Ibid., 57–58.

35 Ibid., 56, 53.

36 Data as reported in Bradford Rennie, "From Idealism to Pragmatism: 1923 in Alberta," in *Alberta Formed, Alberta Transformed*, vol. 2, 446–47. Barlow reported similar findings in his *Report of the Royal Commission*, 5, 9.

37 Rennie, "From Idealism to Pragmatism," 447.

38 Max Foran, "1967: Embracing the Future . . . at Arm's Length," in *Alberta Formed, Alberta Transformed*, vol. 2, 620.

39 Rennie, "From Idealism to Pragmatism," 447.

40 David Bright, "1919: A Year of Extraordinary Difficulty," in *Alberta Formed, Alberta Transformed*, vol. 2, 427. See also Mitchell and Naylor, "The Prairies: In the Eye of the Storm."

41 Rennie, "From Idealism to Pragmatism," 448.

42 Rundle to Stotyn, PAA, PR1990.0245.

43 Later biographical information is derived from the obituary for Mary Beatrice Rundle that was in *The Daily Telegraph* (London), http://announcements.telegraph.co.uk/deaths/ass833/rundle-mary-beatrice-cbe (accessed on 8 August 2011).

8

A Blueprint for Range Management: The Anderson Grazing Rates Report of 1941

Max Foran

> Grass is pleasing to the eye and therefore pleasure giving. It preserves the soil, enriches it and spells the difference between verdure and desert.
>
> —Anderson Grazing Report

As an agent of change, the Great Depression of the 1930s has been a focus of considerable study. The miseries and impasse generated during the long years of the Depression had their impact on federal/provincial relations, the birth of the social welfare state, and even constitutional change. In terms of agriculture, the formation of the Prairie Farm Rehabilitation Administration (PFRA) to deal with the problems of soil erosion and lack of sufficient water resources to enable agricultural development in the crippled dry areas of the Prairie West was a major response to farm abandonment and drought. The impact of the Depression on ranching, or more specifically on the leased grasslands on which it depended, is less appreciated. So, also, is the way that the Western Canadian ranch, always shaped by external techniques and practices, became reconfigured around new management ideas. In many respects, the ranch became more rooted to its place in Western Canada by grassland ecology tested on far distant ranges and locations. In that context, the publication of a document in 1941 entitled the "Grazing Rates Report" (later known as the "Anderson Report") was crucial in that its recommendations represented a radical shift in philosophy and practice. By reinforcing the importance of the range as a fragile variable, and by relating the value of grass to its productivity, the Anderson Report changed the way ranchers did business by adding a monetary bottom line to the emerging principles of range management. Ranching practices, then, applied by newcomers to the region, were reformed by lessons learned elsewhere to allow the rancher and his place in Western Canada to finally find a sustainable home.

Changing land use patterns involving human intervention invariably result in dispossession and alienation, a theme forming a constant in this anthology's contributions. The rolling grasslands and wooded areas of the southern Alberta foothills country were no exception. For centuries, Indigenous peoples interacted with wildlife in a predator-prey relationship, acted out seasonally, rhythmically, and with a balance that barely brushed the landscape. The buffalo were the first to be dispossessed (via near-extermination) by outside human intervention, followed by the Native people, their displacement to reserves rationalized on grounds that mocked who they had been. The incoming ranching frontier, sanctioned by the federal government in the name of proper progress and wise land use, replaced the buffalo with less environmentally adaptable cattle, and replaced the Indigenous peoples with European, eastern Canadian, and American uninformed strangers bent on turning grass to dollars. In this transformation, wildlife was alienated from its habitats. Ungulates consumed grass that was no longer theirs. Raptors and wolves took animals that were not theirs. Both became enemies of the new order. Milling cattle trampled delicate riparian ecosystems, fouling waters and ending the lives of the unnoticed and irrelevant creatures that lived there. Though to the untrained eye the incoming cattle regime simply dotted a pristine landscape with intermittent human activity, it had done much more. The dispossessed, the displaced, and the alienated were of minor consequence in the new age of progress where everything had to earn its keep or get out of the way.

The leasehold system

Unlike the US experience, ranching in Western Canada was founded on the leasehold system. Beginning in 1881, tracts of up to 100,000 acres on Crown land could be leased from the federal government at a cent per acre per year. This availability of cheap, nutritious fescue and other native grasses spawned the big ranches and launched the golden era of the open range industry. Over the next forty-five years the availability of these Crown leases was seen as crucial to the survival of the beef cattle industry. The prime issue with them up to 1925 concerned their security. Besieged by the onslaught of farmers, homesteads, and cash crops, leasehold size and length of tenure suffered curtailment (1892, 1905, and 1920) before being stabilized in 1925. In that year, regulations were amended, setting the maximum leaseholding at 25,000 acres and providing for 21-year closed leases. When Alberta took over the control of grazing leases following the transfer of natural resources by the federal government in October 1930, they numbered 3,778 and occupied 3.22 million acres.[1] They ranged from the foothills country to the west and south of Calgary to the arid areas to the east near the Saskatchewan border, to the short grass country in the south and southeast.

Between 1885 and 1930, when the federal government handed over control of its natural resources to the Prairie Provinces, annual rental rates on grazing land were stabilized at 2¢ an acre, a figure based on an arbitrary assessment of all western grazing land at 25¢ an acre with 8 per cent interest.[2] However, this low figure must be set against the volatility of beef prices which, in addition to the vagaries of the 14-year cattle cycle, were compounded by the uncertain and tariff-prone American market upon which the industry relied after 1913. Leaseholders paid no extra tax to the federal government unless the lease happened to impinge on school lands, in which case a levy was assessed, as high as 10¢ an acre in some cases. Local taxes were involved but only if the lease impinged on a municipal area or an improvement district.

The emergence of problems

In spite of the consolidation of leasehold tenure in 1925, problems began for ranchers in the not-so-roaring twenties. Faced with an unpalatable US tariff, low prices, and drought, the industry hovered at times on the brink of extinction. Two results were evident. Both gathered devastating momentum in the ensuing decade.

The first was the increasing burden of land costs. Lease rentals were only partly to blame. The main cause concerned deeded land. In most cases ranchers carried lease land in addition to their own holdings. Taxes on deeded land rose considerably in the wake of increasing demands for roads, schools, and other institutional amenities. In 1922, A7 ranch owner Alfred Ernest Cross paid $5.20 tax on a quarter of leased land. A deeded quarter in the same township cost him $26.34 in taxes.[3] Especially in the drought-ridden years between 1921 and 1923, tax arrears began to build. In 1922, the Province of Alberta took title to 105 sections of land in forfeiture for unpaid taxes.[4] Uncollected taxes were more than the actual levy in Alberta's municipal districts every year in the 1920s. In 1930 taxation arrears exceeded the levy in municipal districts by $1.6 million.[5] Even before the full onslaught of the Depression, ranchers were in dire straits. One source quoted a rate of return of 0.83 per cent on the typical ranch balance sheet between 1926 and 1931.[6]

The second manifestation of the trying times of the 1920s was an awareness of the vulnerability of the range itself. Through the first quarter of the twentieth century, government officials were ignorant of the principles of effective range management.[7] Reports from federal research stations during this period dealt primarily with experiments designed to improve cash crop farming. Livestock experiments concerned themselves with nutritional studies, mostly involving grain finishing and legume forages.[8]

The negative effects of unrestrained breaking of land to the plough were noted as early as 1915 by the federal inspector of ranches when he wrote in his report of a patch of 20 acres broken in 1885 which "had never grown back to its natural state."[9] However, his warning that ploughed land was forever rendered useless for grazing went unheeded. Furthermore, the stipulations on stocking rates in the various grazing regulations, for example, showed that official interest lay in securing maximum land usage. In the 1914 Regulations, the minister of the interior could compel a rancher to stock more cattle if he felt it necessary. In 1925, the new provisions for 21-year leases contained a clause which prevented renewal if the leasehold was not being used to its fullest extent. All regulations, including the provincial regulations of 1931, referred to 30 as representing the *maximum* number of acres per animal, a ridiculously low figure for much of the semi-arid ranch lands in the south and southeast. In 1928, the federal government rejected a request by the Dry Belt Ranchers Association to set the stocking rate at 60 acres per animal in the short grass country. Clearly, land differentiation according to carrying capacity was not part of official policy.

It is also true that most ranchers agreed with the principle of heavily stocked ranges. Accustomed to an extended period of favourable grazing conditions, they seemed to accept the notion of unlimited grass.[10] All they wanted was cheap and easy access to it. By the early 1920s the visible evidence presented by deteriorating range conditions caused by overgrazing, and the vegetative degradation associated with the reversion of abandoned cropland to its natural state, brought stockmen face to face with the fragility of the land. The ensuing ten years marked the beginnings in understanding the principles and merits of range management.

It was the stockmen, and not the government research stations, who first recognized the implications of range degradation. In 1924, the Western Stock Growers Association (WSGA) appealed to the federal government for assistance in arresting the erosion of grazing lands.[11] The result was the establishment in 1927 of a research station on a private lease in the heart of the short grass country south of Medicine Hat. Located 18 miles south and 9 miles east of Manyberries, and comprising 18,000 acres typical of the 80,000 square miles of short grass country, the station began pioneering the new science of range management.

The Depression of the 1930s

The Great Depression began for the ranching industry in 1930 with the imposition by the United States of the prohibitive Hawley–Smoot Tariff on live cattle.[12] The results for the ensuing ten years were low prices and a surfeit of animals. One led to intolerable financial burdens and an assault on inequitable land costs. The other was manifest in accelerated range degradation due to overgrazing.

Figures released by the federal government during this period showed that ranchers needed a floor price of $6.00 per hundredweight to break even.[13] With this floor price unattainable, many ranchers simply could not cope. Arrears in rentals and taxes piled up while bankruptcies and lease cancellations increased dramatically.[14]

Between 1931 and 1936 the average yearly price paid for good butcher steers in Toronto dropped over 34 per cent from the average in the 1920s.[15] The Alberta livestock commissioner referred to 1931 as recording the lowest prices for livestock in the previous thirty years,[16] a situation exceeded in the following year when good butcher cattle brought a dismal $2.90 per hundredweight at the Calgary Stockyards.[17] Again, in 1933, the livestock commissioner spoke about the lowest prices on record when steers off the range brought less than $2.00 per hundredweight.[18] A Winnipeg cattle dealer told the federal minister of agriculture in January 1933 that more than half the cattle sold at the St. Boniface Stockyards brought less than $1.50 per hundredweight and many went as low as 35¢ per hundredweight.[19] In 1936, low-end cattle were bringing 1¢ per pound in the Lethbridge area while canner cows were selling at 50¢ per hundredweight. Some cattle shipments actually brought less than the cost of transporting them.[20] Grant MacEwan, then Professor of Animal Husbandry at the University of Saskatchewan, recalled low-quality animals being worth more for their hide than for their meat.[21]

The sustained period of low prices pushed ranchers to precarious financial brinks. A survey by Manyberries Research Station of twenty-seven ranches concluded that stockmen barely met their operating costs in 1931 and that ten of the twenty-seven had to use reserve capital or borrowed money to keep afloat.[22] A study involving 10,000 head showed that the production costs were more than double stockyard prices for cattle in 1932–34.[23] According to one authority, the expected rate of return on a calf was a dismal 1.1 per cent.[24] In late 1933, the *Albertan* (Calgary) claimed that ranchers' operating costs exceeded revenues by 240 per cent.[25]

Land costs were thrown into sharper perspective. Put simply, they were far too high in terms of the total costs of production. One expert told the 1935 WSGA Convention that the land charges on beef production were double that of grain.[26] Although statistics varied with year and area, land costs hovered between 15 and 25 per cent of the costs of total production, and the value of his cattle, around 20 per cent of his equity.[27]

It was estimated in 1937 that land taxes, together with water and fencing costs, were over 50 per cent of the cost of production.²⁸ These were ruinous figures.

Under the effect of the appallingly low prices, ranchers could not pay their land taxes and rentals. This now included leasehold rentals, which after 1930 had doubled. When the province took over the management of leaseholds in 1930, it added a further general tax levy of 2¢ per acre to the 2¢ rental already charged by the federal government on its yet unexpired leases. This 4¢ levy in catastrophic times was perceived as too much, unfair, and a prelude to bankruptcy. In desperation, ranchers sought redress in reduced taxes.²⁹ The leasehold rentals angered stockmen more than the local tax burdens. The latter was a universal signifier of bad times; the former was unfair in that the levy on grass had no relation to its worth. The general disquiet over a disproportionate levy marked the beginnings of an attitudinal shift. In the meantime, arrears began to build.

By 1936, the total arrears on uncollected taxes in 1936 totalled $18.22 million.³⁰ Leasehold arrears also showed a significant increase in the period. At the time of transfer of natural resources in 1930, leasehold arrears totalled $39,771.46; eight years later, the corresponding figure was $279,873.44.³¹ In the same year, 813 leases were cancelled. Between 1933 and 1937-37, taxation arrears for municipal districts averaged $6.2 million, more than double the tax levy. The situation in the major leasehold areas was proportionally worse. In 1935 the five districts with the largest leasehold acreage were in taxation arrears of more than half a million dollars, or roughly five times their annual tax levy.³²

Range degradation reached alarming proportions. Rather than sell their cattle at ruinous prices, desperate ranchers kept them on the range hoping for a rise in prices. In 1932, 80,000 fewer cattle were marketed in Alberta due to herd accumulation.³³ Between 1931 and 1936, cattle numbers in the province increased by 430,000 and in the ranching districts by 138,000. The impact of these increased numbers was reflected in chronic overstocking and extensive range deterioration.³⁴ One report found that over a four-year cycle, overgrazing increased weed cover by 250 per cent, and reduced grass cover by 25 per cent and forage yield by 45 per cent.³⁵ The effect of overgrazing on profits was evidenced in a study undertaken in Miles City, Montana, between 1933 and 1939. Researchers found that cows on overgrazed pastures produced fewer calves. Moreover, their lower weaning weight, compared to those bred from cows on moderately grazed pastures, increased the feed costs of finishing them by one third.[36] In 1934 the government was forced to take over three overgrazed leases totalling 223,500 acres.[37] Two years later, the provincial supervisor of grazing warned of the "probability of Alberta grasslands being completely overgrazed and developing into a desert."[38] The situation was not confined to the semi-arid lands of the south and southeast. In 1937 the district agriculturalist in more northerly Camrose also commented on the chronic overgrazing of pastures in his district.[39]

Uncontrolled displacement had wrought its own end: rich fescue grass was dispossessed by weeds and the groundwater regimes displaced by dust and dryness. Everything, it appeared, was alienated from everything else. Farmers fled from land they had violated though ignorance. Ranchers stood by helplessly while their grasses turned against them. Their solution, however, was redress, not reconciliation.

A changing mentality

As indicated, the cumulative effects of rising indebtedness, land degradation, and a growing awareness of range management created an attitudinal shift within the cattle industry. For over fifty years the cost of grass itself was assumed as a constant. Feed, labour, and cattle prices were far more volatile than the cost of grass, especially on leased land. In terms of leasehold rentals, grass was grass; its value, fixed; and its state of health, irrelevant. In referring to the livestock industry in 1936 as "a hazardous occupation which now depends on exceptionally favourable circumstances and good management to save it from financial disaster," the provincial grazing appraiser foretold the events to come.[40] They took two forms. First were the efforts to change the way leasehold rents were structured. Second, some of the principles of range management moved from "good ideas" to regulation.

The issue of changing the entire leasehold structure was broached as early as 1932 by noted agriculturalist L.B. Thomson. In a paper entitled "Economics of the Ranching Industry in Alberta and Saskatchewan," Thomson put forward the notion that taxes and rentals on grazing land should be linked to its carrying capacity.[41] Four years later he reiterated his message to the WSGA Annual Convention, stating that "in the rating capacity of grazing lands, it should be on the basis of production value rather than on acreage alone."[42]

Thomson's points were well taken by short grass rancher George Ross of Aden.[43] Ross, who was already recognized as a leader and innovator in the industry through his work in establishing the Red Label Feeders Association in the late 1920s, was no stranger to the financial difficulties associated with large-scale ranching enterprises.[44] His family had expanded well beyond its original Milk River location before being curtailed by low prices and diminishing returns. Shortly after Thomson's address, Ross initiated the formation of the Short Grass Stock Growers' Association (SGSGA) in Medicine Hat in July 1936. After dividing the short grass country of 30,000 square miles into twelve zones headed by a spokesman, the meeting passed its first resolution calling for the provincial government to rate grazing lands on their earning capacity in relation to livestock values. By January 1937, the association had organized its forces sufficiently to approach Hon. N.E. Tanner, minister of lands and mines.[45] Implicit in its suggestion to Tanner was a promise to submit to a voluntary experiment of a new tax on production should it be approved. Tanner, who was equally interested in a way out of the financial morass that was crippling an important industry, agreed to undertake a survey with a view to classifying leasehold lands in terms of their productive capacity. Four months later, the SGSGA was able to report to its membership that "a signed agreement has been made with the Provincial Government to submit the control of grazing land to a board representing the Government and stockmen ... to administer this land on a production basis.[46]

By the end of 1937, the notion of leasehold rentals being based on production seemed a foregone conclusion. In fact a formula had already been worked out by the SGSGA, one based on several presuppositions. It was assumed that 50 acres per adult animal was a reasonable base rate for grazing cattle on a lease in the short grass country. It was also assumed that this same animal would gain 250 lb. in a year. If these two figures were multiplied (the number of allowable cattle on a lease at a 50:1 ratio × 250), then one would arrive at a figure that correlated with the production capacity of the grass on which the animals had grazed. If this figure was multiplied again by the average market price of cattle (average price in the Calgary Stockyards between July and December), the figure reached would represent what the grass was actually worth that year. The annual lease rental rate or production tax could be established by taking a percentage of that figure. The figure of 10 per cent was suggested as a maximum.[47]

The issue was, of course, was it worth it? This was what the proposed survey was all about. From the outset it was agreed that it should be conducted within a valid time frame, by knowledgeable individuals, and that it should deal with the issue from a scientific and wide-ranging perspective. In July 1939, a special committee consisting of representatives from the SGSGA and the provincial government began its investigation into the best ways of protecting the natural grasslands while ensuring that ranchers paid equitable rentals on their leases.

The special committee was chaired by Graham Anderson, an inspector with the Department of Municipal Affairs at Brooks. Described as "the best man for the job," Anderson was well-qualified, having been assistant supervisor of grazing in the Dominion (federal) Department of the Interior. His 1924 master's thesis at the University of Saskatchewan was on scientific range management. Tanner and his deputy minister, John Harvie, were routed into the process through their addition as non-active committee members. Members of the committee were prominent ranchers George Ross, Rube Gilchrist, and P.A. Minor.

Range management

The impetus for changing the leasehold structure was accompanied by an increasing official awareness in the merits of range management. In 1936, the provincial grazing supervisor, in recommending the adoption of range management principles, implied that there was no alternative if the industry was to survive.[48] Though the science of range management has become more sophisticated with time, its basic principles were as true in the late 1930s as they are today. Range management in the cattle industry involves the integration of land usage with beef production so that both are optimized. The key variables in the range management equation are carrying capacity, or the number of animals that can graze the land without damaging it, and the productive value and ongoing health of the forage they consume. The new production tax was seen as being consistent with these principles.

Agricultural scientists had been carrying the messages of range management principles to the livestock community since the late 1920s. As already mentioned, foremost among these spokesmen for more enlightened grazing practices were L.B. Thomson,[49] superintendent of Manyberries and later Swift Current Dominion Research Stations, and his on-site colleague, S.E. Clarke, an agricultural scientist specializing in Forage Crops and Pasture Studies. Throughout the 1930s both men were regular speakers at the WSGA Conventions.[50] Between them, they hammered home the concept of differentiated ranching practices necessitated by variable topography, climate, and grass cover. By using visual references and statistics based on ongoing research at their own facilities, Clarke and Thomson stressed the need for drastic change in the way grass was managed if the floundering ranching industry was to survive.

The Anderson Grazing Rates Report

The special committee took two years to complete its report, which was released in 1941. Dedicated to former Provincial Grazing Supervisor Albert Helmer, whom it described as "one of Canada's first conservationists," the Anderson Report was extensive and wide ranging. The report covered 237 pages and was based on over 100 interviews with ranchers, government experts and administrators, stock associations, co-operative marketing organizations, cattle companies, banks, breeders, packers, and veterinarians in both Canada and the United States. It also received seventy written briefs on a wide range of scientific and economic topics. The Grazing Rates Report was a solid, insightful document with important implications for both the government and the livestock industry. Anderson himself described it as far reaching in scope and ground breaking in its implications.[51]

He was right. Though the report's primary focus was on a survey of sixteen ranches in the short grass country, it gave much more. It opened with a solid historical review of the leasehold system, which was put in further perspective by a scientific analysis of the short grass area in terms of soils, vegetation, topography, and fitness for economic use. The range management work at Manyberries Research Station was highlighted as a source and guide for all ranchers, and a detailed analysis of production costs identified how short grass ranchers were facing challenges beyond their control. The report also dwelt on marketing and beef grading issues.

Government grazing policies were studied in British Columbia, Saskatchewan, South Africa, Argentina, New Zealand, three Australian, and a half a dozen US states. Here, the report found a diverse range of policy and several conciliations to leaseholders. In Australia, tenure was longer and some states offered to pay for improvements. Argentinean leaseholders paid very low taxes while South Africa included provision for buying leases. None offered a production tax. The report found that state grazing policies in the United States were similar to Alberta's in terms of their defects. However, the National Forest Service, a branch of the US federal Department of Agriculture, which administered grazing policies in national forest reserves, provided guidance. Here, a form of production tax had been in place since the early 1930s, when lease rentals were set against current prices in proportion to those in the 1920s, when the average price of cattle was $6.62 per hundredweight. The fact that this policy had been well received by American leaseholders was a further vindication of the direction the Anderson Report wanted to take.[52]

The report directed its recommendations separately to government, individuals, and livestock associations. Its common message to all three was to recognize and become more sensitive to the intrinsic value of grass as an invaluable and vulnerable resource. It advised the government to adopt the new formula for assessing leasehold rentals and justified the various standards upon which it was based. The report also recommended 20-year leases, the division of the province into three areas of differing carrying capacities, a herd limit of 500 in the short grass region, and a relaxation in arrears repayments.

In terms of range management, the report provided direction. In recommending that the province adopt a policy of conservation, it suggested the formation of a Grasslands Commission comprised of government officials and representatives of the stock associations to direct grazing policy and to act as a clearing house for information. It recommended that at least 25 per cent of grazing revenues be turned back into range improvement programs. The report was critical of agricultural practices in the short grass area and felt that all crop lands yielding averages of less than 12 bushels of wheat per acre should be allowed to revert to grazing.

The report did not let ranchers "off the hook." They were advised to be more efficient in their record keeping and management practices, and proactive when it came to marketing their product. The report felt that ranchers were too resistant to scientific range management principles and warned them that continued reliance on the old ways would not be tolerated. The stock associations were encouraged to show the way in education and co-operative marketing. Above all, the report charged them to become "the foremost proponents of conservation in all its forms including wild life."

While the Anderson Report was under preparation, two significant events occurred – events that combined to undermine its impact. The first concerned the revised lease regulations issued by the provincial government in 1940 which, in addition to guaranteeing a 20-year leases, also froze the maximum flat rental rate at 4¢ per acre.[53] Second were cattle prices. They were on the rise. In 1941 they were 8.62¢ per pound. It takes no arithmetical wizardry to realize that under the new formula, cattle prices over 8¢ per pound translated into a production tax in excess of 4¢ an acre. Also of note is that it was anticipated that any change to a production tax was to be on a voluntary basis. Yet the tenor of the Anderson Report and the fact that Anderson, a government employee, authored it suggested a wider application. The recommendation to accept the new formula made no mention of its voluntary nature.

Thus, for all its farsightedness and validity, its strong plea for the widespread adoption of range management principles, and its recommendation that, under conditions of drought and low prices, 3¢ an acre should be the maximum leasehold rental, the Anderson Report was in for a rough ride upon its release.

The outcome

In 1940, in reference to the Anderson Report under preparation, the WSGA had noted that "the need for a permanent land policy ... is felt by the grazing industry," and that the results of the investigation were "awaited with keen interest." Upon the release of the report in early 1941, this "keen interest" was replaced with dismay. Rising cattle prices and a fixed flat rate of 4¢ an acre in the short grass country had negated the need for a production tax. After claiming that it had achieved that which it had set out to do, the SGSGA merged with the WSGA. When the provincial government called on its members to honour their agreement to try out the new production-based leasehold rentals on an experimental basis, it was met with indifference and non-compliance. Only two ranchers of the original fifty-four volunteered, and no one else from outside the SGSGA.[54] The *Canadian Cattlemen*, the official voice of the WSGA, after giving the report a brief mention in the back page of its September 1941 issue, proceeded to ignore it completely.[55]

In some ways, the stockmen's reluctance to accept the Grazing Rates Report is understandable. The new formula was supposed to be voluntary. Yet this does not explain the reluctance of SGSGA members to test it on an optional basis. After all, it was they who initiated it in the first place. It could also be argued that some WSGA members, especially those in higher carrying capacity zones, preferred a flat rate. However, the WSGA was worried about more than a production tax. It mistrusted the government and feared that the new formula might be replaced by a wider levy on all production.[56] It was also concerned about the implications for government interference in the recommended Grazing Commission.[57] The fact that the Anderson Report was essentially about the need to stabilize the ranching industry was ignored.

The Anderson Report, however, had a much different impact on the provincial government. The Hon. N.E. Tanner, the provincial minister of lands and mines, was impressed with its wider implications for stabilizing the beef cattle industry and, more specifically, by linking range carrying capacity with the costs of production. To him, the Anderson Report's recommendations should have been applicable to the whole province and warranted much more than a tepid voluntary response. He began by dividing the province into carrying capacity zones as recommended in the Grazing Rates Report.[58] Three such zones were demarcated. A 50:1 ratio (one animal per 50 acres) delineated the short grass country of southern Alberta and the drier areas of the east. Along the heavily grassed foothills, 24:1 was considered a fair allocation, while most of central Alberta and a narrow trough extending south through High River and opening up in the Milk River country south of Lethbridge were designated at 32:1.[59]

On 14 January 1944, Tanner wrote to the WSGA asking for its recommendations on government grazing policies in the postwar period.[60]

He followed up by going public in an article published in the *Canadian Cattlemen*. He referred to the government's commitment to the ranching industry through its recently enacted regulations providing for security of tenure, and to the co-operation between his ministry and the ranchers in devising the new production tax on leaseholds. He then castigated the short grass ranchers, saying that "this plan has been submitted to the members of the Short Grass Stock Growers' Association, but to date it is regretted that the plan has not received more favourable consideration."[61] Tanner left no illusions about his perception of the situation:

> It is well remembered by all that during the 1930s the present flat rental rate was high in comparison to the price of beef and drought conditions that prevailed at that time. It was during this period that many of the ranchers got in arrears in their rental which made it very difficult to carry on both from the standpoint of ranchers, as lessees, and the Department, as lessor. Today the same flat rate of rental is charged as in the late nineteen thirties, yet the price of livestock has increased considerably during the same period. The ranching industry will never become stabilized as long as the rental costs are fixed and the selling price of livestock and the quantity of grass vary from year to year.[62]

The WSGA was not impressed. Faced with cattle prices that were still rising, it attempted to counter Tanner by advocating a policy that would allow ranchers to gradually become owners of their leases. In pressing for a continuation of the old flat rate, the WSGA stalled for time, suggesting that any new production tax "should be thoroughly tested by experienced operators before being considered as a general policy."[63] Bolstered by the support of its membership at the WSGA Annual Convention, the WSGA Grazing Committee journeyed to Edmonton in October 1944 to present the above views.

The Grazing Committee met on 12 October with a government that had clearly made up its mind.[64] After flatly rejecting the committee's recommendation for outright lease purchases, Department of Lands and Mines officials were equally unreceptive to other suggestions, which included a universal experimentation period and the isolation of the southeast area of the province for a longer trial period. When the Grazing Committee continued to hedge on accepting a tax based on production, the deputy minister responded by hinting strongly at substantial increases in the flat rate. Only then did the Grazing Committee bow to the inevitable. The production tax on leaseholds was accepted for a period of ten years commencing in 1945 and subject to review at the end of a five-year period. In the same year, new Grazing Lease Regulations were implemented. They tied the leases to carrying capacity more closely by limiting cattle numbers on any lease to 1,000 and bound lessees to specific conservation provisions.

WSGA President Thomas Usher told the membership that the decision came as no surprise, and that "it was apparent that the Department favoured basing grazing charges on the production method." He exhorted members to give the new measure their full support,[65] and indicated the fact that carrying rates had been conservatively appraised and ultimately would be established on an individual lease basis. He also referred to an appeal process which protected ranchers from inaccurate carrying capacity appraisals.[66]

Still, it was a bitter pill to swallow. From a maximum flat rate of 4¢ per acre between 1940 and 1944, ranchers in the 24:1 carrying capacity zone were levied 9.25¢ per acre in 1945; those in the 32:1 zone paid 7¢ per acre while even those in the 50:1 zone accepted a rate of 4.5¢ per acre, a figure higher than the previous maximum. Over the next seven years, the levies continued to rise until 1951, when the three rates were 25.25¢, 19¢ and 12¢ an acre, respectively, based on a market price of $25.24 per hundredweight.

Conclusion

The Anderson Report was a crucial document in that it provided the scientific rationale and the authoritative voice to convince the provincial government to take further steps respecting leaseholds. Its recommendations identified principles of range management that sought to manipulate grazing in the interests of both livestock and grass. The regulations that were in place by 1945 set the stage for the maintenance of healthy rangelands under lease and for equitable rentals that were linked with cattle prices and grass consumption.

The ranchers' negative reaction to the Anderson Report showed that they were not really interested in relating leasehold taxes with the cost of production as advertised in their rhetoric. It was more about the need to correlate lease rentals with low prices but not about the same correlation when cattle prices were higher. That the new system presupposed the need to adopt range management strategies did not seem to matter.

With some modifications this process for leasehold management and rentals remained in place for the next fifty years. By 1997, there were 5,600 leases covering 5.3 million acres. In that year, they were subject to review.[67] Under the new regulations, the lease rental structure remained largely intact, though subject to changes in terminology and other refinements.[68] However, the responsibilities of the leaseholder with respect to range management were increased. Range management has expanded. The leaseholder's stewardship includes the integrated management not only of cattle and grass but other plants, microflora, and mineral, nutrient and water cycles: in other words, the entire grazing ecosystem.[69] Moreover, leasehold lands are interpreted more strictly as being in the public realm and access to them has been widened to include oil and gas activity, trapping, and recreational use.

The Anderson Report recognized the importance of grass as a vulnerable resource. It was not the first to do so. However, in tying its use to consumption, the Anderson Report made the first statement about distancing grass from the most dangerous word that can be associated with any natural resource: "inexhaustible."

The Anderson Report, its rationale, pragmatic reception, and subsequent limited impact on deeded grazing lands emphasized an entrenched human-centred perception of the land. History by its very nature deals exclusively with human activity, with change and adaptation being measured solely in terms of which humans will be affected and how. The evolution of the ranching industry in Alberta is a typical example. It has been discussed almost solely in human terms rather than as an environmental interplay between human and non-human actors. Cattle made money and provided jobs for humans. Scholarly interest, and indeed this discussion, has concerned itself primarily with how this process unfolded, and how best it could be maintained and enhanced for a wider range of humans. The land and the wildlife it sustained were instrumental to these human interests. The dispossession of Indigenous peoples, the displacement of small farmers and squatters, and the alienation of wildlife had all been accomplished by the 1930s when prime grasslands became alienated from their natural state. The drama of the Anderson Report and the events that led up to it had only one set of actors and a miserable backdrop they had largely fashioned themselves.

Notes

1. Gross leasehold acreage had been steadily rising since the formation of the province in 1905, partly as a result of farm abandonments after 1920, but mostly because of the increasing amount of marginal land being sought after for grazing purposes: 1.551 million acres were under lease in 1906; 1.737 million acres in 1910; 2.563 million acres in 1918, and 2.925 million acres in 1923. See Max Foran, "The Impact of the Depression on Grazing Lease Policy in Alberta," in *Cowboys, Ranchers, and the Cattle Business: Cross-Border Perspectives on Ranching History*, ed. Simon Evans, Sarah Carter, and Bill Yeo (Calgary and Boulder: University of Calgary Press and University Press of Colorado, 1990), 123–25.

2. The source of this statement was Albert Helmer, federal Supervisor of Grazing. See C. Graham Anderson, Grazing Appraiser, Department of Lands and Mines, Province of Alberta, in *Grazing Rates Report, Short Grass Area of Alberta* (hereafter Anderson Report) compiled with the co-operation of the Short Grass Stock Growers' Association (Edmonton: A. Shnitka, King's Printer, 1941), 71.

3. See A.E. Cross fonds, box 114, file folder 918, Glenbow Archives (hereafter GA). cited in Foran, "The Impact of the Depression on Grazing Lease Policy in Alberta," 126.

4. *Edmonton Bulletin*, 24 February 1923.

5. Alberta, *Department of Municipal Affairs Annual Reports*, 1921–29 (Edmonton: Department of Municipal Affairs, 1921–30). Arrears on Dominion lease rentals amounted to $39,771.44 at the time of the transfer of natural resources to the provinces. See L.B. Thomson, "Costs of Beef Cattle Production," *Canadian Cattlemen*, June 1938, 126; *Edmonton Bulletin*, 24 February 1923; and Foran "The Impact of the Depression on Grazing Lease Policy in Alberta," 126.

6. F. Albert Rudd, "Production and Marketing of Beef Cattle from the Short Grass Plains Area of Canada" (master's thesis, University of Alberta, 1935), 63.

7. S.E. Clarke, "Pasture Investigations in the Short Grass Plains of Saskatchewan and Alberta," *Scientific Agriculture* 10, no. 10 (June 1930): 731–49.

8. One has only to read the *Sessional Papers* during the period. Heavy emphasis was placed on crop experiments. In fact, all forage experimentation was discontinued during World War I.

9. See "Annual Report of the Department of the Interior for the year 1916," No. 25, Report of the Inspector of Ranches, *Sessional Papers* 52, no. 1 (Ottawa: King's Printer, 1917). In his report for the year 1916, the inspector wrote that "owing to the exceptional crop of 1915, the granting of leases for grazing purposes is getting more difficult to settle satisfactorily as much land that was heretofore looked upon as worthless from an agricultural standpoint is now being entered for that purpose." Cited in Foran, "The Impact of the Depression," 127.

10 Clarke, "Pasture Investigations," 733.

11 See S.E. Clarke, J.A. Campbell, and J.B. Campbell, *An Ecological and Grazing Capacity Study of the Native Grass Pastures in Southern Alberta, Saskatchewan and Manitoba*, Publication No. 738, Technical Bulletin 44, Department of Agriculture, Division of Forage Crops, Dominion, Experimental Station, Swift Current, Saskatchewan, 4; Resolution passed at 31st Annual Conference, Calgary, 30 March 1927, Western Stock Growers Association Papers (hereafter WSGA Papers), box 1, file folder 9, GA.

12 This crushing tariff exceeded the already burdensome Fordney–McCumber tariff of 1922 and amounted to a 30 per cent levy on exported cattle to the United States. Shipments to the United States from Canada dropped from over 160,000 in 1929 to less than 10,000 in 1931. In Alberta the reductions were even more dramatic. From 27,650 in 1929, the number dropped to just 48 in 1931, and a year later no cattle left Alberta for the United States. According to the Alberta Department of Agriculture, prices immediately dropped after the imposition of the tariff by between $1.00–2.50 per cwt, followed by another decline a few months later of between $2.00–2.50 per cwt. See *Annual Report for the Department of Agriculture of the Province of Alberta for the Year 1930* (Edmonton: King's Printer, 1931), and *Canadian Cattlemen*, June 1938.

13 "Brief on Grazing Lands," Short Grass Stock Growers Association, 1937. WSGA Papers, box 13, file folder 121, GA. Another economic survey in 1938–39 put land charges and rentals as 19 per cent of production in the short grass country. See also *Canadian Cattlemen*, December 1940.

14 Figures abstracted from the Department of Lands and Mines Annual Reports suggest that well over 1,000 leases were cancelled between 1935 and 1940. One result of these cancellations was the establishment of Provincial Grazing Reserves. By 1944 there were three such reserves totalling 223,500 acres running 3,933 head of cattle, plus another ten reserves run by approved grazing associations. In Foran, "The Impact of the Depression," 130.

15 "Monthly Average Price Good Butcher Steers, Toronto, 1920–1938," *Canadian Cattlemen*, September 1938, 91. The average price of $19.59 in 1920 dropped dramatically the following year to $7.58, and fell below $7.00 in 1923 and 1924 before recovering slightly and then exceeding $10.00 in 1928–29. In sharp contrast, the average price between 1931 and 1938 was $5.50. These Toronto prices were higher than what would have been realized in regional markets such as Calgary.

16 "Report of the Livestock Supervisor," *Annual Report of the Department of Agriculture of the Province of Alberta for the Year 1931* (Edmonton: King's Printer, 1932).

17 Ibid., 1932.

18 Ibid., 1933.

19 Harry Vosper to Robert Weir, 11 January 1933, "Correspondence Between G.G. Serkau and Department of Agriculture Respecting the Exchange of Canadian Cattle for Russian Oil Products," No. 238, *Sessional Papers* 1932–33, 52 (Ottawa: King's Printer, 1934).

20 The low prices received for agricultural products during the Depression has spawned a host of stories, most apocryphal but all making a tragic point about the economic miseries of a world gone crazy. The story is told about a farmer who, after bringing his wheat to the elevator, received less the cost of getting it there. He resolved the situation by promising the elevator operator a turkey to make up the differential. A month later he brought in two turkeys as payment. When reminded by the elevator operator that he only owed one

turkey, the farmer replied that the other turkey was to cover the second load of wheat he had just brought in.

21 "Interview with Dr. J.W. Grant MacEwan, Professor of Animal Husbandry, University of Saskatchewan, 1928–46, Dean of Agriculture, University of Manitoba, 1956–61," Calgary, 20 August 1997. MacEwan himself was heavily involved in animal nutrition research at the time, and frequently published his findings in *Scientific Agriculture* in the early 1930s. He later published extensively in *Canadian Cattlemen*, where he served for a time as associate editor. "Canner cow" was used to describe those low-grade animals whose meat was to be used for canning purposes. See also Foran, "Impact of the Depression," 130.

22 L.B. Thomson, "Costs of Beef Cattle Production," *Canadian Cattlemen*, June 1938, 42. Thomson at the time of writing was superintendent of the Experimental Station at Swift Current, but was referring to experiments undertaken at Manyberries during his tenure as superintendent. The survey represented cattle numbers in excess of 50,000.

23 "The Livestock Industry of Alberta," WSGA Papers, box 13, file folder 112, GA.

24 L.B. Thomson, "An Economic Study of Beef Cattle Raising on the Range Areas of Alberta and Saskatchewan," Preliminary Report, 1932, WSGA Papers, box 13, file folder 112, GA.

25 The editorial gave a selling price of 2.5¢ per pound and a production cost of 6¢ per pound. *Calgary Albertan*, 27 November 1933. See also Foran, "Impact of the Depression," 127.

26 See "Address" by L.B. Thomson, then superintendent of Manyberries Research Station, 11 May 1935, WSGA Papers, box 2, file folder 11, GA. According to Thomson, land costs on producing 100 lb. of beef represented 12 per cent of total costs; a similar figure for grain was 6 per cent.

27 L.B. Thomson, "Costs of Beef Cattle Production," *Canadian Cattlemen*, June 1938, 42. Thomson at the time was superintendent of the Dominion Experimental Farm, Swift Current, Saskatchewan. It was felt that profits were assured only when ranchers had over 50 per cent of their equity in cattle.

28 Discussion on Range Rehabilitation, 4 July 1937, WSGA Papers, box 4, file folder 23, GA.

29 In 1935, the WSGA successfully negotiated for a reduction in rentals and taxes. Then in January 1937, leasehold arrears in rentals and taxation were amalgamated. *Canadian Cattlemen*, September 1938.

30 "Federal Survey of Living Conditions on Alberta Farms," *Brooks Bulletin*, 23 April 1936. See also Foran, "Impact of the Depression," 140.

31 The above statistics were abstracted from Alberta, *Department of Municipal Affairs, Annual Report*, 1927–42.

32 WSGA Papers, box 13, file folder 112, GA.

33 Reports of Grazing Supervisor, 1931, 1935, 1936, *Annual Report of the Department of Lands and Mines of the Province of Alberta* (Edmonton: King's Printer). It was held that overgrazing could reduce the market weight of a yearling by as much as 55 lb.

34 See J.A. and J.B. Campbell, "Grasslands Investigations in Alberta, Saskatchewan and Manitoba," in *Canadian Cattlemen*, March, June, September, December 1942.

35 The report was quoting an article by Louis C. Hurt, Senior Range Examiner, "Overgrazing Increases Production Costs by Reducing Number and Weight of Range Calves," Anderson Report, 151–52.

36 *Department of Lands and Mines Annual Report for the Province of Alberta*, 1944.

37 Ibid., 1936.
38 *Annual Report of the Department of Agriculture for the Province of Alberta*, 1937.
39 Report of the Grazing Supervisor, *Annual Report for the Department of Agriculture of the Province of Alberta*, 1936.
40 Likely Thomson was influenced by the recent move toward a production-type tax by the US Forest Service, which administered grazing leases in national forest reserves. WSGA Papers, box 13, file folder 112, GA.
41 Thomson's words were echoed by Clarke in an address to the 1937 Convention. WSGA Papers, box 2, file folder 10, GA.
42 Ross is a fascinating figure. The son of a rancher, he learned to fly during World War I and afterward became one of the first, if not the first cattleman to use his own plane for business activities. He served for several years on the executive of the WSGA, including a term as president. He was also chairman of the Canadian Council of Beef Producers and a member of the federal advisory Wartime Prices and Trade Board. Ross died at his Milk River ranch in 1956. See also Foran, "Impact of the Depression," 132,.
43 In the late 1920s, Ross conducted what many thought was a foolish experiment when he shipped several feeders to farms around Saskatoon to be tended by rural children. The success of the experiment confounded his critics. One carload sold at 17¢ per lb., well over the current market price.
44 George Ross to N.E. Tanner, 20 January 1937, WSGA Papers, box 2, file folder 11, GA. See also *Farm and Ranch Review*, July 1936, and *Canadian Cattlemen*, July 1939, for SGSGA's President George Ross regarding the reasons for founding the organization. Also see Foran, "Impact of the Depression," 132.
45 Proceedings of WSGA 41st Convention, 25–27 May 1937, WSGA Papers, box 2, file folder 10, GA. See *Farm and Ranch Review*, July 1936; *Canadian Cattlemen*, July 1939; and Foran, "Impact of the Depression."
46 On a 2,000-acre lease with a carrying capacity of 50:1 and an average price of 5¢ per pound, the formula would look like this: Carrying capacity: 2,000 divided by 50 equals 40 animals. Multiply this by 250 lb. to compute 10,000 lb. of gain, 10,000 lb. x 5¢ equals $500. This represents the total value of the grass that year. Production tax or levy on this grass at 10 per cent is $50, or 2.5¢ per acre over the 2,000 acres under lease. Report of the Grazing Supervisor, *Annual Report of the Department of Agriculture of the Province of Alberta*, 1936.
47 Known as "LB," Thomson, according to Grant MacEwan, was a no-nonsense, very capable, and highly respected administrator. MacEwan remembers him as the only Western agriculturalist "who Jimmy Gardiner [federal agriculture minister] would ever listen to." See also Foran, "Impact of the Depression," 135.
48 Report of the Grazing Supervisor, *Annual Report of the Department of Agriculture of the Province of Alberta*, 1936.
49 L.B. Thomson, "Costs of Production and Land Charges," 1935, "Carrying Capacities and Beef Production," 1936; S.E. Clarke, "A Study of Our Range Pastures," 1929, "The Differences Between Grass in the East and in the Foothills," 1932, "Providing Feed for Range Livestock," 1935, "Leaseholds and Production Costs," 1937.
50 Anderson Report, 17.
51 Ibid., 50

52 Ibid., 91–93; *Canadian Cattlemen*, March 1940.

53 See "Revised Alberta Lease Regulations," *Canadian Cattlemen*, March 1940, 359; and *Annual Report of the Department of Lands and Mines of the Province of Alberta*, 1940. It is interesting that while the three-year cancellation clause remained in effect, this long-contentious issue had ceased to be of concern. The soil surveys which had followed the provisions of the new Land Act in 1939 had clearly classified the true agricultural potential of land.

54 "N.E. Tanner to WSGA Board of Directors, 14 January 1944." WSGA Papers, box 2, file folder 12, GA. The 54 members who had originally said they would be part of the production tax experiment represented 1,045,000 acres of leased land. See "Grazing Rates Report," p. 9, in the same file. Though not documented, it is likely that George Ross was one of the two who did volunteer.

55 The report's lack of mention in subsequent issues indicated that it had been conveniently forgotten.

56 "Resolution passed at 42nd Convention, 2–3 June, 1938," WSGA Papers, box 2, file folder 11, GA.

57 "Board of Directors Meeting, 22 October 1941," ibid.

58 On 3 April 1939, the legislature of the Province of Alberta had assented to an important new Act, "An Act to Amend and Consolidate the Provincial Lands Act," Chapter 10, *Statutes of Alberta, 1939* (Edmonton: King's Printer, 1939). This Act abolished the old Homestead System and replaced it with an Agricultural Leasing policy. The Act also directed the minister of lands and mines to divide the province for land utilization purposes.

59 Later a 40:1 animal zone was added to include most of the area north of Edmonton. See Map, "Alberta, Grazing Capacity and Grazing Rates, 1951," GA.

60 "Tanner to Chairman of WSGA Grazing Committee, 14 January 1944," WSGA Papers, box 2, file folder 12, GA.

61 N.E. Tanner, "Alberta's Grazing Policy," *Canadian Cattlemen*, March 1944, 172–73.

62 Ibid.

63 "Report of Grazing Committee, WSGA Annual Convention, 15–16 June 1944," WSGA Papers, box 2, file folder 13, GA.

64 For more details, see "Meeting with Government and Grazing Committee, 12 October 1944," WSGA Papers, box 2, file folder 13, GA.

65 Usher's words were conciliatory: "This may seem a pretty drastic change for some, but I would ask all our members to give the plan a fair trial before passing judgment on it." See *Canadian Cattlemen*, December 1944.

66 Following the first year of the new arrangement, the Department of Lands and Mines reported on its satisfactory implementation, noting that very few ranchers had resorted to the appeal process: *Annual Report of the Department of Lands and Mines of the Province of Alberta*, 1946. The department was correct up to a point in that objections were expressed mainly in terms of carrying capacity appraisals. The real issue at stake was not so much the objections as the fact that ranchers realized that the era of flat rates was gone forever and that the production tax was a *fait accompli*.

67 "Review Focuses on Grazing Leases, Public Lands," *Western Producer*, 12 June 1997, http://www.producer.com/1997/06/review-focuses-on-land-use-grazing-leases/, (accessed 7 August 2016); "Grazing Leases Discussed with Thurber Commission," *Western Stock Grower*, July 1997, 4.

68 Government of Alberta, *Alberta Lease Review Report* (November 1998) (Edmonton: Alberta Agriculture, Food and Rural Development, 1997). The basis for assessment rests on Animal Units and Animal Unit Months.

69 *Grazing Lease Stewardship Code of Practice* (Edmonton: Alberta Sustainable Resource Development, 14 December 2007).

9

Mountain Capitalists, Space, and Modernity at the Banff School of Fine Arts

PearlAnn Reichwein and Karen Wall

Introduction

Why is a school for the arts located in Banff, Alberta? Such an obvious question can lend insight to social relations taken for granted as natural in everyday life. Today's Banff Centre occupies a privileged space in Banff National Park. Its iconic location on Tunnel Mountain in the Alberta Rockies is synonymous with the image and reputation of an international destination for professional arts and management programs in Western Canada. Situated in the Town of Banff, it is further encompassed within the Canadian Rocky Mountain Parks World Heritage Site designated by UNESCO in 1984. Its spatial design, architecture, and landscape emerged from a modernist legacy of postwar campus development for the Banff School of Fine Arts, an adult extension outreach program started by the University of Alberta in 1933. A permanent campus to position Alberta's public university in Canada's premier national park was a postwar strategic initiative led by school director Donald Cameron. The spatial imaginary of the school and campus as it emerged designed in international modernist style was produced by multiple agents. Negotiation, contestation, and construction rendered the Banff School campus as a distinct space in a prominent national park townsite. In this paper, we explore the postwar campus in terms of spatialization based on Henri Lefebvre's ideas about space as a social product and Jody Berland's ideas about modernism in postwar Canada.

Banff's urban history as a federally designed townsite is commonly obscured by tendencies to conflate it with readings of Banff National Park as a "natural" space rather than as a cultural landscape. Urban development and select land use were integral to constructing the Banff townsite as a park destination and tourist economy. Federal leasehold records indicate how cumulative decisions led the Banff School to become a significant space and cultural institution within a national park. Architectural sketches, plans, drawings, and correspondence suggest how the Banff School campus mapped postwar international modernism onto Banff's place identity and urban heritage. Architecture and landscape design were facets of constructing the postwar park environment and its viewscapes. Although its postwar visual arts programs were strong in older traditions of realist and impressionist landscape painting,[1] artists at the school gazed through the frames of architectural modernism that prevailed in its built form. The postwar campus was also a spatial manifestation of 1950s democratic liberalism in its idealization of education and travel as a means of social engagement among citizens. The state and capital were actors in the production of urban space and modernism at the school, along with the agency of university staff and students. Private donors were central to its postwar capital projects for campus construction. Both education and culture were structured as assets in national park urban space and national policy. The urban–nature matrix involved in constructing the early Banff campus is pertinent to today's issues of urbanization, cultural landscapes, and place making. We argue that the growth of the postwar Banff School campus points to processes of urban spatialization and the reproduction of capitalism during the influence of the modernist state in Canada.

Henri Lefebvre's ideas about space as a social product theorized processes of urban spatialization and the reproduction of capitalism. Space is understood as a cultural production and process of social relations, a site of struggle to produce and reproduce meanings, particularly in everyday life. Lefebvre's triad of spatial practices, representations of space, and spaces of representation were central tenets in his work *The Production of*

Space.[2] Lukasz Stanek highlighted how Lefebvre's understanding of space emerged with emphasis on "the shift of the research focus from space to processes of its production; the embrace of the multiplicity of social practices that produce space and make it socially productive; and the focus on the contradictory, conflictual, and, ultimately, political character of the processes of production of space."[3] This chapter focuses on the Banff School as a site for the production of space through social relations, with specific interest in the postwar Tunnel Mountain campus, where the dialectical interactions of state, capital, design, and environment merged to produce a modernist urbanized landscape in Banff townsite. This is a story of art and nature written in the spatial relations of power.

Jody Berland examined how the state fostered democratic liberalism through cultural policy and artistic modernism in postwar Canada. Public institutions and public policy frameworks played a direct role in the formation of modernist liberal democracy and social values that aimed to generate a new and better world after World War II. Berland argued that "Canada's nationalist modernists were informed by a constellation of interdependent ideas expressing strong social as well as cultural purpose."[4] Scott McLean observed that, under its director Donald Cameron, the University of Alberta's Department of Extension explicitly aligned itself with a postwar internationalist ideology to foster "social and economic progress."[5] Educated people and tourism were considered assets to social progress in the form of economic success in postwar Alberta. Spaces of the Banff School helped to produce the modernist project as a social product that aligned with liberal capitalism under the welfare state.

Notably, the University of Alberta located the Banff School of Fine Arts in Canada's first national park, Banff National Park. A distant 400 kilometres from the university main campus in the provincial capital of Alberta, Edmonton, the Banff School campus emerged as a cultural landscape situated within the larger cultural landscape of a world-famous national park in the Canadian Rockies. The Department of Extension began the summer school as a program for educational holidays during the depths of the Great Depression. The first Banff School was a populist outreach community theatre program conducted by Extension with Carnegie grant support in 1933, but it took place in borrowed space without its own campus. Academic course offerings expanded, as well as the name of the school (from the Banff School of Drama to the Banff School of Fine

Arts), and subsequently several hundred students enrolled each summer in theatre, painting, music, dance, plastic arts, photography, and various other adult extension classes conducted by the university's Department of Extension. Why was the mountain park holiday townsite of Banff chosen as the environment for the University of Alberta's summer education venture, and what story does the early history of urban spatialization on the Banff School campus have to tell about the production of postwar modernist landscapes, design, and cultural capital? The original entity of the Banff School of Fine Arts no longer exists, its former campus is home to the current Banff Centre, a learning centre devoted to professional arts, leadership, and mountain culture where the production of space as urbanization and capitalism is ongoing and indicative of more recent federal and provincial policy directions under the neoliberal state.

"The Salzburg of America"

Banff and Salzburg were joined in the imagination of a man who had expansive plans for the University of Alberta's role in adult extension education, liberal democratic citizenship, and internationalism, long before these urban hubs were designated UNESCO World Heritage Sites. Envisioned as an educational institution and world centre for art and culture in the Canadian Rockies, the Banff School was conceived as "the Salzburg of America" by its long-time director Donald Cameron (1901–1989). Cameron was a proponent of adult education who worked in the Department of Extension in Edmonton and ran the summer school in Banff. The school was located, he explained, based on the premise that "in Banff we had a great natural asset and a natural setting for a school in the Fine Arts."[6] By naturalizing the idea of a mountain national park as the right place for creating and consuming fine arts, education, and tourism, he promoted the potential for the Banff School to combine scenery with artistic capital in a symbolic landscape, much like the Austrian Salzburg Festival.[7] Cameron held that the Banff School was a growing tourism concern, as he noted in 1946: "the school is becoming important, not only for its own sake but as a major tourist attraction in the Province of Alberta."[8] Establishing the new province of Alberta in 1905 was an outgrowth of late nineteenth-century agricultural settlement in Western Canada; tourism in the region had long capitalized on national parks in the Rockies as a prime attraction, as illustrated by the highly successful Canadian Pacific Railway tours and Banff Springs Hotel beginning in the 1880s, and by official tourism promotions undertaken by the Alberta government through Cameron's era.[9] Construction of the Banff School's postwar campus moved another step further in the spatialization of urban capitalism in Banff. Cameron promoted internationalism after the war and maintained that Banff's beauty radiated a universal appeal, as he wrote in 1951: "Banff doesn't belong to Alberta alone, or to Canada; it belongs to America and the world.... Wherever they live, people feel that Banff belongs to them. That feeling is a great asset to Banff, to Alberta and to the Banff School of Fine Arts."[10] Reflecting on Banff's global appeal, Cameron in some ways foreshadowed the currency of world heritage designation and notions of "world class" tourism attractions.

Contrary to Donald and Peggy Leighton's institutional and historiographic myths that the school was destined to be "on a mountainside overlooking the Bow Valley in the Rocky Mountains," the current campus on Tunnel Mountain was *not* the initial site for the permanent campus, nor was the modernist architectural design of the school's signature buildings a foregone conclusion.[11] Examination of federal leasehold records, university correspondence, and architectural designs tells another story about making cultural landscapes as capital through urban spatialization at the Banff School of Fine Arts

Moving to the "Campus in the clouds"

Cameron was intent on creating a distinctive physical space for the Banff School in keeping with his grand vision for nation building and international educational presence. The University of Alberta first operated its month-long summer sessions in shared space, in particular that belonging to the local school board, where classes were held in the public Banff High School and later in a public auditorium on Banff Avenue jointly funded by the university and the local school board. The latter is now a well-recognized historic building that serves as the Parks Canada Information Centre. By the mid-1940s, overcrowded summer enrolments and a lack of residence accommodation led to expansion plans in anticipation of postwar growth. University President Robert Newton justified the need for a permanent campus to Banff's national park superintendent in 1944 by claiming that "there is surely no finer way of capitalizing the beauties of Banff National Park in the interests of the whole country than by sending art students steeped in its atmosphere into every community."[12]

Facility development was foremost in Donald Cameron's mind as the Banff School approached postwar reconstruction, and he formed an alliance with a key private donor and others to fund capital for construction costs. Leonora Christine Woods (1875–1960) was the widow of Lt. Col. James H. Woods (1868–1941), the late publisher of the *Calgary Herald* newspaper and a noted Western Canadian patron of the arts and the university; she aimed to commemorate her husband through investment in both. Mrs. Woods was also an active Calgary leader in philanthropic organizations and boards, such as the Victorian Order of Nurses and the Red Cross. From 1922, Gables Securities was her personal financial corporation administered by Eric Harvie through his company Managers Limited; after her death, her fortune endowed the Woods Foundation.[13] Eric Harvie, a prominent Calgary lawyer and investor, represented Mrs. Woods as a benefactor in dealings with Cameron in relation to the Banff School. Harvie also became a prominent Alberta benefactor to arts, culture, and education based on his success in the petroleum industry, endowing the Devonian Foundation, Glenbow Foundation, and other institutions.[14] Cameron and Harvie joined forces to pursue the construction of a permanent university campus within the Banff townsite. The federal government proved instrumental in providing the land to establish a school of fine arts on prime public property in Banff National Park in concert with proposals to spatialize the arts and culture in Banff as a Salzburg in the Rockies. With the support of private capital and the state, the Banff School opened a new permanent campus on Tunnel Mountain in 1947.

Historically, national parks in Canada are federal Crown lands, and properties in Banff were typically occupied on the basis of long-term leaseholds rather than private land ownership. Federal townsite surveys in the nineteenth century subdivided blocks and lots along the Bow River near the confluence of the Spray River at Banff, which remained a federally administered townsite until town governance status was attained in 1990. When Cameron approached local Banff National Park Superintendent P.J. Jennings, the school was permitted to obtain a leasehold for a townsite lot on Cougar Street situated low in the valley on boggy land along Whiskey Creek. It was an area zoned for low-priced tourist accommodation with room to accommodate 300 people. Higher-level negotiations subsequently ensued to raise the profile of the proposed site. By October 1945, Cameron considered the Whiskey Creek land inadequate for his purposes and entered discussions with Ottawa through Dr. Charles Camsell, deputy minister of mines and resources responsible for national parks and his executive administrators, whereby the Whiskey Creek site was exchanged for three blocks situated on slightly higher ground on Deer Street near the main commercial street of Banff Avenue. "It was a good small site and John Rule's sketch [of the School] had helped greatly in its acquisition because for the first time this gave physical form to what had previously been only a dream," as Cameron wrote in later years.[15] National park officials were persuaded that the new site was more suitable for Cameron's growing plans for a grand campus.

As President Newton submitted to Roy Gibson, director of the Lands, Parks, and Forests Branch, the university felt justified asking the branch for substantial co-operation in obtaining the lots because "the School draws students from all over Canada and is therefore performing a national service. It is rapidly becoming one of the major attractions of the Banff National Park."[16] Cultural tourism, as well as natural attractions, added to Banff's capital as a tourist destination for adults seeking to further their arts education, as well as for general tourists wishing to sightsee and consume the arts while visiting the park.[17] A permanent campus space would capitalize on all of it. Subsequently, Cameron and Eric Harvie, acting on behalf of Calgary donor Mrs. Woods, scouted out the potential of a third site, on Tunnel Mountain, during the winter of 1945–46, as Cameron recounted:

> We then went over the St. Julien site, situated immediately above the town on Tunnel Mountain and just across the river from the Banff Springs Hotel. Without question this was the finest site in Banff. It consisted of about thirty acres of land, part of which would always be a natural park. It had the finest view in Banff. It was only six minutes' walk from the centre of the town but by virtue of its location was separate and private. Major Jennings indicated that he personally would be in favour

of letting us have this site but he didn't hold out much hope that Ottawa would agree.[18]

Superintendent Jennings favoured advancing the project on the St. Julien site, a far superior block of land zoned for expensive realty development, and he pushed his recommendation forward to National Parks officials in Ottawa based on the rationale that "what the University of Alberta Extension Department now has in mind is essentially a national project … such being the case it is felt that favourable consideration should be given to this request."[19] Cameron's vision of the Salzburg of North America was a dream of cultural capital that turned a provincial educational outreach program into an expansive project that enticed national supporters. It was an optimistic ambition that predated Alberta's booming postwar oil and gas economy of the late 1940s with its headquarters in Calgary, a growing city 130 kilometres east of Banff townsite.

Ottawa officials agreed to grant the prestigious St. Julien lot on a perpetual lease for one dollar a year and contributed the development of municipal services to the project following Cameron's persistent lobby for the site.[20] The landlease transaction was indicative of Cameron's ability to generate federal support for his vision of an adult education facility in Banff National Park because it was seen as a prestigious amenity for public education and tourism in the scheme of park townsite planning and national development. At the time, officials believed that a fine arts school could directly benefit the interpretation of Banff to the public, in harmony with the mandate of national parks for public education and enjoyment.[21]

Cameron shared his campus building plans in summer 1946 at a public picnic staged on the new St. Julien grounds with a turnout of 500 Banff School summer students and 30 staff. "Some very distinguished Canadians" attended among the school's painting instructors, including A.Y. Jackson, J.W.G. Macdonald, Lawren Harris, H.D. Glyde, and W.J. Phillips. A bagpiper skirled on the hill throughout the evening to entertain the crowd. Superintendent Jennings spoke to offer the co-operation of his office "in furthering what he said the Government of Canada considered to be an important and unique development in the history of the national parks."[22] Obtaining the exclusive St. Julien block on Tunnel Mountain signified a substantial realty upscaling for adult education in Banff. The grand site became the spatial manifestation of postwar national development discourse espoused by the school and federal officials as they consciously designed the urban landscape of Banff National Park.

Designs for a campus landscape

The Banff School's first permanent buildings on the St. Julien campus site were opened between 1947 and 1953. They consisted of the first residential chalet, occupied in 1947, two more chalets in 1949, and an administration building in 1953.[23] Designed in an international-modernist style, the chalets featured flat-roofed sundecks and broad windows overlooking the "finest view in Banff." The view was a panorama of Cascade Mountain, Mount Norquay, Sulphur Mountain, and Mount Rundle, with direct sightlines spanning over Banff townsite and up the Bow Valley to Mount Bourgeau and the Massive Range. Construction of the school's first buildings on Tunnel Mountain was typically fast-tracked ahead of financing and opened for summer guests before total completion. Cameron improvised as host, and, likewise, insisted residents make do as tradesmen finished windows, doors, and plumbing. When Donald Cameron Hall opened in June 1953 – without hot water for guests attending the National Conference of the Canadian Association for Adult Education – visitors dubbed it the "CCC" for "Cameron's Cold-water Chalet."[24]

Design concepts for the Banff School's first buildings evolved through several stages that began with a vernacular Canadian national park aesthetic and ended with international modernism.[25] Historical photographs of concept drawings and other extant archives depict the shifting process. Canada's famous golf expert and landscape designer Stanley Thompson agreed to serve the Banff School for a dollar a year after striking up a collegial friendship with Cameron and Harvie following a meeting at Banff's Mount Royal Hotel, while he was consulting with the Parks Department in 1946.[26]

The first known Banff School design concepts were produced in the mid-1940s by Thompson Jones and Company, Thompson's Toronto firm of engineers and landscape architects renowned for golf course and landscape design; notably, it had designed golf courses in Banff, Jasper, and Cape Breton Highlands national parks. A perspective drawing by Thompson Jones situated the proposed Banff School campus as a tightly massed low-profile

9.1 Banff School campus first imagined by Thompson Jones and Company for fundraising in the mid-1940s. University of Alberta Archives, UAA 78-17-2-230.

area tucked amid dense forestation, overlooking the Banff Springs Hotel and Banff townsite (see fig. 9:1).[27] The drawing emphasized Tunnel Mountain, the Bow River, and the Canadian Pacific Railway's prominent hotel as the dominant features on the landscape. Tunnel Mountain was depicted in exaggerated dimensions relative to its actual environs. The concept for the main school building was sketched in the retro style of a manor house, with gabled rooflines, stone arches, and a great hall.

Similar traditionalist concepts for a grand school building with a steeple,[28] revised later as a turret,[29] arose in separate 1940s drawings by Rule Wynn and Rule, an Edmonton architectural firm often engaged by the University of Alberta to design building plans for its main campus in Edmonton. John Rule's early drawings for a Colonel Woods Memorial building (see fig. 9:2) later led Cameron to describe its style as "a miniature of

9.2 "Colonel Wood[s] Memorial" building in a revised sketch by John Rule in 1946. University of Alberta Archives, UAA 78-17-2-240.

the Banff Springs Hotel."[30] Clearly the proposed name of the hall appealed to the donor, Mrs. Woods. Drawings also emerged for student residence buildings designed as rustic alpine chalets, constructed in rough-sawn British Columbia cedar timber and stucco (see fig. 9:3).[31] Elements in these early designs denote features such as fieldstone detailing, steep-gabled rooflines, Tudor Revival elements, Craftsman accents, and rustic Swiss alpine motifs that were already common to the Canadian national park architectural vernacular, particularly in Banff, where this look was first encouraged by park authorities.[32]

The school's art instructors, however, objected to the traditionalist design concepts first proposed by Rule Wynn and Rule and used in Donald Cameron's footwork for negotiations. Correspondence dating from September 1946 reveals certain tensions at work behind the design changes, as James Smart, controller of the National Parks headquarters office in Ottawa, responded to Cameron:

9.3 A rustic Student Chalet, $12,000 cost for summer occupancy, drawn by Rule Wynn and Rule. University of Alberta Archives, UAA 78-17-2-235.

> I am rather surprised that your art staff are critical of the design of the buildings submitted by Messrs. Rule, Wynn and Rule. No doubt the artists would prefer something a little more modern in design. However, I take a rather dim view of modern art and I would hate to see any buildings of a modern design built in one of our National Parks, that is, of the severe lines that is [sic] usually seen in modern architecture. In my opinion they would not fit in at all with the mountain resort. Modern methods of construction would be all right but the architectural design should be entirely suitable for the environment, which is not always the case in modern design.[33]

Establishing the mountain resort aesthetic and design qualities understood as "suitable for the environment" relied on the determination of National Parks officials in such distinctions of taste.

A major change diverted the design direction in late 1946, and the designs ultimately implemented on the Banff School campus shifted to express international modernism rendered by Alberta architects. The university produced a 1947 prospectus with drawings by Rule Wynn and Rule imagining an expansive campus amalgam of flat-roofed modernist buildings spread across a broad open hillside on the St. Julien site, with plans for twenty to thirty chalets and accommodation for a thousand students (see fig. 9:4).[34] These drawings suggest a forest cut back to open the vistas to and from a small urban complex distinct from the main Banff townsite. A hall for the Colonel Woods Memorial, re-rendered as a modernist horizontal structure for a "Studio Building," then appeared in the prospectus as an "Administration Building," suggesting fluid design concepts for the campus capital campaign. Likewise, drawings for a "Typical Chalet" for student residences, with various sizes and estimated costs, also took on the modernist look and a range of price tags for donors (see figs. 9:5 and 9:6). Newspaper reports from as far away as Vancouver indicated intentions that the proposed campus would "set a distinctive new style for indigenous Canadian architecture" and employ local Rundle stone and timber.[35] Landscaping designs and planting later emphasized native Rocky Mountain vegetation species and hardy exotics to accentuate the campus environment.[36]

In time, Emma Read Newton, wife of the university president, also weighed into the debate over the new modernist architectural design. "To me the flat squat buildings are too much like lumbermen's shacks," she wrote to Eric Harvie, in January 1947, while acknowledging admiration for flat-top architecture in the southern United States and France in the Basses-Alpes. It was not suitable for the mountains, however, and she looked to Norway as a better example:

> In Norway, I observed the houses very tall and narrow and knew the Norwegians had felt the height of their pines and peeks [sic] in their souls – the height is a matter of aspiration that reaches skyward and summit-ward: perfectly consistent architecture for mountain country.
>
> Imagine how dull and prosaic the Banff Springs Hotel would have been with a flat roof like the Banff shops!

Composite Layout Showing Approximate Relationship of the Banff School Buildings

The ultimate plan calls for an Administration Building, a Music and Drama Building, a Studio Building and between 20 and 30 Chalets. Later on a central heating plant and Gymnasium should be added. In the meantime, the heating will be done from the Administration Building.

Sketches and drawings in this brochure by Rule, Wynn & Rule, Architects—Edmonton, Alberta

9.4 "Composite Layout Showing Approximate Relationship of the Banff School Buildings" in campus concepts by Rule Wynn and Rule for capital campaign in 1947. University of Alberta Archives, UAA 78-17-7-5-47, Prospectus, p. 8.

> This passion for doing something purely Canadian overlooks doing something perfectly nature-all, or natural. The scenery is everything in Banff, not mortals.[37]

Harvie responded that it was "most interesting" hearing from various people among specialists and others in discussion of the new plans. He thanked her for her candid feedback. "With few exceptions the artist and architects favored the modern designs without qualification or hesitancy. Others, like myself, were somewhat shocked when we first saw these, but in a great many of these cases they later swung around to rather favour them," he suggested. The cost of construction and maintenance was another merit of the modern designs according to his inquiries for qualified advice.[38]

Cameron meanwhile shrugged off Mrs. Newton's opinion in a letter to Harvie, indicating that he was not surprised and would not take it seriously.

"Canvassing the opinions of leading artists and architects," Cameron had found the new design was unanimously preferred, while they were "very critical of the style of the Banff Springs Hotel." Moreover, he suspected Newton would be hoisted with her own petard by artists with regard to doing something Canadian and overlooking something natural: "It is just because the artists and the architects believe that the horizontal lines will blend into the scenery better than the peaks that they recommend that type; also as a matter of record, all of the new buildings of any size in Switzerland and in Norway to-day feature the flat or horizontal lines."[39] Their correspondence offers insights into the design process shifting between differing spatialized representations of the new campus through the relations of architectural design and critique. These letters also underscore exposure to internationalist designs in other countries and aspirations for the Banff School to keep up with trends, despite lagging regional diffusion,

9.5 A modernist design for "Colonel Wood[s] Memorial" was relabelled in pencil as "Studio Building, Banff School of Fine Arts" and later appeared as "Administration Building." University of Alberta Archives, UAA 78-17-2-243.

informed by artists and architects as cultural mediators and authorities. To speak of originating a Canadian architectural form would have overstated the impact of the design but recognized, at least, intentional use of local materials. Cost was never far from mind, however, as Harvie's recourse to pragmatics, in his role as a fundraiser, suggests.

By March 1947, the National Parks administration was "pretty well convinced that the modern type of buildings should be quite satisfactory as depicted in the plans," with some minor adjustments. Smart noted, however, that the general manager of the luxurious Banff Springs Hotel across the river from the development site had expressed concerns about the Banff School campus not blending in with the scenery.[40] Such concern was indicative of the CPR's corporate investment in park viewscapes seen from its hotel. The social relations of "fit" within the mountain resort community and nature were a key issue in designing the campus, as they were in designing the park.

9.6 Modern flat-top design of a "Typical Chalet" proposed in 1947. Three were constructed as the first Banff School buildings. University of Alberta Archives, UAA 78-17-7-5-47, Prospectus, p. 10.

Modern design had begun to interest Cameron on tours of other institutions as early as October 1945. Visiting the art studios and workshops at the Cranbrook Academy in Bloomfield Hills, Michigan, he observed and approved the modern simplicity of Scandinavian aesthetics in weaving, furniture, and sculpture produced at the school. "They were beautiful in their simplicity and were very modern in design," he commented about tables and chairs made in the woodworking shop.[41] Cameron had previously travelled to Denmark and Sweden, in the context of his adult extension work, and noted the Scandinavian ethnicity of the Midwestern instructors he met.

Modernist architecture also piqued the director's interest. In the midst of Cameron expanding his campus building program, interaction with the Kansas City Art Institute and School of Design's Executive Vice-President W.M. Symon, who visited the Banff School session in 1948, led to an exchange of photos and drawings of the American campus by early

September. New buildings on the Kansas campus were clearly defined in international modernist style with flat roofs, long horizontal lines, and windows for north light where students and teachers were shown in studio and classroom instruction. "Modern is the style for new buildings, with the design intended to give students the utmost in their work," reported an accompanying news clipping headlined "Making Art Pay Off in Cash: Kansas City Industries Now Look to Institute Students for Ideas That Can Be Turned into Profits." Symon advised Cameron, "You really have an excellent set-up and the future possibilities are excellent. I see no reason why you should not be able, under present conditions, to get the million dollars you are seeking for the physical plant in Banff, particularly since the tuition and other income takes care of itself."[42] Capital projects relied on capital donors, attested senior university administrators between themselves.

Relations between architect John Rule and Donald Cameron were not as warm. They were at odds throughout the design process for the postwar Banff campus. Cameron pushed to receive drawings and sketches on time to pursue donor funding and advance construction. His many letters to Eric Harvie complained about Rule being inaccurate and behind schedule with drawings and cost estimates, despite Cameron's repeated requests sent frequently to Rule, every second day at some points.[43] "Rule does not pay any attention to the amount he was told to consider as to the maximum cost of the building, and I think we have simply got to tell him that he is work [sic] within the figures we give him or we will have to get someone else who will.... On top of that his supervision is a joke."[44] Meanwhile Rule worked to produce a shifting design concept influenced by budgetary limitations and Cameron's client demands, while juggling many other institutional and commercial projects that included the Rutherford Library opening in 1948 and other buildings on the growing university's main campus in Edmonton.[45] Rutherford Library, in particular, was grand monumental public architecture in neo-Georgian style; as a major construction project, it far outpaced the scale and grandeur of the first small Banff School summer cottage built off the main campus in 1947. Cameron saw it differently from his perspective as head of the Banff School.

The historiographic retelling of the Banff School campus design period is a noteworthy indication of polarity and lingering tensions on both sides. In his commemorative monograph, *Campus in the Clouds* (1956),

Cameron recounted that to obtain the first sketch for fundraising, he went straight to the university architects Rule Wynn and Rule, a local firm of former graduates, as advised by President Newton, and told John Rule, "I have fifty thousand dollars for a start on a building for the Banff School ... Fifty thousand is not enough. Pay no attention to that; this is what I need":

> I told him that I wanted a building that would provide a dining-room for 300, sleeping quarters for at least 150 and classrooms for the same number. That was where I made my first mistake. I have since learned that you don't tell architects to pay no attention to costs, they will do that without being told ... He presented me with a sketch of a building that looked like a miniature of the Banff Springs Hotel. I hesitantly asked what he thought that building would cost and he airily said "Oh, about $350,000."[46]

Nonetheless, dealings with Cameron posed practical challenges to design and execution, according to a commemorative history of the architectural firm Rule Wynn and Rule published in 1988:

> Senator Cameron's book [*The Impossible Dream*] reproduced John Rule's sketch of his original concept for the Banff Centre, showing John's love of mediaeval forms, but made no further mention of the architects. Had he done so, there would surely have been hints of disharmony. Donald Cameron had strong ideas which John felt infringed upon the architect's realm. For instance, the four-storey [administration] building offered no elevator. When a panting climber asked for an explanation, Mr. Cameron would laugh: "There are 60,000 reasons and each one costs a dollar.[47]

Rule was bound by interpersonal tensions and economics behind the scenes, along with his client's fundraising campaigns and thrift. These divergent stories reflected conflicts that shaped the production of architectural representations of space and the resulting campus.

Architecture students at other Canadian universities contacted Cameron to inquire about design projects in hopes of future work opportunities.

On more than one occasion, he encouraged concepts for future buildings and obtained sketches and models derived from senior student projects. University of British Columbia architecture student Albert J. Church designed a recreation centre for the Banff School for his 1954–56 BA honours thesis in architecture. He sent photographs of his models depicting a flat-topped international modernist complex with an L-shaped outdoor swimming pool to Cameron, after ongoing correspondence seeking potential contract work to realize the design. It was a few years premature according to the director, who mentioned that potential funding from the new Canada Council might assist future development.[48] Similarly, UBC student George Leishman expressed his plans to design a "Festival Theatre" with an outdoor amphitheatre in a natural bowl in 1956. Cameron specifically lectured Leishman to prepare his assignment with careful consideration to "the economics of the project" involving capital costs, operations and maintenance, as well as transportation to the site. "These are all factors which are quite frequently overlooked and my own view is that if I was marking the thesis of a graduating student, I would certainly lower his grading if factors such as I have mentioned were not taken into consideration." Leishman was also advised that while Cameron might be able to find time to meet with him in Banff, "under no circumstance should you come there expecting to see me without a definite appointment, because while I am in the west I shall be extremely busy and part of the time I shall be in places other than Banff."[49] Designs obtained free of charge optimized Cameron's ability to visually represent space to support his fundraising efforts, but exploited student labour with fewer direct benefits to these early career architects. As early as the postwar construction boom in 1946, Cameron asked Cecil Burgess, head professor of architecture at the University of Alberta where Rule and Wynn had trained, about potential to hold a design competition open to professional architectural firms interested in the Banff School, and in 1953 he inquired with architecture professors about a student competition at the University of Manitoba. Academics in architecture did not consider Cameron's proposals for design competitions pragmatic because he lacked a proper understanding of protocols and cost.[50]

Later plans for campus expansion and more land acquisition considered by Cameron became problematic in national park townsite planning and environmental terms, as Parks officials made clear. In 1960, Ottawa put the brakes on Cameron's notions to develop a liberal arts university on Tunnel

Mountain. Although Banff seemed to belong to everyone and attracted visitors from around the world, it could not sustain infinite development, a point stressed by National Parks Director J.R.B. Coleman in correspondence to Cameron with regard to the unsuitability of full-scale university operations on the Banff campus.[51]

Accelerated postwar growth transformed built form in Alberta towns and cities. As a federally administered national park townsite, Banff was an outlier in certain respects of urban planning and governance in Alberta, but not isolated from new trends and economic factors. A major oil strike in 1947 near Edmonton at Leduc, Alberta, triggered a building boom. Tourism demands in the Rockies escalated with postwar prosperity. Modernist aesthetics in the design and construction of buildings rapidly became the new normal in Alberta, as elsewhere after World War II, with the influence of the International Style. Trends were further accentuated by the scope of accelerated postwar construction in the province. Rule Wynn and Rule, along with other Alberta architects, were active in this transformation by 1947.[52]

Reading the sketches suggests a preference for a postwar modernist architectural form rather than the vernacular common to existing buildings in Canada's Rocky Mountain parks. The long and low horizontal lines of the Banff School administration building may have had something vaguely in common with Frank Lloyd Wright's Banff Pavilion (1911–1938), but, overall, the new school introduced a flat-top design concept unusual in Banff National Park at the time and one that was forward thinking for the local area.[53] Commercial building designs for several Banff hotels in a similar style soon followed. Designs by Rule Wynn and Rule went on to produce many examples of modernist architecture after World War II, particularly evident in commissions in Edmonton and throughout Alberta.

Did the shift toward international modernism in the school design privilege universalism over the local and the particular? The Rocky Mountain Salzburg was by definition a borrowed concept, yet the school design might have appeared anywhere and certainly did not grow organically out of Tunnel Mountain as implied by founding myths advanced by Leighton and Leighton. Cameron claimed the campus gave "a physical body to what was before only a dream,"[54] but was the dream rendered in such a way that the local vernacular, albeit one shaped by imported influences, succumbed to the assimilation of globalizing trends and omnibus universalism?

Universalism was in keeping with Cameron's sense that Banff belonged to everyone. Modernism had found a place alongside nostalgic traditionalism and rusticism in contemporaneous Canadian designs in national parks, and, given Canada's internationalist style of postwar citizenship, the campus suggested bringing home a worldly, forward look at art and design.

Ultimately, students came to the Banff School campus on Tunnel Mountain to study and live in its spaces. Residence buildings were occupied as chalets for students who lived together and ate together in the dining room. Working at the school and playing in Banff were combined spatially through learning spaces in classrooms and in various locales surrounding the townsite and park. Educational programs were produced by the University of Alberta and hundreds of students occupied these spaces, territorialized the new campus, and gradually added to the urbanization of the park townsite. The town looked upward to the distinct Tunnel Mountain campus, but Banffites also gazed on a seasonal enclave of academic migrants and business competition. A burgeoning trade in conferences at the Banff School led to emergent tensions between "town and gown" as local hotels objected to a public educational facility cutting into its tourist markets.[55] Tourists as well as students came to see the campus and its vistas, as noted in the student newspaper: "the sight-seeing tours take up visitors to point out the school and its almost ideal location, perched upon the mountainside; three brown and white chalets overlooking the Bow River, the boathouse in the distance and the mountains behind."[56] Likewise, paintings such as "View from the Director's Window" by instructor Janet Middleton, and various school promotional photographs, illustrate how the architectural design of the campus and buildings framed a landscape view of Banff National Park. Functioning as a magisterial viewpoint overlooking the townsite and Bow Valley, the Banff School embodied a museological gaze that presented Banff National Park on display.[57] Notably, it showcased an urbanized cultural landscape as mountain beauty.

The Banff campus also served as a stage with a mountain backdrop for presenting the arts in the open air, not unlike the real Salzburg. The cover photos from the 1953 University of Alberta Faculty of Extension publications featured the Banff School signature buildings and mountain campus, effectively merging the cultural landscape of the campus into the iconographic identity of Banff National Park, producing a double attraction in the equation of cultural capital and international tourism for national development.⁵⁸ The social relations of space nested the educational and economic functions of the Banff School into the Banff townsite, which in turn nested inside Banff National Park as a reproduction of urbanization and capitalism. Today the three postwar modernist chalets continue to function on the campus of the Banff Centre, enjoined with new spaces.

Conclusion

Why did the Banff School of Fine Arts modernist campus come to exist as an urbanized landscape in the heart of Canada's first national park? Canadian public policy makers fostered a place for artists and art institutions in postwar Banff because art was considered essential to notions of cultural capital that linked education and tourism to the promotion of liberal democratic citizenship during Donald Cameron's era. Making cultural landscapes in the Canadian Rockies was a complex spatial and social interaction that involved many agents in dialectical tension. The Banff School, operated by the University of Alberta, was influential in creating and reproducing common understandings of Banff as a landscape wherein nature and culture met.

Understanding the Banff campus as an ongoing process of power through territory, imagination, and daily life points to Lefebvre's dialectics of space. "Spatial practices" of education constituted a "school" in Banff for the performance of learning and teaching fine arts along with the touristic relations of dwelling.⁵⁹ Art was valued as an important way of knowing. Institutionalizing nature through a campus landscape and design was central to generating ideas of Canadian national identity and postwar internationalism.⁶⁰ "Representations of space" re/produced Banff as land subdivided by leaseholds for numbered lots and blocks zoned within a federal townsite in a national park, then shaped by architectural design projects into a campus with buildings and landscaping. The conceptualization of the Banff School campus framed Banff National Park as Salzburg, with a cosmopolitan gaze on iconic Canadian nature expressed spatially and stylistically through the architecture of postwar international modernism. The Banff School produced "spaces of representation" through the lived and imaginative dwelling of residents and visitors in the liminal educational/touristic spaces of a holiday at school; it was simultaneously a residence, hermitage, classroom, playground, studio, and stage for dialectics of space and counterspace. Work and leisure at the Banff School merged in transformative and reiterative interactions through the spatial relations of the state and capital in Canada's postwar liberal democracy.

The Province of Alberta's public university in Edmonton reached out to colonize its mountain park satellite in the Bow Valley, yet Calgary capital was a driving force to leverage and build the Banff campus. "The connection of the avant-garde, progressive ideals of the Modern Movement with the corporate mode of business and design in North America is one of the stranger and most influential turns of fate in the entire history of architectural ideas," noted Trevor Boddy in his study of Alberta architecture, which underscored that most of urban Alberta was influenced by modernism's functionalist forms and philosophies.[61] Alberta's national parks and townsites were also influenced by modernism and linked within a larger spatial matrix of urban corporate capital integrated with local resources and labour.

Interrogating the production of a modernist cultural landscape in a Canadian national park uncovers the art of design at work, denaturalizes and historicizes culturally specific constructs of nature, parks, and tourism, and points to extant material culture of the modernist legacy as a symbolic artifact and heritage resource as time moves forward. The urbanized campus serves as a reminder of the politics of educational space as well as the long-standing and contested history of people and design active in Banff National Park in the midst of a contemporary UNESCO World Heritage Site. The Banff School was represented through urban design as internationalist modernism at work within the spatio-political boundaries of Canada's first national park, making park urban space, and producing art and nature as a landscape of spatialized capital.

Donald Cameron Hall was demolished in February 2011 to make way for new spaces imagined and concretized on the Banff Centre campus. Kinnear Centre for Creativity and Innovation opened in 2010, complete with a royal visit, brass fanfare, and vertical dancers suspended from its roof. Kinnear is a long three-storey retro Bauhaus modernist building designed by Diamond Schmitt. It was constructed in glass and steel to LEED Silver standards. It features a BMO Financial Group Galleria and windows with "sweeping views down the slope of Tunnel Mountain toward the Bourgeau mountain range." Mountain views in other directions are partly visible beyond the walls of urban densification on campus. Outdoor performances for 1,600 spectators are staged in the new Shaw Amphitheatre opened simultaneously below the Kinnear. Banff Centre's largest ever capital campaign, spearheaded by Calgary securities entrepreneur James Kinnear, raised $100 million for the Banff Centre Revitalization Project from 2007 to 2010. The length of the commemorative donor wall witnesses this neoliberal effort of corporate and community support. "Here, exceptional artists and leaders from around the world will be inspired to create and perform new works of art, share skills and knowledge in an interdisciplinary environment, explore ideas and develop solutions in the arts and leadership," stated Banff Centre President and CEO Mary E. Hofstetter, in media releases for the opening. "The programs taking place in the Kinnear Centre will build Alberta and Canada's cultural repertoire, advance global creativity, and contribute to a robust economy and sustainable communities."[62] Aspirations for Western Canadian "pioneer" spirit with global impact through a marriage of entrepreneurial and public support expanded in 2012 under Banff Centre's next CEO, Jeff Melanson, who aimed at capital campaigns for infrastructure renewal worth "hundreds of millions."[63] But new architecture was still in progress as he left for Toronto two years later, and economic downturn confronted the Banff Centre much as it did Alberta's public education sector overall.

Federal policies for neoliberal development under Stephen Harper steered the course of Canada's national parks to be branded as products for trade, profit, and transnational globalization, even as Alberta's government under Alison Redford situated postsecondary education and research as "Campus Alberta." Signature architectural structures for education, such as the new Kinnear Centre, represent and reproduce capitalist spatialization in the Canadian Rockies.[64] Ongoing processes of urban spatialization and the reproduction of capitalism are visible in the growth of the contemporary Banff Centre campus landscape, much as it was in the liberal modernist era under Cameron seventy years earlier. Its origins also hint at the potential to define arts and education as capital to enrich lives and diversify economies as a public space of late modernity in the contemporary West.

Notes

1. Karen Wall and PearlAnn Reichwein, "Climbing the Pinnacle of Art: Learning Vacations at the Banff School of Fine Arts, 1933–1959," *Canadian Historical Review* 92, no. 1 (March 2011): 70–105.

2. Henri Lefebvre, *The Production of Space* (Oxford: Basil Blackwell, 1991), 38–39; Gordon Waitt, "Playing with Sydney: Marketing Sydney for the 2000 Olympics," *Urban Studies* 36, no. 7 (1999): 1064.

3. Lukasz Stanek, *Henri Lefebvre on Space: Architecture, Urban Research, and the Production of Theory* (Minneapolis: University of Minnesota Press, 2011), xi.

4. Jody Berland, "Nationalism and the Modernist Legacy: Dialogues with Innis," in *Cultural Capital: A Reader on Modernist Legacies, State Institutions, and the Value(s) of Art*, ed. Jody Berland and S. Hornstein (Montreal: McGill-Queen's University Press, 2000), 28, and see 14–38.

5. Sean McLean, "'A Work Second to None': Positioning Extension at the University of Alberta, 1912–75," *Studies in the Education of Adults* 39, no. 1 (Spring 2007): 85.

6. Donald Cameron, *Campus in the Clouds* (Toronto: McClelland and Stewart, 1956), 51.

7. The Historic Centre of the City of Salzburg World Heritage Site was inscribed in 1996. UNESCO World Heritage, http://whc.unesco.org/pg.cfm?cid=31&id_site=784 (accessed 2 May 2012). Michael Steinberg, *The Meaning of the Salzburg Festival: Austria as Theatre and Ideology, 1890–1938* (Ithaca, NY: Cornell University Press, 1990), 76, 78, 224.

8. Annual Reports, Banff School of Fine Arts, 1946, accession 78-17, box 3, 2-22, University of Alberta Archives (hereafter UAA).

9. Sheila Campbell, "Branding the Last Best West: Regionalism, Tourism, and the Construction of the Tourist Gaze in Alberta, 1905–1940" (MA thesis, University of Alberta, 2005).

10. Cameron, *Campus in the Clouds*, 51.

11. Donald Leighton and Peggy Leighton, *Artists, Builders and Dreamers: 50 Years at the Banff School* (Toronto: McClelland and Stewart, 1982), 155.

12. Newton to Jennings, 4 August 1944, RG 84, A-2-a, vol. 515, file B317-2, Library and Archives Canada (hereafter LAC).

13. Leonora C. Woods Fonds, Glenbow Archives (hereafter GA), Archives Main Catalogue description, http://ww2.glenbow.org/search/archivesMainResults.aspx?XC=/search/archivesMainResults.aspx&TN=MAINCAT&AC=QBE_QUERY&RF=WebResults&DL=0&RL=0&NP=255&%0AMF=WPEngMsg.ini&MR=5&QB0=AND&QF0=-Main%20entry+%7C+Title&QI0=Leonora+C.+Woods+fonds (accessed 1 May 2012).

14. Eric L. Harvey Fonds, GA, Archives Main Catalogue description, http://ww2.glenbow.org/search/archivesMainResults.aspx?XC=/search/archivesMainResults.aspx&TN=MAINCAT&AC=QBE_QUERY&RF=WebResults&DL=0&RL=0&NP=255&MF=WPEngMsg.ini&MR=5&QB0=AND&QF0=Main%20entry%2B%7C%2BTitle&QI0=Eric%20Harvie%20fonds (accessed 1 May 2012).

15. Cameron, *Campus in the Clouds*, 64.

16. Newton to Gibson, 20 November 1945, RG 84, A-2-a, vol. 515, file B317-2, LAC.

17. PearlAnn Reichwein, "Holiday at the Banff School of Fine Arts: The Cinematic Production of Culture, Nature, and Nation in the Canadian Rockies, 1945–1952," *Journal of Canadian Studies* 39, no. 1 (Winter 2005): 49–73.

18   Cameron, *Campus in the Clouds*, 71.
19   Jennings to Smart, 7 March 1946, RG 84, A-2-a, vol. 515, file B317-2, LAC.
20   Smart to Banff National Park Superintendent, 1 April 1946; and Gibson to Jackson, 19 March 1946, RG 84, A-2-a, vol. 865, file B21-41-11 to 28, LAC.
21   Laing to Cameron, 13 July 1964, RG 84, A-2-a, vol. 897, file B21-42-1 to 20, LAC.
22   Cameron, *Campus in the Clouds*, 82–83.
23   Cameron to Robertson, 14 November 1960, accession 78-17, box 15, item 13-42, UAA. Cameron, *Campus in the Clouds*, 81–82.
24   Leighton and Leighton, *Artists, Builders and Dreamers*, 121–23.
25   Photographs of design sketches, passim, accession 78-17, box 2, UAA.
26   Cameron, *Campus in the Clouds*, 75.
27   For Fig. 9:1, perspectivist drawing of Banff School on Tunnel Mountain by Thompson Jones and Company, see accession 78-17, box 2, image 230, UAA.
28   Rule Wynn and Rule rendered more than one extant drawing of a grand hall depicted with different wings and rooftop elements. For a scanned historical photograph identified as "The first conceptual sketch for the permanent Banff School by John Rule," see Image A 43 01 32, http://archives.banffcentre.ca/ics-wpd/exec/icswppro.dll?AC=GET_RECORD&XC=/ics-wpd/exec/icswppro.dll&BU=http%3A%2F%2Farchives.banffcentre.ca%2Fphotos%2Fadvsearch.aspx-%3Fremember%3Dtrue&TN=photocat&SN=AUTO6601&SE=1626&RN=2&M-R=9&TR=0&TX=1000&ES=0&CS=1&XP=&RF=WebGallery&EF=&DF=Web-FullImages&RL=0&EL=0&DL=0&NP=255&ID=&MF=GENERICENGWPMSG.INI&MQ=&TI=0&DT=&ST=0&IR=28&NR=0&NB=0&SV=0&SS=0&BG=&F-G=&QS=&OEX=ISO-8859-1&OEH=ISO-8859-1 (accessed 1 February 2016), Paul D. Fleck Library and Archives. It shows a grand building with two steeples. For a similar rendering of a smaller grand building with one steeple, see accession 78-17, box 2, image 234, UAA.
29   For Fig. 9:2, "Colonel Wood Memorial" [sic] hall revised with a turret in 1946 sketch by John Rule, accession 78-17, box 2, image 240, UAA.
30   Cameron, *Campus in the Clouds*, 64. The various extant concept drawings of a grand hall depicted with stonework, gables, and steeples/turret match his reference to the Canadian Pacific Railway's Banff Springs Hotel architecture.
31   For Fig. 9:3, rustic "Typical Chalet," see accession 78-17, box 2, image 235, UAA.
32   Edward D. Mills, *Rustic Building Programs in Canada's National Parks, 1887–1950* (Ottawa: National Historic Sites Directorate, Parks Canada, 1994).
33   Smart to Cameron, 16 September 1946, RG 84, A-2-a, vol. 515, file B317-2, reel T-10457, LAC.
34   For Fig. 9:4, see page 8 and for Fig. 9:6, see page 10 in University of Alberta Banff School of Fine Arts and the Banff Foundation Prospectus, 1947, accession 78-17, box 7, item 5-47, UAA. For Fig. 9:5 see accession 78-17, box 2, image 243, UAA; this design concept reappears in the 1947 Prospectus, labelled as "Administration Building" on page 2.
35   Wilfrid Bennett, "College of the Rockies," *Vancouver Daily Province* (5 July 1947), 1, accession 78-17, item 6-11, box 7, UAA.
36   Memoranda to Proposals for Ground Development at Banff School of Fine Arts, c. 1953, accession 78-17, box 16, item 13-57, UAA.

37 E. Newton to Harvie, 17 January 1947, accession 78-17, box 4, item 28, UAA.
38 Harvie to Newton, 18 January 1947, accession 78-17, box 4, item 28, UAA.
39 Cameron to Harvie, 21 January 1947, accession 78-17, box 4, item 28, UAA.
40 Smart to Cameron, 4 March 1947, RG 84, A-2-a, vol. 515, file B317-2, T-10457, LAC.
41 Cameron, Memorandum of the interview at the Cranbrook Academy, 8 October 1945, accession 78-17, box 5, item 2, UAA.
42 Symon to Cameron, 31 August 1948; 13 September 1948, with attachments, including "Making Art Pay Off in Cash: Kansas City Industries Now Look to Institute Students for Ideas That Can Be Turned into Profits," accession 78-17, box 5, item 2, UAA.
43 Cameron to Harvie, 13 Nov. 1945; 22 April 1947; and other letters in this box, passim, accession 78-17, box 4, UAA.
44 Cameron to Harvie, 8 August 1947, accession 78-17, box 4, item 28, UAA.
45 For list of the U of A commissions, see Kathy E. Zimon, ed., *The Rule Wynn and Rule (Edmonton) Architectural Drawings* (Calgary: University of Calgary Press, 1997), 302–3.
46 Cameron, *Campus in the Clouds*, 63.
47 Tony Cashman and Norman H. Croll, *50 Years in Architecture: A History Published by Schmidt Feldberg Croll Henderson to Mark the 50th Anniversary of the Firm Founded in 1938 as Rule Wynn Rule* (Edmonton: Schmidt Feldberg Croll Henderson, 1988), 6.
48 Cameron offered to house Church at the Banff School and meet with him in August: see Church to Cameron, 7 August 1954; Cameron to Church, 29 December 1956, with photographs of models for Recreation Centre, accession 78-17, box 14, item 12-5, UAA.
49 Feistmann to Cameron, 30 December 1956; Cameron to Feistmann, 16 January 1957; accession 78-17, box 14, item 12-5, UAA.
50 For discussion with Professor Burgess, see Cameron to Newton, 3 October 1946; UAA, accession 78-17, box 4, item 28, UAA; Russell to Cameron, 2 March 1953, accession 78-17, box 14, item 12-11, UAA. Note that John A. Russell was director of the School of Architecture at University of Manitoba.
51 Coleman to Cameron, 28 June 1960, accession 78-17, box 16, item 13-42, UAA.
52 Donald G. Wetherell, *Architecture, Town Planning and Community: Selected Writings and Public Talks by Cecil Burgess, 1909–1946* (Edmonton: University of Alberta Press, 2005), lxviii; Trevor Boddy, *Modern Architecture in Alberta* (Regina: Alberta Culture and Multiculturalism and the Canadian Plains Research Centre, 1987), 77–89; Donald G. Wetherell and Irene R.A. Kmet, *Town Life: Main Street and the Evolution of Small Town Alberta, 1880–1947* (Edmonton: University of Alberta Press and Alberta Community Development, 1995).
53 Regarding the Banff Pavilion, see Boddy, *Modern Architecture in Alberta*, 36–38. Although heavy snowfall is noted as a local environmental design consideration that generally leads to a preference for angled rooflines in the Canadian Rockies, flat-topped slab structures emerged in various commercial and public buildings in Banff after the Banff School campus was built, for example the Timberline Hotel and the Banff High School.
54 Cameron to Mrs. J. H. Woods, 9 November 1948, accession 78-17, box 15, item 12-38, UAA.
55 Leighton and Leighton, *Artists, Builders and Dreamers*, 122–25.

56 Lakshmi Rao, "Whispering Pines," *The Art Spark*, 15 August 1950, 1, accession 78-17, box 24, item 18-47, UAA.

57 For how national parks in the United States frame the gaze on nature by design, see Tom Patin, "Exhibitions and Empire: National Parks and the Performance of Manifest Destiny," *Journal of American Culture*, 22, no. 1 (2000): 45, 48.

58 Annual Reports Banff School of Fine Arts, 1953, accession 78-17, box 3, item 2-24, UAA.

59 Lefebvre, *The Production of Space*, 38–39; Rob Shields, *Places on the Margin: Alternative Geographies of Modernity* (London: Routledge, 1991), 50–58.

60 Lynda Jessup comments on the work of Canadian landscape painters in this regard. See Lynda Jessup, "The Group of Seven and the Tourist Landscape in Western Canada, or The More Things Change…," *Journal of Canadian Studies* 37, no. 1 (Spring 2002): 144–79.

61 Boddy, *Modern Architecture in Alberta*, 111.

62 Kinnear Centre for Creativity and Innovation, The Banff Centre, Banff, Grand Opening, 2010, http://www.kinnearcentre.org/KinnearCentre_Final.pdf (accessed 2 May 2012), 30; Media Release, "The Banff Centre Opens the Kinnear Centre for Creativity and Innovation, 24 July 2010," http://www.banffcentre.ca/media-release/1029/the-banff-centre-opens-the-kinnear-centre-for-creativity-and-innovation-july-24-2010centre-completes-100-million-revitalization-project-by-architects-diamond-schmitt/ (accessed 2 May 2012).

63 Marsha Lederman, "Meet Jeff Melanson, the Arts Impresario even Conservatives can Love," *Globe and Mail*, 14 September 2012, http://www.theglobeandmail.com/arts/meet-jeff-melanson-the-arts-impresario-even-conservatives-can-love/article4545088/?page=all (accessed 1 February 2016); CBC News, "Banff Centre expansion on hold: Ambitious $900 million plan scrapped in favour of focusing on existing assets," 17 June 2015, http://www.cbc.ca/news/canada/calgary/banff-centre-expansion-on-hold-1.3116915 (accessed 1 February 2016).

64 The Kinnear "Banff Conference Centre" (Source: Canadian Tourism Commission), as well as main street Banff Avenue, Glacier Discovery Walk, Chateau Lake Louise, and nearby ski runs, were images used to illustrate news reports about a shift toward pro-development national park policies announced under federal Environment Minister Peter Kent: see Jen Gerson, "Mountain of Change in Store as Canada's National Parks Aim to Attract Mass-tourism," *National Post*, 31 May 2013, http://news.nationalpost.com/news/canada/mountain-of-change-in-store-as-canadas-national-parks-aim-to-attract-mass-tourism (accessed 1 February 2016).

Bibliography

Akenson, Donald. *The Irish Diaspora: A Primer.* Toronto: Meany, 1993.
Allen, Ann Taylor. "Feminism and Eugenics in Germany and Britain, 1900–1940: A Comparative Perspective." *German Studies Review* 23, no. 3 (October 2000): 477–505.
Anderson, C. Graham. *Grazing Rates Report, Short Grass Area of Alberta.* Edmonton: A. Shnitka, King's Printer, 1941.
Anderson, Frank. *The Frank Slide Story.* Calgary: Frontier, 1979.
Ashcroft, Bill. *Post-Colonial Studies: The Key Concepts.* New York: Routledge, 2000.
Avery, Cheryl. "The Reticent Archives: Preserving LGBTTIQ Histories." *Comma* 2013, no. 1 (2014): 69–77.
Banton, Martin, and Gurnam Singh. "'Race,' Disability and Oppression." In *Disabling Barriers, Enabling Environments.* 2nd ed., edited by John Swain, Sally French, Colin Barnes, and Carol Thomas, 111–18. London: Sage, 2000.
Barlow, Montague. *Report of the Royal Commission Respecting the Coal Industry of the Province of Alberta, 1935.* Edmonton: A. Shnitka, King's Printer, 1936.
Barman, Jean. "Ethnicity in the Pursuit of Status: British Middle and Upper-Class Emigration to British Columbia in the Late Nineteenth and early Twentieth Centuries." *Canadian Ethnic Studies* 18, no. 1 (1986): 32–51.
Barr, John J. *The Dynasty: The Rise and Fall of Social Credit in Alberta.* Toronto: McClelland and Stewart, 1974.
Barriault, Marcel. "Hard to Dismiss: the Archival Value of Gay Male Erotica and Pornography." *Archivaria* 68 (Fall 2009): 219–46.

Barron, E. Laurie. *Walking in Indian Moccasins: The Native Policies of Tommy Douglas and the CCF*. Vancouver: University of British Columbia Press, 1997.

Bartley, Paula. *Emmeline Pankhurst*. London: Routledge, 2002.

Bell, Catherine, and Val Napoleon, eds. *First Nations Cultural Heritage and Law: Case Studies, Voices and Perspectives*. Vancouver: University of British Columbia Press, 2008.

Belyea, Barbara. "Mapping the Marias: The Interface of Native and Scientific Cartographies." *Great Plains Quarterly* 17, no. 3–4 (1997): 165–84.

———, ed. *A Year Inland: The Journal of a Hudson's Bay Company Winterer*. Waterloo: Wilfrid Laurier University Press, 2000.

Benson, Nathanial A. *None of It Came Easy: The Story of James Garfield Gardiner*. Toronto: Burns and MacEachern, 1955.

Berland, Jody. "Nationalism and the Modernist Legacy: Dialogues with Innis." In *Cultural Capital: A Reader on Modernist Legacies, State Institutions, and the Value(s) of Art*, edited by Jody Berland and S. Hornstein, 14–38. Montreal: McGill-Queen's University Press, 2000.

Berry, Susan, and Jack Brink. *Aboriginal Cultures in Alberta: Five Hundred Generations*. Edmonton: Provincial Museum of Alberta, 2004.

Binnema, Theodore. "How Does a Map Mean?: Old Swan's Map of 1801 and the Blackfoot World." In *From Rupert's Land to Canada: Essays in Honour of John E. Foster*, edited by Theodore Binnema, Gerhard Ens, and Roderick C. Macleod, 201–24. Edmonton: University of Alberta Press, 2001

———, and Melanie Niemi. "'Let the Line Be Drawn Now': Wilderness, Conservation, and the Exclusion of Aboriginal People from Banff National Park in Canada." *Environmental History* 11, no. 4 (2006): 724–50.

Bird, Isabella. *A Lady's Life in the Rocky Mountains*. 1879. Reprint. London: Virago, 1986.

———. *The Englishwoman in America*. London: John Murray, 1856.

Blumhofer, Edith L. *Aimee Semple McPherson: Everybody's Sister*. Grand Rapids, MI: W.B. Eerdmans, 1993.

Boddy, Trevor. *Modern Architecture in Alberta*. Regina: Alberta Culture and Multiculturalism and the Canadian Plains Research Center, 1987.

Braz, Albert. *The False Traitor: Louis Riel in Canadian Culture*. Toronto: University of Toronto Press, 2003.

Bridgman, Wellington. *Breaking Prairie Sod: The Story of a Preacher in the Eighties*. Toronto: Musson, 1920.

Briggs, Julia. "'Almost Ashamed of England Being so English': Woolf and Ideas of Englishness." In *At Home and Abroad in the Empire: British Women Writers in the 1930s*, edited by. Robin Hackett, Freda Hamer, and Gay Wachman, 97–118. Newark, DE: University of Delaware Press, 2009.

Bright, David. "1919: A Year of Extraordinary Difficulty." In *Alberta Formed, Alberta Transformed*, vol. 2, edited by Michael Payne, Donald Wetherell, and Catharine Cavanaugh, 413–43. Edmonton: University of Alberta Press, and Calgary: University of Calgary Press, 2006.

Brownlie, Robin. *A Fatherly Eye : Indian Agents, Government Power, and Aboriginal Resistance in Ontario, 1918–1939*. Don Mills ON: Oxford University Press, 2003.

Buckley, Karen. *Danger, Death, and Disaster in the Crowsnest Pass Mines, 1902–1928*. Calgary: University of Calgary Press, 2004.

Bumsted, J.M. "Trying to Describe the Buffalo: An Historiographical Essay on the Red River Settlement." In *Thomas Scott's Body: And Other Essays on Early Manitoba History*, 11–36. Winnipeg: University of Manitoba Press, 2000.

Cameron, Donald. *Campus in the Clouds*. Toronto: McClelland and Stewart, 1956.

Campbell, John Duncan. *Catalogue of Coal Mines on the Alberta Plains (Research Council of Alberta Preliminary Report*. Edmonton: Research Council of Alberta, 1964.

Campbell, Sheila. "Branding the Last Best West: Regionalism, Tourism, and the Construction of the Tourist Gaze in Alberta, 1905–1940." MA thesis, University of Alberta, 2005.

Canadian Human Rights Commission, "Women's Rights," *Human Rights in Canada: A Historical Perspective*. http://www.chrc-ccdp.ca/en/browseSubjects/womenRights.asp.

Caragata, Warren. *Alberta Labour: A Heritage Untold*. Toronto: Lorimer, 1979.

Carpenter, David. *"Private Life." Lights to Each Other*. Saskatoon: University of Saskatchewan, 2004.

Carter, Sarah. "Britishness, 'Foreignness,' Women and Land in Western Canada, 1890s–1920s," *Humanities Research* 13, no. 1 (2006): 43–60.

———. "Creating 'Semi-Widows' and 'Supernumerary Wives': Prohibiting Polygamy in Prairie Canada's Aboriginal Communities to 1900." In *Contact Zones: Aboriginal and Settler Women in Canada's Colonial Past*, edited by Katie Pickles and Myra Rutherdale, 131–60. Vancouver: University of British Columbia Press, 2005.

———. *Lost Harvests: Prairie Indian Reserve Farmers and Government Policy*. Montreal: McGill-Queen's University Press, 1990.

———. "The Missionaries' Indian: Publications of John McDougall, John Mclean, and Egerton Ryerson Young." *Prairie Forum* 9, no. 1 (1984): 27–44.

———. "Man's Mission of Subjugation: The Publications of John Maclean, John McDougall and Egerton R. Young, Nineteenth-Century Methodist Missionaries in Western Canada." Master's thesis, University of Saskatchewan, 1980.

———,Walter Hildebrandt, and Dorothy First Rider, *The True Spirit and Original Intent of Treaty 7*. Montreal: McGill-Queen's University Press, 1996.Cashman, Tony, and Norman H. Croll, *50 Years in Architecture: A History Published by Schmidt Feldberg Croll Henderson to Mark the 50th Anniversary of the Firm Founded in 1938 as Rule Wynn Rule*. Edmonton: Schmidt Feldberg Croll Henderson, 1988.

CBC News. "Banff Centre expansion on hold: Ambitious $900 million plan scrapped in favour of focusing on existing assets," 17 June 2015. http://www.cbc.ca/news/canada/calgary/banff-centre-expansion-on-hold-1.3116915.

Chan, Sucheng. "Western American Historiography and People of Color." In *Peoples of Color in the American West*, edited by Sucheng Chan, Douglas Henry Daniels, Mario T. Garcia, and Terry P. Wilson, 1–14. Lexington, MA: D.C. Heath, 1994.

Cherwinski, W.J.C. " 'Misfits,' 'Malingerers,' and 'Malcontents': The British Harvester Movement of 1928." In *The Developing West*, edited by J.E. Foster, 271–302. Edmonton: University of Alberta Press, 1983.

Clarke, S.E. "Pasture Investigations in the Short Grass Plains of Saskatchewan and Alberta." *Scientific Agriculture* 10, no. 10 (June 1930): 731–49.

Clapperton, Jonathan. "Naturalizing Race Relations: Conservation, Colonialism, and Spectacle at the Banff Indian Days." *Canadian Historical Review* 94, no. 3 (2013): 349–79.

Cleverdon, Catherine L. *The Woman Suffrage Movement in Canada*. Toronto: University of Toronto Press, 1974.

Clifford, James. *Routes: Travel and Translation in the Late Twentieth Century*. Cambridge, MA: Harvard University Press, 1997.

Coates, Donna, and George Melnyk, "The Struggle for an Alberta Literature." In *Wild Words: Essays on Alberta Literature*, edited by Donna Coates and George Melnyk, vii–xi. Edmonton: Athabasca University Press, 2009.

Cole, Douglas. *Captured Heritage: The Scramble for Northwest Coast Artifacts*. Vancouver: University of British Columbia Press, 1995.

Conaty, Gerry. "Glenbow's Blackfoot Gallery: Working Towards Coexistence." In *Museums and Source Communities: A Routledge Reader*, edited by Laura Peers and Alison Brown, 227–41. London: Routledge, 2003.

Conrad, Margaret. "A Brief Survey of Canadian Historiography." In *Possibilities for the Past: Shaping History Education in Canada*, edited by Penney Clark, 33–54. Vancouver: University of British Columbia Press, 2011.

Cowie, Isaac. *The Company of Adventurers*. Toronto: W. Briggs, 1914.

Currie, Philip J., and Eva B. Koppelhus, eds., *Dinosaur Provincial Park: A Spectacular Ancient Ecosystem Revealed*. Bloomington: Indiana University Press, 2005.

De Trémaudan, A.H. *Histoire de la Nation Métisse dans L'Ouest canadien*. Montreal: Albert Lévesque, 1936. In English translation by Elizabeth Maguet, *Hold High Your Heads*. Winnipeg: Pemmican, 1982.

Deloria, Vine, Jr. *Red Earth, White Lies: Native Americans and the Myth of Scientific Fact*. New York: Scribner, 1995.

Dempsey, Hugh. *Indian Tribes of Alberta*. Repr. and rev. ed.. Calgary: Glenbow-Alberta Institute, [1979] 1988.

——. *The Great Blackfoot Treaties*. Calgary: Heritage House, 2015.

——. "One Hundred Years of Treaty Seven." In *One Century Later: Western Canadian Reserve Indians Since Treaty 7*, edited by Ian Getty and Donald B. Smith, 20–30. Vancouver: University of British Columbia Press, 1978.

Devereux, Cecily. *Growing a Race: Nellie L. McClung and the Fiction of Eugenic Feminism*. Montreal: McGill-Queen's University Press, 2006.

Devine, Heather. "After The Spirit Sang. Aboriginal Canadians and Museum Policy in the New Millennium." In *How Canadians Communicate III: Contexts of Canadian Popular Culture*, edited by Bart Beaty, Derek Briton, Gloria Filax, and Rebecca Sullivan, 217–40. Edmonton: Athabasca University Press, 2010.

Dick, Lyle. "Vernacular Currents in Western Canadian Historiography: The Passion and Prose of Katherine Hughes, F.G. Roe, and Roy Ito." In *The West and Beyond: New Perspectives on an Imagined Region*, edited by Alvin Finkel, Sarah Carter, and Peter Fortna, 13–46. Edmonton: Athabasca University Press, 2010.

——. "Red River's Vernacular Historians." *Manitoba History* 71 (Winter 2013): 3–15.

Dickason, Olive Patricia. *Canada's First Nations: A History of Founding Peoples from Earliest Time*, 3rd ed. Don Mills, ON: Oxford University Press, 2002.

Dowling, D.B. *Canada Department of Mines Geological Survey: The Coal Mines of Manitoba, Saskatchewan, Alberta and Eastern British Columbia*. Ottawa: Canada Department of Mines, 1909.

Duberman, Martin Bauml. *About Time: Exploring the Gay Past*. New York: Sea Horse, 1986.

Dunae, Patrick A. *Gentlemen Emigrants: From the British Public Schools to the Canadian Frontier*. Vancouver: Douglas & McIntyre, 1981.

Dyck, Erika. *Facing Eugenics: Reproduction, Sterilization and the Politics of Choice*. Toronto: University of Toronto Press, 2013.

Elections Canada, *A History of the Vote in Canada*. Ottawa: Office of the Chief Electoral Officer, 2007.

Emberley, Julia V. *Defamiliarizing the Aboriginal: Cultural Practices and Decolonization in Canada*. Toronto: University of Toronto Press, 2007.

———. "Epistemic Heterogeneity: Indigenous Storytelling, Testimonial Practices, and the Question of Violence in Indian Residential Schools." In *Reconciling Canada: Critical Perspectives on the Culture of Redress*, edited by Jennifer Henderson and Pauline Wakeham, 143–58. Toronto: University of Toronto Press, 2013.

Ens, Gerhard J., and Joe Sawchuk. *From New Peoples to New Nations: Aspects of Métis History and Identity from the Eighteenth to Twenty-first Centuries*. Toronto: University of Toronto Press, 2015.

Epstein, Daniel Mark. *Sister Aimee: The Life of Aimee Semple McPherson*. New York: Harcourt Brace, 1994.

Evans, Sterling. "Badlands and Bones: Towards a Conservation and Social History of Dinosaur Provincial Park, Alberta." In *Place and Replace*, edited by Leah Morton, Essylt Jones, and Adele Perry, 250–70. Winnipeg: University of Manitoba Press, 2013.

———. *Bound in Twine: The History and Ecology of the Henequen-Wheat Complex for Mexico and the American and Canadian Plains, 1880–1950*. College Station: Texas A&M University Press, 2007.

———, ed. *The Borderlands of the American and Canadian Wests: Essays on Regional History of the Forty-ninth Parallel*. Norman: University of Nebraska Press, 2006.

Faragher, John Mack. "The Frontier Trail: Rethinking Turner and Reimagining the American West." *American Historical Review* 98, no. 1 (February 1993): 106–17.

Fiamengo, Janice. "Rediscovering our Foremothers Again: Racial Ideas of Canada's Early Feminists, 1885–1945." In *Rethinking Canada: The Promise of Women's History*. 5th ed., edited by Mona Gleason and Adele Perry, 144–63. Don Mills, ON: Oxford University Press, 2006.

Field, Monica, and David McIntire, *On the Edge of Destruction: Canada's Deadliest Rockslide*. Crowsnest Pass, AB: Frank Slide Interpretive Centre, 2003.

Finch, David. *Hell's Half Acre: Early Days in the Great Alberta Oil Patch*. Victoria: Heritage House, 2005.

Finkel, Alvin. "1935: The Social Credit Revolution." In *Alberta Formed, Alberta Transformed*, vol. 2, edited by Michael Payne, Donald Wetherell, and Catharine Cavanaugh, 490–512. Edmonton: University of Alberta Press, and Calgary: University of Calgary Press, 2006.

———. "Alberta Social Credit Reappraised: The Radical Character of the Early Social Credit Movement." In *The Prairie West: Historical Readings*, edited by R. Douglas Francis and Howard Palmer, 661–81. Edmonton: Pica Pica Press, 1992.

———. *The Social Credit Phenomenon in Alberta*. Toronto: University Press of Toronto, 1989.

Fischer, Suzanne. "Nota Bene: If You 'Discover' Something in an Archive, It's Not a Discovery." *Atlantic*, 19 June 2012. http://www.theatlantic.com/technology/archive/2012/06/nota-bene-if-you-discover-something-in-an-archive-its-not-a-discovery/258538/.

Flores, Dan. "Place: Thinking about Bioregional History." In *The Natural West: Environmental History in the Great Plains and Rocky Mountains*, 89–106. Norman: University of Oklahoma Press, 1984.

Foran, Max. "1967: Embracing the Future . . . at Arm's Length." In *Alberta Formed, Alberta Transformed*, vol. 2, edited by Michael Payne, Donald Wetherell, and Catharine Cavanaugh, 613–43. Edmonton: University of Alberta Press, and Calgary: University of Calgary Press, 2006.

———, "The Impact of the Depression on Grazing Lease Policy in Alberta." In *Cowboys, Ranchers, and the Cattle Business: Cross-Border Perspectives on Ranching History*, edited by Simon Evans, Sarah Carter and Bill Yeo, 123–38. Calgary and Boulder: University of Calgary Press and University Press of Colorado, 1990.

Forster, E.M. *Howards End*. 1910. Reprint, New York: Longman, 2010.

———. *A Passage to India*. 1924. Reprint, New York: Meiers, 1979.

Frank, Gloria Jean. "That's My Dinner on Display: A First Nations Reflection on Museum Culture." *BC Studies* 125/126 (2000): 163–78.

Friesen, Gerald. "Critical History in Western Canada: 1900–2000." In *The West and Beyond: New Perspectives on an Imagined Region*, edited by Alvin Finkel, Sarah Carter, and Peter Fortna, 3–12. Edmonton: Athabasca University Press, 2010.

———. "Space and Region in Canadian History." *Journal of the Canadian Historical Association* 16 (2005): 1–48.

———. Afterword. In *Rural Life: Portraits of the Prairie Town, 1946*. By James P. Giffen, 202–8. Winnipeg: University of Manitoba Press, 2004.

———."Defining the Prairies: or, Why the Prairies Don't Exist." In *Toward Defining the Prairies: Region, Culture and History*, edited by Robert Wardhaugh, 13–28. Winnipeg: University of Manitoba Press, 2001.

———. *The West: Regional Debate, National Ambitions, Global Age*. Toronto: Penguin, 1999.

———. *River Road: Essays on Manitoba and Prairie History*. Winnipeg: University of Manitoba Press, 1996.

———. *The Canadian Prairies: A History*. Toronto: University of Toronto Press, 1987.

Fudge, Judy, and Erick Tucker, *Labour before the Law: The Regulation of Workers' Collective Action in Canada, 1900–1948*. Toronto: Oxford University Press, 2001.

Ganapathy, Sandhya. "Imagining Alaska Local and Translocal Engagements with Place." *American Anthropologist* 115, no. 1 (March 2013): 96–111.

Ganaway, Brian. Review of Carolyn Steedman's *Dust: The Archive and Cultural History*. http://h-net.msu.edu/cgi-bin/logbrowse.pl?trx-=vx&list=h-german&month=0307&week=b&msg=w3TdA-IzWE3ofD77HMaHe5w&user=&pw=.

Gerson, Jen. "Mountain of Change in Store as Canada's National Parks Aim to Attract Mass-Tourism." *National Post*, 31 May 2013. http://news.nationalpost.com/news/canada/mountain-of-change-in-store-as-canadas-national-parks-aim-to-attract-mass-tourism.

Gibbons, Sheila Rae. "'The True [Political] Mothers of Today': Farm Women and the Organization of Eugenic Feminism in Alberta." MA thesis, University of Saskatchewan, 2012.

———. "'Our Power to Remodel Civilization': The Development of Eugenic Feminism in Alberta 1909–1921." *Canadian Bulletin of Medical History* 31, no. 1 (2014): 123–42.

Goldsborough, Gordon. "Memorable Manitobans: Francis Marion Beynon (1884–1951), *Manitoba Historical Society*. http://www.mhs.mb.ca/docs/people/beynon_fm.shtml.

Golebiowski, Laura. "Oil Discovery in Turner Valley: Press Reactions," *Alberta History* 55, no. 3 (2007): 20–28.

Gray, Charlotte. *Nellie McClung*. Toronto: Penguin Canada, 2008.

Gray, James H. *Men against the Desert*. Saskatoon: Western Producer Prairie Books, 1978.

Grekul, Jana, Harvey Krahn, and Dave Odynak. "Sterilizing the "Feeble-minded": Eugenics in Alberta, Canada, 1929–1972." *Journal of Historical Sociology* 17, no. 4 (December 2004): 358–84.

Griffiths, Alison, *"Shivers Down Your Spine": Cinema, Museums, and the Immersive View*. New York: Columbia University Press, 2008.

Gwyn, Richard. *Nation Maker – Sir John A. Macdonald: His Life, Our Times, Volume 2: 1867–1891*. Toronto: Random House Canada, 2011.

Hackett, Robin, Freda Hamer, and Gay Wachman, eds., *At Home and Abroad in the Empire: British Women Writers in the 1930s*. Newark, DE: University of Delaware Press, 2009.

Haney, Chuck. *Badlands of the High Plains*. Helena, MT: Farcountry Press, 2001.

Hart, Genevieve, and Ncumisa Mfazo. "Places for all? Cape Town's Public Library Services to Gays And Lesbians." *South African Journal of Library and Information Science* 76, no. 2 (2010): 81–90.

Hawkes, John. *The Story of Saskatchewan and Its People*, 3 vols. Regina: S.J. Clarke, 1924.

Henderson, Jennifer. *Settler Feminism and Race Making in Canada*. Toronto: University of Toronto Press, 2003.

Hill, Tom, and Trudy Nicks, eds. *Turning the Page: Forging New Partnerships Between Museums and First Peoples*. 2nd ed. Ottawa: Assembly of First Nations and the Canadian Museums Association, 1992.

Huseman, Jennifer, and Damien Short. "'A Slow Industrial Genocide': Tar Sands and the Indigenous People of Northern Alberta." *International Journal of Human Rights* 16, no. 1 (2012): 216–37.

Isern, Thomas D. *Bull Threshers and Bindlestiffs: Harvesting and Threshing on the North American Plains*. Lawrence: University Press of Kansas, 1990.
Jackel, Susan, ed. *A Flannel Shirt and Liberty: British Emigrant Gentlewomen in the Canadian West, 1880–1914*. Vancouver: University of British Columbia Press, 1982.
Jacknis, Ira. "Repatriation as Social Drama: The Kwakiutl Indians of British Columbia, 1922–1980." In *Repatriation Reader: Who Owns American Indian Remains?*, edited by Devon Mihesuah, 266–81. Lincoln: University of Nebraska Press, 2000.
Jagodinsky, Katrina. "A Tale of Two Sisters: Family Histories from the Strait Salish Borderlands," *Western Historical Quarterly* 47, no. 1 (Summer 2016): 1–23.
Jennings, Rosalind. "Disappearing Doubles and Deceptive Landscapes in the Writing of Robert Kroetsch." *London Journal of Canadian Studies* 12 (1996): 20–27.
Jessup, Lynda. "The Group of Seven and the Tourist Landscape in Western Canada, or The More Things Change…" *Journal of Canadian Studies* 37, no. 1 (Spring 2002): 144–79.
Johnson, Jean L. ed. *Big Hill Country*. Cochrane, AB: Cochrane and Area Historical Society, 1977.
Jonatis, Aldona. *Art of the Northwest Coast*. Seattle: University of Washington Press, 2006.
Jones, David C. *Empire of Dust: Settling and Abandoning the Prairie Dry Belt*. Edmonton: University of Alberta Press, 1987.
Kaye, Francis W. *Good Lands: A Meditation and History on the Great Plains*. Edmonton: Athabasca University Press, 2011.
———. *Hiding the Audience: Viewing Arts & Arts Institutions on the Prairies*. Edmonton: University of Alberta Press, 2003.
———, and Robert Thacker. "'Gone Back to Alberta': Robert Kroetsch Rewriting the Great Plains." *Great Plains Quarterly* 1, no. 1 (1994): 167–83.
Kinnear Centre for Creativity and Innovation, The Banff Centre, Banff, Grand Opening, 2010. http://www.kinnearcentre.org/KinnearCentre_Final.pdf.
Kinsman, Gary. *The Regulation of Desire: Homo and Hetero Sexualities*. 2nd ed., rev. Montreal: Black Rose Books, 1996.

Kirshenblatt-Gimblett, Barbara. *Destination Culture: Tourism, Museums, and Heritage*. Berkeley: University of California Press, 1998.

Kroetsch, Robert. *The Last Narrative of Mrs. David Thompson*. Windsor, ON: Wrinkle Press, 2007.

LaRocque, Joseph (as told to Robert Tyre). "I Saw Saskatchewan's Bloody Rebellion." *Liberty*. July 1955.

Lately, Thomas. *Storming Heaven: The Lives and Turmoil of Minnie Kennedy and Aimee Semple McPherson*. New York: Morrow, 1970.

Lederman, Marsha. "Meet Jeff Melanson, the Arts Impresario even Conservatives can Love." *Globe and Mail*, 14 September 2012. http://www.theglobeandmail.com/arts/meet-jeff-melanson-the-arts-impresario-even-conservatives-can-love/article4545088/?page=all.

Lefebvre, Henri. *The Production of Space*. Oxford: Basil Blackwell, 1991.

Leighton, Donald, and Peggy Leighton. *Artists, Builders and Dreamers: 50 Years at the Banff School*. Toronto: McClelland and Stewart, 1982.

Li, Peter S. "Visible Minorities in Canadian Society: Challenges of Racial Diversity." In *Social Differentiation, Patterns and Processes*, edited by Danielle Juteau Lee, 117–54. Toronto: University of Toronto Press, 2003.

Library and Archives Canada. "Modernization – Myth Busters." http://www.bac-lac.gc.ca/eng/about-us/modernization/Pages/Myth-Busters.aspx.

Lowen, Royden, and Gerald Friesen. *Immigrants in Prairie Cities: Ethnic Diversity in Twentieth-Century Canada*. Toronto: University of Toronto Press, 2009.

Lukenbill, Bill. "Modern Gay and Lesbian Libraries and Archives in North America: A Study in Community Identity and Affirmation." *Library Management* 23, no. 1/2 (2002): 93–100.

Lund, John. "Representation of Homosexuality in the *Alberta Report*." Paper presented at the annual meeting for the Association of Canadian Archivists, Calgary, Alberta, 15–17 May 2009.

Macdougall, Brenda, and Nicole St-Onge."Rooted in Mobility: Metis Buffalo Hunting Brigades." *Manitoba History* 71 (Winter 2013): 21–32.

———, Carolyn Podruchny, and Nicole St-Onge, eds. *Contours of a People: Métis Family, Mobility and History*. Norman: Oklahoma University Press, 2012.

Mackinnon, Doris Jeanne. *The Identities of Marie Rose Delorme Smith, Portrait of a Métis Woman, 1861–1960*. Regina: University of Regina Press, 2012.

Maclean. John. *McDougall of Alberta: A Life of Rev. John McDougall, D.D., Pathfinder of Empire and Prophet of the Plains*. Toronto: Ryerson, 1927.

Mair, Kimberly. "Putting Things in their Place: The Syncrude Gallery of Aboriginal Culture at the Royal Alberta Museum and the Idiom of Majority History." In *Canadian Literature and Cultural Memory*, edited by Cynthia Sugars and Eleanor Ty, 39–52. Don Mills, ON: Oxford University Press, 2014.

Mason, Courtney. *Spirits of the Rockies: Reasserting an Indigenous Presence in Banff National Park*. Toronto: University of Toronto Press, 2014.

Massie, Merle. *Forest Prairie Edge: Place History in Saskatchewan*. Winnipeg: University of Manitoba Press, 2014.

Maynard. Steven. "'The Burning, Wilful Evidence': Lesbian/Gay History and Archival Research." *Archivaria* 33 (Winter 1991–92): 195–201.

McClung, Nellie. *In Times Like These*. Toronto: University of Toronto Press, 1972.

McCormak, A. Ross. "Networks Among British Immigrants and Accommodation to Canadian Society: Winnipeg, 1900–1914." *Histoire sociale – Social History* 17, no. 34 (November 1984): 357–74.

McCrady, David G. *Living with Strangers: The Nineteenth-Century Sioux and the Canadian-American Borderlands*. Norman: University of Nebraska Press, 2006.

McDougall, John. *Pathfinding on Plain and Prairie*. Toronto: William Briggs, 1898.

McKay, Ian. "The Liberal Order Framework: A Prospectus for a Reconnaissance of Canadian History." *Canadian Historical Review* 81, no. 4 (November 2000): 617–45.

McLaren, Angus. *Our Own Master Race: Eugenics in Canada 1885–1945*. Toronto: McClelland and Stewart, 1990.

McLaren, John. "Maternal Feminism in Action – Emily Murphy, Police Magistrate." *Windsor Yearbook of Access to Justice* 8 (1988): 234–52.

Mclean, Sean. "'A Work Second to None': Positioning Extension at the University of Alberta, 1912–75." *Studies in the Education of Adults* 39, no. 1 (Spring 2007): 77–91.

McLeod, Neal. "Plains Cree Identity: Borderlands, Ambiguous Genealogies and Narrative Irony." *Canadian Journal of Native Studies* 20, no. 2 (2000): 437–54.

McLoughlin, Moira. *Museums and the Representations of Native Canadians: Negotiating the Borders of Culture.* New York: Garland, 1999.

Meijer Drees, Laurie. "'Indians' Bygone Past': The Banff Indian Days, 1902–1945." *Past Imperfect* 2 (1993): 7–28.

Miller, J.R. *Skyscrapers Hide the Heavens: A History of Indian-White Relations in Canada.* Toronto: University of Toronto Press, 1991.

———. "From Riel to the Métis." *Canadian Historical Review* 69, no. 1 (1988): 1–20.

Milloy, John S. *A National Crime: The Canadian Government and the Residential School System, 1879 to 1986.* Winnipeg: University of Manitoba Press, 1999.

Mills, Edward D. *Rustic Building Programs in Canada's National Parks, 1887–1950.* Ottawa: National Historic Sites Directorate, Parks Canada, 1994.

Mitchell, David. *The Fighting Pankhursts: A Study in Tenacity.* London: Jonathan Cape, 1967.

Mitchell, Tom, and James Naylor, "The Prairies: In the Eye of the Storm." In *The Workers' Revolt in Canada, 1917–1925,* edited by Craig Herron, 176–231. Toronto: University of Toronto Press, 1998.

Monto, Tom. *Solidarity and Anger: History of the Alberta Labour Movement.* Edmonton: Crang, 1989.

Moore, Stephen L. "Refugees from Volstead: Cross-Boundary Tourism in the Northwest during Prohibition." In *The Borderlands of the American and Canadian Wests: Essays on Regional History of the Forty-Ninth Parallel,* edited by Sterling Evans, 246–62. Lincoln: University of Nebraska Press, 2006.

Moss, Erin L., H.J. Stam, and Diane Kattevilder. "From Suffrage to Sterilization: Eugenics and the Women's Movement in 20th Century

Alberta." *Canadian Psychology / Psychologie canadienne* 54, no. 2 (2013): 105–14.

Murphy, Emily. *The Black Candle*. Toronto: Thomas Allen, 1922.

———. *Janey Canuck in the West*. Toronto: McLelland and Stewart, 1975.

Murton, James. *Creating a Modern Countryside: Liberalism and Land Resettlement in British* Columbia. Vancouver: University of British Columbia Press, 2007.

Neufeld, David. "Learning to Drive the Yukon River: Western Cartography and Athapaskan Story Maps." In *Big Country, Big Issues: Canada's Environment, Culture and History*, edited by Nadine Klopfer and Christof Mauch, 16–43. Munich: Rachel Carson Center for Environment and Society, 2011).

Newton, Janice. *The Feminist Challenge to the Canadian Left, 1900–1918*. Montreal: McGill-Queen's University Press, 1995.

Nix, Ernest. "McDougall, John Chantler." *Dictionary of Canadian Biography Online*, vol. 14. University of Toronto/Université Laval, 2003–. http://www.biographi.ca/en/bio/mcdougall_john_chantler_14E.html.

Noble, Brian, and Glenn Rollans, *Alberta, the Badlands*. Toronto: Reidmore Books, 1981.

O'Byrne, Nicole. "Challenging the Liberal Order Framework: Natural Resources and Métis Policy in Alberta and Saskatchewan (1930–1948)." PhD diss., University of Victoria, 2014.

Oetelaar, Gerald A., and D. Joy Oetelaar. "The Structured World of the *Niitsitapi*: The Landscape as Historical Archive among Hunter-Gatherers of the Northern Plains." In *Structured Worlds: The Archaeology of Hunter-Gatherer Thought and Action*, edited by A. Cannon, 69–94. Sheffield, UK: Equinox, 2011.

Owram, Doug. "1951: Oil's Magic Wand." In *Alberta Formed, Alberta Transformed*, vol. 2, edited by Michael Payne, Donald Wetherell, and Catharine Cavanaugh, 566–87. Edmonton: University of Alberta Press, and Calgary: University of Calgary Press, 2006.

———. *The Government Generation: Canadian Intellectuals and the State, 1900–1945*. Toronto: University of Toronto Press, 1986.

Parris, Brittany Bennett. "Creating, Reconstructing, and Protecting Historical Narratives: Archives and the LBGT Community." *Current Studies in Librarianship* 29, no. 1/2 (2005): 5–25.

Patin, Tom. "Exhibitions and Empire: National Parks and the Performance of Manifest Destiny." *Journal of American Culture* 22, no. 1 (2000): 41–60.

Pettipas, Katherine. *Severing the Ties that Bind: Government Repression of Indigenous Religious Cultures on the Prairies*. Winnipeg: University of Manitoba Press, 1994.

Pettit, Jennifer Loretta Jane. "'To Christianize and Civilize': Native Industrial Schools in Canada." PhD diss., University of Calgary, 1998.

Pickles, Katie. *Female Imperialism and National Identity: Imperial Order Daughters of the Empire*. Manchester: Manchester University Press, 2002.

Podruchny, Carolyn. *Making the Voyageur World: Travelers and Traders in the North American Fur Trade*. Lincoln: University of Nebraska Press, 2006.Pratt, Mary Louise. *Imperial Eyes: Travel Writing and Transculturation*. 2nd ed. London: Routledge, [1992] 2008.

Prefontaine, Darren R., Lean Dorion, Patrick Young, and Sherry Farrell Racette. "Métis Identity," at the Gabriel Dumont Institute. *The Virtual Museum of Métis History and Culture*. http://www.metismuseum.ca/media/db/00726.

Purvis, June. *Emmeline Pankhurst: A Biography*. London: Routledge, 2002.

Pylypchuk, Mary Ann. "The Value of Aboriginal Records as Legal Evidence in Canada: An Examination of Sources." *Archivaria* 32 (Summer 1991): 51–77.Radford, Megan Cécile. "How Canadian Newspaper Women Won the Vote." *Walrus,* July/August 2011. http://walrusmagazine.com/articles/2011.07-dalton-camp-award-how-canadian-newspaper-women-*won*-the-vote/.

Ramirez, Bruno, and Donald Avery. "Immigration and Ethnic Studies." In *A Thematic Guide to Canadian Studies*, edited by A. Artibise, 77–116. Montreal; McGill-Queen's University Press, 1990.

Rawson, K.J. "Accessing Transgender // Desiring Queer(er?) Archival Logics." *Archivaria* 68 (Fall 2009): 123–40.

Reichwein, PearlAnn. "Holiday at the Banff School of Fine Arts: The Cinematic Production of Culture, Nature, and Nation in the

Canadian Rockies, 1945–1952." *Journal of Canadian Studies* 39, no. 1 (Winter 2005): 49–73.

Rennie, Bradford. "From Idealism to Pragmatism: 1923 in Alberta." In *Alberta Formed, Alberta Transformed*, vol. 2, edited by Michael Payne, Donald Wetherell, and Catharine Cavanaugh, 443–63. Edmonton: University of Alberta Press, and Calgary: University of Calgary Press, 2006.

Robertson, John Palmerston. *A Political Manual of the Province of Manitoba and the North-west Territories.* Winnipeg: Call Printing, 1887.

Robinson, Zac, and Stephen Slemon. "Deception in High Places." *Canadian Alpine Journal* 94 (2011): 12–17.

Rollyson, Carl. "A Conservative Revolutionary: Emmeline Pankhurst, 1857–1928." *Virginia Quarterly Review* 79, no. 2 (Spring 2003): 325–35.

Root, Robert. *Following Isabella: Travels in Colorado Then and Now.* Norman: University of Oklahoma Press, 2009.

Rothman, Hal. *Devil's Bargains: Tourism in the Twentieth-Century American West.* Lawrence: University Press of Kansas, 2000.

———. *Neon Metropolis: How Las Vegas Started the Twenty-First Century.* New York: Routledge, 2003.

Rudd, F. Albert. "Production and Marketing of Beef Cattle from the Short Grass Plains Area of Canada," Master's thesis, University of Alberta, 1935.

Rutherdale, Myra. *Women and the White Man's God : Gender and Race in the Canadian Mission Field.* Vancouver: University of British Columbia Press, 2002.

Samson, Amy. "Eugenics in the Community: The United Farm Women of Alberta. Public Health Nursing, Teaching, Social Work, and Sexual Sterilization in Alberta, 1928–1972." PhD diss., University of Saskatchewan, 2014.

———. "Eugenics in the Community: Gendered Professions and Eugenic Sterilization in Alberta, 1928–1972." *Canadian Bulletin of Medical History* 31, no. 1 (2014): 143–63.

Sanders, Bryne Hope. *Emily Murphy Crusader ("Janey Canuck").* Toronto: Macmillan Canada, 1945.

Scott, Bonnie Kime. "Rebecca West: Construction of a Public Intelligence through Letters of the 1930s." In *At Home and Abroad in the Empire: British Women Writers in the 1930s*, edited by Robin Hackett, Freda Hamer, and Gay Wachman, 187–202. Newark, DE: University of Delaware Press, 2009.

Sharp, Paul F. *The Agrarian Revolt in Western Canada*. Winnipeg: Hignell, 1997.

Sharpe, Robert J., and Patricia I. McMahon. *The Persons Case: The Origins and Legacy of the Fight for Legal Personhood*. Toronto: University of Toronto Press, 2007.

Shields, Rob. *Places on the Margin: Alternative Geographies of Modernity*. London: Routledge, 1991.

Simon, Roger I. "The Terrible Gift: Museums and the Possibility of Hope without Consolation," *Museum Management and Curatorship* 21 (2006): 187–204.

Smith, David E., and Norman Ward. *Jimmy Gardiner: Relentless Liberal*. Toronto: University of Toronto Press, 1990.

———. *Prairie Liberalism: The Liberal Party in Saskatchewan, 1905–71*. Toronto: University of Toronto Press, 1975.

Smith, Henry Nash. *Virgin Land: The American West as Symbol and Myth*. Cambridge, MA: Harvard University Press, 1950.

Smith, Keith. *Liberalism, Surveillance, and Resistance: Indigenous Communities in Western Canada, 1877–1927*. Edmonton: Athabasca University Press, 2009.

Snow, John. *These Mountains Are our Sacred Places: The Story of the Stoney People*. Toronto: Fitzhenry & Whiteside, 2005.

Stanek, Lukasz. *Henri Lefebvre on Space: Architecture, Urban Research, and the Production of Theory*. Minneapolis: University of Minnesota Press, 2011.

"Star Blanket." In *Saskatchewan First Nations: Lives Past and Present*, edited by Christian Thompson, 125–27. Regina: Canadian Plains Research Center, 2004.

Steinberg, Michael. *The Meaning of the Salzburg Festival: Austria as Theatre and Ideology, 1890–1938*. Ithaca, NY: Cornell University Press, 1990.

Stepney, Philip H.R., "Development of the Syncrude Canada Aboriginal Peoples Gallery." *Alberta Museums Review* 23, no. 3 (1997).

———, and David J. Goa, eds. *The Scriver Blackfoot Collection: Repatriation of Canada's Heritage*. Edmonton: Provincial Museum of Alberta, 1990.

Stewart, David A. "The First Half Century: A Sketch of the Early Years of the Historical and Scientific Society of Manitoba." *Manitoba Pageant* 24, no. 3 (Spring 1979). http://www.mhs.mb.ca/docs/pageant/24/firsthalfcentury.shtml.

Stoler, Ann Laura, and Frederick Cooper. "Between Metropole and Colony: Rethinking a Research Agenda." In *Tensions of Empire: Colonial Cultures in a Bourgeois World*, edited by Frederick Cooper and Ann Laura Stoler, 1–59. Berkeley: University of California Press, 1997.

Stote, Karen. "An Act of Genocide: Eugenics, Indian Policy and the Sterilization of Aboriginal Women in Canada." PhD diss., University of New Brunswick, 2012.

Strong-Boag, Veronica. "'The Citizenship Debates': The 1885 Franchise Act." In *Contesting Canadian Citizenship: Historical Readings*, edited by Robert Adamoski, Dorothy Chunn and Robert Menzies, 69–94. Toronto: University of Toronto Press, 2002.

———. *The New Day Recalled: Lives of Girls and Women in English Canada, 1919–1939*. Toronto: Copp Clark Pitman, 1993.

Stunden Bower, Shannon. *Wet Prairie: People, Land, and Water in Agricultural Manitoba* Vancouver: University of British Columbia Press, 2011.

Taylor, Andrew. "'The Same Old Sausage': Thomas Carlyle and the James Family." In *The Carlyles at Home and Abroad: Essays in Honour of Kenneth J. Fielding*, edited by D. Sorensen and R. Tarr. London: Ashgate, 2004.Thomas, Lewis H. "Riel, Louis (1844–85)." In *Dictionary of Canadian Biography*, vol. 11.University of Toronto/Université Laval. 2003–. http://www.biographi.ca/en/bio/riel_louis_1844_85_11E.html.

———, ed. *William Aberhart and Social Credit in Alberta*. Vancouver: Copp Clark, 1977.

Thorne, Duncan. "Native Anger Rising over Murals." *Edmonton Journal*, 19 February 1997.

Titley, Brian. *The Frontier World of Edgar Dewdney*. Vancouver: University of British Columbia Press, 1999.

———. *A Narrow Vision: Duncan Campbell Scott and the Administration of Indian Affairs in Canada*. Vancouver: University of British Columbia Press, 1986.

Tobias, John. "AHCHUCHWAHAUHHATOHAPIT (Ahchacoosacootacoopits, Star Blanket)" in *Dictionary of Canadian Biography*, vol. 14, University of Toronto/Université Laval, 2003–. http://www.biographi.ca/en/bio/ahchuchwahauhhatohapit_14E.html.

Turkel, William J. *The Archive of Place: Unearthing the Pasts of the Chilcotin Plateau*. Vancouver: University of British Columbia Press, 2007.

Valverde, Mariana. "'When the Mother of the Race Is Free': Race, Reproduction and Sexuality in First-Wave Feminism." In *Gender Conflicts*, edited by Franca Iacovetta and Mariana, 3–26. Toronto: University of Toronto Press, 1992.

Van Herk, Aritha. Introduction. In *The Studhorse Man*, by Robert Kroetsch, Edmonton: University of Alberta Press, 2004.

Verrette, Michel. "Trémaudan, Auguste-Henri De." In *Dictionary of Canadian Biography*, vol. 15. University of Toronto/Université Laval, 2003–, http://www.biographi.ca/en/bio/tremaudan_auguste_henri_de_15E.html.

Voisey, Paul. *Vulcan: The Making of a Prairie Community*. Toronto: University of Toronto Press, 1988.

Von Heyking, Amy. *Creating Citizens: History and Identity in Alberta's Schools, 1905 to 1980*. Calgary: University of Calgary Press, 2006.

Waitt, Gordon. "Playing with Sydney: Marketing Sydney for the 2000 Olympics." *Urban Studies* 36, no. 7 (1999): 1055–77.

Wall, Karen, and PearlAnn Reichwein. "Climbing the Pinnacle of Art: Learning Vacations at the Banff School of Fine Arts, 1933–1959." *Canadian Historical Review* 92, no. 1 (March 2011): 70–105.

Walters, Margaret. *Feminism: A Very Short Introduction*. Oxford: Oxford University Press, 2005.

Westman, Clinton N. "Social Impact Assessment and the Anthropology of the Future in Canada's Tar Sands." *Human Organization* 72, no. 2 (2013): 111–20.

Wetherell, Donald G. *Architecture, Town Planning and Community: Selected Writings and Public Talks by Cecil Burgess, 1909–1946*. Edmonton: University of Alberta Press, 2005.

———, and Irene R.A. Kmet. *Town Life: Main Street and the Evolution of Small Town Alberta, 1880–1947.* Edmonton: University of Alberta Press and Alberta Community Development, 1995.

White, James. *Power in Alberta: Water, Coal and Natural Gas.* Ottawa: Canada, Commission on Conservation, 1919.

Wickenhauser, Joseph. "Finding Ourselves: LGBTQ Archives and the Small Urban Centre." Paper presented at the Knotty Encounters Interdisciplinary Graduate Student Conference, Toronto, Ontario, 3 March 2012.

Wilkie Historical Society, *Wilkie, Saskatchewan, 1908–1988*, vol. 1. Wilkie: Wilkie History Society, 1989.

Woodward, Rocky. "Scriver Accused of Violating Trust." *Windspeaker* 8, no. 7 (1990). http://www.w.ammsa.com/publications/windspeaker/scriver-accused-violating-trust.

Wright, Donald A. *The Professionalization of History in English Canada.* Toronto: University of Toronto Press, 2005.

Zeigler, Mary. "Eugenic Feminism: Mental Hygiene, the Women's Movement, and the Campaign for Eugenic Legal Reform, 1900–1935." *Harvard Journal of Law and Gender* 31, no. 1 (Winter 2008): 211–36.

Zimon, Kathy E., ed. *The Rule Wynn and Rule (Edmonton) Architectural Drawings.* Calgary: University of Calgary Press, 1997.

Contributors

CHERYL AVERY has been an archivist since 1985, and joined the University of Saskatchewan Archives & Special Collections in 1991. She served as the vice-chair of the Canadian Council of Archives, was co-chair of the Canadian Archival Information Network steering committee, and was co-editor of *Better Off Forgetting?*, a book on archives and public policy.

SARAH CARTER, FRSC, is professor and Henry Marshall Tory Chair in the Department of History and Classics and the Faculty of Native Studies at the University of Alberta. She specializes in the history of Western Canada. Her book, *Imperial Plots: Women, Land, and the Spadework of British Colonialism on the Canadian Prairies* was published by the University of Manitoba Press in fall 2016. She also recently co-edited a collection (with Maria Nugent), *Mistress of Everything: Queen Victoria in Indigenous Worlds* (Manchester University Press, 2016).

GEORGE COLPITTS, is a professor of history in the Department of History at the University of Calgary. He specializes in environmental history with a focus on the fur trade and plains history. His books include *Game in the Garden: A Human History of Wildlife to 1940* (UBC Press, 2002), and *Pemmican Empire: Food, Trade, and the Last Bison Hunts in the North American Plains, 1780–1882* (Cambridge University Press, 2015).

HEATHER DEVINE is an associate professor in the Department of History at the University of Calgary. Her publications, research, and teaching specialties focus on Canadian Native History, Museum and Heritage Studies, and Western Canadian ethnic history, with a particular focus on

Métis ethnohistory. She has worked in curatorial and consulting capacities with the Archaeological Survey of Alberta, the Royal Alberta Museum, the Nickle Arts Museum, and the Canadian Museum of History. She is author of *The People Who Own Themselves: Aboriginal Ethnogenesis in a Canadian Family, 1660–1900,* winner of the Harold Adams Innis Prize for 2004–5.

STERLING EVANS is Louise Welsh Professor of History at the University of Oklahoma. His interests include the transnational, environmental, and agricultural history of North America and Latin America, as evidenced by his book *Bound in Twine: The History and Ecology of the Henequen-Wheat Complex for Mexico and the American and Canadian Plains, 1880–1950* (2007). He has published on conservation and tourism in Costa Rica and is at work on similar projects for Cuba and for the badlands of the North American West.

MAX FORAN has been researching and writing on various Western Canadian historical topics for almost fifty years. Originally from Australia, he was an administrator with the Calgary Board of Education for many years before joining the Faculty of Communication and Culture at the University of Calgary. He has published widely in both urban and rural history, and has recently completed a manuscript on Canadian wildlife policies. He currently resides in Priddis near Calgary with his wife, Heather.

KIMBERLY MAIR is an assistant professor of sociology at the University of Lethbridge. Her research is concerned with the spatialization and aesthetics of communication.

WILL PRATT received his PhD in history from the University of Calgary in 2015, submitting a dissertation on Canadian Army medicine and morale in the Second World War. His research interests are First Nations history and Canadian military history. He is a sessional lecturer at the University of Calgary, Mount Royal University, and the University of Lethbridge.

PEARLANN REICHWEIN is an associate professor at the University of Alberta. Her research focus is the environmental, leisure, and public history of Western Canada. A winner of the Canadian Historical Association's Clio Prize and other book awards, she studies cultural landscapes, governance, and commemoration of outdoor life, parks, and heritage.

MALLORY ALLYSON RICHARD is a policy analyst for the Winnipeg Police Board. She wrote her contribution to this volume while working on the inaugural exhibits of the Canadian Museum for Human Rights. She has a Master's degree in history from the University of Manitoba/University of Winnipeg.

SHELLEY SWEENEY has been Head, University of Manitoba Archives & Special Collections, in Winnipeg, Canada, since 1998. She was in the first class of the Master of Archival Studies program at the University of British Columbia, receiving her degree in 1985 and acquiring her PhD in Archival Enterprise from the University of Texas at Austin in 2002. She has worked closely with a number of donor communities in Manitoba, including the LGBTTTIQ community, to ensure the preservation of their unique histories.

KAREN WALL is associate professor in Communication Studies and Heritage Resource Management at Athabasca University. She has worked as an archivist and museum researcher as well as an educational illustrator. Her current research interests involve visual culture, travel and tourism, and urban Indigenous representation.

Index

A

A. B. C. Mine, 165
Aberhart, William "Bible Bill," 159, 169
agricultural research stations (federal government), Manyberries, 183, 184, 189; Swift Current, 189
Alberta: coal, 151, 152–53, 154, 161, 165. *See also* coal industry
Alexandra Club (Victoria, BC), 137
All Peoples' Mission (Winnipeg), 117
Anderson, Graham, 11, 188
Anderson Grazing Rates Report, 11–12; 179–80, 188, 189, 190–91; impact of, 190, 194; rancher reaction to, 190, 194
Architecture, 12
Armour, William, 151, 154, 155, 165, 166, 203
Asian Canadians: discrimination and franchise, 114–16, 122, 129, 143; J. S. Woodsworth's views of, 116

B

Bahktin, Michail, 6
Baldwin, Stanley, 145, 153
Banff, 12, 9, 160, 166, 203–204, 207, 208–209, 218, 223, 224; Mount Royal Hotel, 211; as UNESCO World Heritage Site, 203, 206, 226
Banff Centre, 203, 206, 225; Donald Cameron Hall, 226; instructor painters, 2010; Kinnear Centre, 226–27; Shaw Amphitheatre, 227; sightlines and mountain views, 211; St. Julian grounds, 210; Woods Memorial building, 208, 212, 213, 215
Banff Indian Days, 104
Banff School of Fine Arts, 12
Banff Springs Hotel, 207, 209, 212, 213, 215, 217, 218, 221
Barlow, Sir Clement Anderson Montague, 10, 151, 153, 154, 155, 158, 162, 171, 172, 174. *See also* Royal Commission on the Coal Mining Industry of Alberta (1935)
Barriault, Marcel, 49
Bartley, Paula, 135, 139, 140
Belyea, Barbara, 27, 33
Bennett, R.B., 158, 163, 170
Berland, Jody, 3
Beynon, Francis Marion, 120, 126, 127
Bill C-150. *See* LGBT official Canadian policy towards
Binford, Lewis, 32

259

bioregions, 3
Bird, Isabella, 155
Blackfoot (Niitsitapi), 1–2, 60. *See also* First Nations
Blairmore, Alberta 154
Boag, Veronica Strong, 113
Boddy, Trevor, 226
Bolshevism, 133, 136, 138, 139, 142
Borden, Robert and Wartime Elections Act, 125–26
Bow River, 94, 96, 97, 208, 212, 224
Brazeau, Alberta, 154
Bridgman, Wellington, 133–34
buffalo, 95, 97, 180
Buffalo Bow (Chief), 75
Burgess, Cecil, 222

C

Cadomin, 154
Calgary, 154, 160, 161, 162–63, 164, 167–68, 184, 187, 208, 210, 226; stockyards, 184, 187
Cameron, Donald, 12, 203, 205, 206–10, 211, 212, 213, 219–22, 223, 225
Camrose, Alberta, 186
Canadian Cattlemen, 192, 193
Canadian Lesbian and Gay Archives, 40, 47–48
Canadian National Council for Combating Venereal Disease (CNCCVD), Toronto, 133, 134, 139–40, 141, 144, 147. *See also* Canadian Social Hygiene Council, Toronto
Canadian National Task Force on Museums and Indigenous communities, 22
Canadian Pacific Railway (CPR), 156, 207, 212. *See also* Banff Springs Hotel
Canadian Social Hygiene Council, Toronto, 144
Canadian Women's Club, 137
Cascade Mountain, 211
cattle industry, 181–85; during Depression years 183–88; post-1940s, 189–94
Chapman, Ethel. M, 139

Chief Kwakwabalasami's House. *See* First Peoples Gallery
Church, Albert J., 222
Clarke, S. E., 189
Clifford, James, 19, 34
Coalspur, Alberta, 154
Colonel Woods Memorial, Banff Centre, 212, 215
community histories, 64
Cranbrook Academy, Michigan, 219
Cree, 25, 60, 61, 93; language, 67, 81
Cross, Alfred Ernest, 182
Crowsnest Pass, Alberta, 160, 164, 166

D

Dendy, Mary, 5
Denny, Cecil, 98
Desjarlais family, 68
De Trémaudan, August-Henri, 65
Devereux, Cecily, 123, 127, 140–41
Devine, Heather, 22, 34, 67, 68
Devine, Mary, 68, 69
Devonian Foundation, 208
Dick, Lyle, 62, 64, 82
Dinosaur Provincial Park, Alberta, 160
District of Assiniboia, 73
Dominion Lands Policy, 4,7
Douglas, Tommy, 85
Doukhobor land claims, British Columbia, 96
Drumheller, 154, 155, 160, 161, 165, 170, 171, 173
Duberman, Martin, 46
Duggan, Lisa, 46
Dunning, Charles Avery, 84
Dry Belt Ranchers Association, 183

E

Edmonton, 153, 154, 155, 157–59, 161, 163–64, 165–70
Edmonton Equal Franchise League, 118, 137, 138
Electoral Franchise Act, tabled 1885, 114–17
Emberley, Julia, 33

Emerald Lake, Alberta, 160
eugenics, 10, 134, 135–37, 140; and sterilization, 134, 137

F

Falcon, Pierre Jr., 64
feminism, 121, 126, 135; and imperialism, 135, 139–41; and eugenics, 135, 136, 140
Fidler, Peter, 2
File Hills, 75; chiefs, 75; reservations, 75; reserve, 81
First Nations: Cree, 25; debate on suffrage, 117; discrimination, 123; elders, 67; enfranchisement with Indian Status (1960), 129; exclusion from franchise, 115–16; experiential mapping, 2–3; Kainai, 2; Niitsitapi, 1–2; Niitsitapi and *The Spirit Sings*, 21–22; Piikani, 2; Siksika, 2, 5; Stoney, 8–9, 93, 96–105
First Peoples Gallery, Chief Kwakwabalasami's House, 5–6, 20–32
Fisher, Art, 67
Fisher, George, 75
Fort Garry, 59
Fort Qu'Appelle, 75, 78, 81
Fort Qu'Appelle Sanatorium, 68
Fort San, 68
Frank, Gloria Jean, 21. *See also* First Peoples Gallery, Chief Kwakwabalasami's House
Friesen, Gerald, 12–13; 169
fur trade, 2, 5–6, 13–14

G

Ganapathy, Sandhya, 3
Gardiner, James G. "Jimmy," 66, 71
George Ross, 187. *See also* Red Label Feeders Association
Gilchrist, Rube, 188

Glenbow Foundation and Museum, 208; *Niitsitapiisinni: Our Way of Life*, 23; planning of *The Spirit Sings*, 22, 23
Glyde, H. D., 210
Grain Growers' Association, Manitoba and Saskatchewan, 118
Grain Growers' Guide, 111–12, 113, 118–19, 121, 124
Grasse, P. L., 99
Gunn, Donald, 64
Gwyn, Richard, 116

H

Hargrave, Joseph James, 64
Harris, Lawren, 210
Harvie, Eric, 208, 209, 211, 215, 216, 218, 220
Harvie, John, 188
Haultain, Sir Frederick, 80
Haultain, Wilmot, 80
Hawkes, John, 77, 81, 82, 83, 84, 91
Helmer, Albert, 189
Henday, Anthony, 5, 24–28. *See also* Royal Alberta Museum
High River, Alberta, 192
Hofstetter, Mary E., 227
Hotel Macdonald (Edmonton) 157, 164, 166, 167, 168
Hudson's Bay Company, 59, 65, 75, 167
Hugonard, Father, 74, 75, 77
Hunter, Rev. James, 64

I

Icelandic women and suffrage association, 118
Independent Labour Party (ILP), 135
Indian Act (1876), 60, 99; amendment, 103
Indo-Canadians excluded from franchise, 129
International Council of Museums: resolution on exhibition of cultural materials, 22

International Labour Organization, 155
Inuit Canadians 1950 enfranchisement, 129
Is-koo-ches, 78

J

Jackson, A. Y., 210
Jackson, T. W., 76
Japanese Canadians, 123; enfranchisement (1947), 129
Jennings, P. J., Banff parks superintendent, 208–10

K

Kainai (Blood), 170. *See also* First Nations
Kansas City Art Institute and School of Design, 219
Kee-was-stoo-tin, 78
Kicking Horse Pass, 160
King, William Lyon Mackenzie, 71, 158
Kinnear, James, 227. *See also* Banff Centre
Kinnikinnick, 61, 68
Kinsman, Gary, 46
Kipp, George, 22
Kroetch, Robert, 12–14
Kwakwa̱ka̱'wakw: and National Museum policy, 22; political mobilization, 21–22

L

Lac Qu'Appelle. *See* Qu'Appelle
Lady Barlow (D. L. Read), 151, 153, 158, 164, 165
Lake Louise, Alberta, 160
LaRocque, Alexander, 76
LaRocque, Antoine, 73, 74; arrest, 73, 74, 75, 76, 81, 82, 84, 85; visit from Star Blanket, 76, 77, 78
LaRocque family, 68, 75, 76, 85
LaRocque, John, 81
Larocque, Joseph Zépherin (J. Z.), 8–9, 59, 66; as community historian, 67, 68, 70; correspondence, 71; correspondence with J. G. Gardiner, 71, 73; correspondence with Native activists, 71; correspondence with Hon. W.J. Patterson; 72, 74, 90; dairy farm, as fish and wildlife field officer, 66, 67, 80; 75; papers, 67, 68, 80; political activist, 66; as public *persona*, 87; in Liberal Party, 77, 84, 86; vernacular writing, 67, 73, 86
LaRocque, Lucy, 67, 68, 69, 70, 88
LaRocque, Robert James "Jimmy," 67, 68, 71; death, 68
LaRocque, Rosalie LaPlante, 73, 75
La Union Nationale Métisse; Saint-Joseph de Manitoba, 65
Laurier, Sir Wilfrid, 76, 85; visit to Lebret, 76; visit to Regina, 84
Lavendar Legacies Guide: Society of American Archivists, 41
Law, Andrew Bonar, 153
leasehold system, 181–183, 185, 186, 187, 188, 189–94; Australian, Argentinian and American, 190
Lebret, Saskatchewan, 8, 66, 67, 69,73, 74, 76,78, 80
Lefebvre, Henri, 204–05, 225
Leishman, George, 222
Lemberg, Saskatchewan, 71
Lesbian, gay, bisexual, transgender, transsexual, two spirit, intersex and queer (LGBTTTIQ) archives. *See* LGBT archives
Lethbridge, Alberta, 154, 155, 157, 161, 162, 169, 184
LGBT archives, 6; Archives Canada collections, 40, 50; survey to archivists, 41, 45–48; University of Manitoba, 43; University of Saskatchewan, 43; University of Victoria, 45; University of Winnipeg, 45
LGBT, official Canadian policy towards, 41–42
Liberal government; federal, 71; Saskatchewan, 71, 86, 87
Liberal Party, 77, 86
Library and Achives Canada, 54

Loewen, Royden, 13
Lubicon Lake Cree: boycott of *The Spirit Sings*, 22

M

McClung, Nellie, 121–23, 127, 134, 138; eugenic feminism, 140–41
MacDonald, J. W. G., 210
Macdonald, John A., 59; and the Electoral Franchise Act, 115–16
McDonald, Archibald, 75
McDougall, George, 94
McDougall, John, 8–9; brief history of career, 94–95; criticism of government economic policy, 97–99; First Nations assimilation and government policy, 96–97, 102–3; orphanage, 101; 103
MacEwan, Grant, 184
Maguire, William Charles, 80, 81, 82
McKay, Ian, 114
McLaren, John, 134, 136
McPherson, Aimee Semple, 168
Manitoba Equal Franchise Club, Suffrage League, 118
Manning, Ernest J., 152
Manyberries. *See* agricultural research stations
Martin, Chief Justice W.W., 80
Mason, Courtney, 94
Maynard, Stephen, 46, 52
Medicine Hat, Alberta, 183, 187
Melanson, Jeff, 227. *See also* Banff Centre
Methodism: missions, 94, 98; Methodist Mission Society, 102; Reverand John Shaw, 98; Saskatchewan District, 95. *See also* McDougall, John
Métis, 7–8, 59, 60, 61, 64, 62, 66; cart trains, 65; culture, 61, 62; educated and affluent, 61, 86; elders, 70; folklore, 62; Métis Society of Saskatchewan, 66, 86, 87 Northwest Rebellion, 78
Middleton, Janet, 224
Miles City, Montana, 185
Milk River, Alberta, 187

Mine Workers of Canada, 173
Minor, P.A., 188
Mitchell, David, 145
Montreal Canadiens, 168
Morleyville, Alberta, 9, 94, 97
Mount Royal Hotel, Banff, 211
Mount Rundle, 160, 211
Murphy, Emily, 9, 122; *The Black Candle*, 122, 143; immigration and venereal disease, 142; as Janey Canuck, 123, 136, 146; as police magistrate, 136; race and eugenics, 134, 141
Museums: collecting and policy, 21–22; spatial organization, 19. *See also* Royal Alberta Museum; Royal British Columbia Museum

N

Natural Resources Transfer Agreement (1930), 89
Newton, Emma Read, 215
Newton, Robert, 208, 209
Nix, Ernest, 102
North West Council, 76
North West Mounted Police, 94, 97, 101,
North West Territories, 88
Northwest Rebellion of 1885, 6, 60, 65, 73, 80, 83, 84, 85, 97; alternative accounts, 86; French Métis in, 78; Star Blanket's Account of, 77, 84

O

One Big Union (OBU), 173
oral history, 83
Ottawa, 156, 157, 158

P

Pankhurst, Christabel, 135, 140; with Canadian Social Hygiene Council, 144; *The Great Scourage and How to End it*, 140
Pankhurst, Emmeline, 10, 133–35; on Bolshevism, 136, 138, 139, 142; and the Great War, 135; speaking tours

in the West, 134; 135–36; 138–44; stands as Conservative Party MP, 145; Women's Social and Political Union, 135
Pass System, 88, 103
Patterson, W.J., 73; aboriginal name, Ka-Nee-Nan Otaeu, 75
Peace Hills Reserve, 99
Perceptions magazine, 51
Phillips, W.J., 210
Piikani (Peigan), 170. *See also* First Nations
Poitras, Jane Ash, 23
Ponoka Asylum, 146
Prairie Farm Rehabilitation Administration (PFRA), 179
Pratt, Mary Louise, 2, 9
prohibition, 159
Purvis, June, 135, 139
Pylypchuk, Mary Ann, 83

Q

Qu'Appelle Valley and mission, 65, 67, 80; Métis Elders, 70; Northwest Rebellion, 73, 78

R

Rabbit Hill, 155, 165
racial purity, 133, 134, 137, 142–43, 144
Rainbow Resource Centre, 45
range management, 180, 182, 186, 188–89, 190–91, 194–95
Rawson, K.J., 52
Red Label Feeders Association, 187
Red River Resistance, 64, 73
Red River settlement, 64, 73; elites, 65
Redford, Alison, 227
Regina, Saskatchewan , 75, 80, 81, 82, 84, 85
Riel, Louis, 60, 65, 75
Riel Rebellion. *See* Northwest Rebellion of 1885
Rocky Mountains, 1–2, 161, 169, 203, 207, 215
Roman Catholic Church; clerics, 65; religious histories, 65
Roosevelt, Franklin, 155
Rosedale Mine: strike, 171
Ross, Alexander, 64
Rossville mission. *See* McDougall, George
Royal Alberta Museum (RAM), 5, 22
Royal British Columbia Museum (RBCM), 5, 20–21
Royal Canadian Mounted Police, 81
Royal Commission on the Coal Mining Industry of Alberta (1935), 10–11, 151–52, 153, 154–55, 165–66, 171–73, community meetings and tours, 154–55
Rule, John, and Rule, Wynn and Rule architects, 209, 212, 215, 216, 220–21, 222–23
Rundle, Mary Beatrice, 10–11, 151, 153–54, 173–74; class, 163–64; cultural observer, 167–68; as diary writer: 155–56; gender, 164–66; observations, 158–603
Rupert's Land, 59
Rutherdale, Myra, 94
Rutherford Library, University of Alberta, 220

S

Saddle Lake Reserve, 99
Saleeby, Caleb, 142–43
Salzburg, as design inspiration, 12, 206, 208, 210, 223, 224
Saskatchewan Provincial Equal Suffrage Board, 118
Saskatchewan, 60, 65, 66, 70, 84; historical society, 67; Liberal Party, 66
Saskatoon Star-Phoenix, 91
Saulteaux, 61; language 67
Saunders Creek, 154
Scrip, 60, 87
Scriver Blackfoot collection. *See* Royal Alberta Museum (RAM)
Selkirk Settlers, 64
Sexual Steriliztion Act, Alberta (1928), 134, 146
Shaw Amphitheatre, Banff Centre, 227

Short Grass Stock Growers' Association (SGSGA), 187, 188, 192; merger with WSGA, 192
Siksika (Blackfoot Confederacy), 170. *See also* First Nations
Simon, Roger, 35
Small, Sarah, 13–14
Smith, Henry Nash, 9
Smith, Keith, 93
Snow, Chief John, 96
Social Credit Party, Alberta, 152, 159, 169
Springhill Grain Growers in Manitoba, 121
St. François-Xavier, parish, 73
St. Julien site, Banff Centre, 210
Stanek, Lukasz, 205
Star Blanket (*Ahchacoosahcotatakoopit*), 75, 91; account of Northwest Rebellion, 77, 78, 79, 80, 82, 83, 84;
Steinhauer, Abigail, 95
Stepney, Philip, 26
Stoney, Nakoda, 170. *See also* First Nations
Stoney Plain Reserve, 99
Strong-Boag, Veronica, 113
Suffrage movement, 9–10; 111–14
Swift Current Dominion Research Station. *See* agricultural research stations
Symon, W.M. *See* Kansas City Art Institute and School of Design
Syncrude Gallery of Aboriginal Culture (SGAC), 5, 20–21; 23–29

T

Tanner, Hon. N.E., 192–93, 187–88
Thompson, Christian, "Thoughts, Fancies and Facts," 80, 91
Thompson, David, 13–14
Thompson Jones and Company, architects, 211, 212
Thompson, Stanley, 211
Thomson, L.B., 186, 189. *See also* agricultural research stations
Toronto, 80, 156, 157, 168; *Maple Leafs*, 168
Treaties, No. Four, 77; No. 6, 96; No. 7, 96–97, 100, 170
Trudeau, Pierre: as Justice Minister, 41

Turner Valley, 155, 162, 163, 164, 165
Tyre, Robert, 85

U

UNESCO World Heritage Site, Banff, 203, 206, 226
unions, labour organization, 145, 155, 166, 172, 173
United Farm Women of Alberta: views on sterilization, 9
United Farmers of Alberta, 121, 146
University of Manitoba: Archives and Special Collections, LGBT collections, 42–43
University of Saskatchewan Archives & Special Collections: LGBT collections, 43
University of Toronto Homophile Association, 42
University of Victoria: Transgender Archives, 45
University of Winnipeg Archives: Two-Spirited Collection, 45
Usher, Thomas, 194

V

Vankoughhnet, Lawrence, 98
Vermilion Lakes, 160
vernacular history and architecture, 62, 64, 65
Victoria Settlement, 95
Von Heyking, Amy, 118

W

Walsh, William L., 152
Weekes, Mary, 81
Welsh, Norbert, 81
Western Stock Growers Association (WSGA), 183, 184, 186, 189, 191, 192–94
White Buffalo Calf (Chief *Wahpiimoosetoosis*), 77
Willey, Anna Marie, 66
Winnipeg Political Equality League, 118

Winnipeg, 66, 80, 143, 156, 161; General Strike, 173
Winnipeg: Gay and Lesbian Reource Centre, 47
Women's Christian Temperance Union, 118
Women's franchise, 137, 146; Asian and First Nations, 112–13; in Britain, 137; Electoral Franchise Act (1885) 115–17; federal Wartime Elections Act 1917, 125–27; Manitoba, Saskatchewan and Alberta, 113–14. *See also* suffrage movement
Women's Social and Political Union (WSPU), 135
Woods, Leonora Christine, 208, 209, 213
Woods, Lt. Col. James, 208; Woods Memorial building, 208, 212, 213, 215
Woodsworth, J.S., 117–18
Wright, Frank Lloyd: Banff Pavilion, 12

Y

Young, Egerton Ryerson, 104

www.ingramcontent.com/pod-product-compliance
Lightning Source LLC
Chambersburg PA
CBHW061254230426
43665CB00027B/2938